Acclaim
for the first three editions!

"L... your
foo... ...rol
to ...lls
com... ...

—*Detroit Free Press*

"A no-nonsense, no-frills compendium, conveniently organized by subject. There's advice on everything from cutting grocery bills to investing in mutual funds."
—*Kiplinger's Personal Finance Magazine*

"The perfect '90s pocket book for people who want to keep more than pocket change."
—*The Atlanta Journal*

Featured on *Oprah!*

Now *Penny Pinching* is bigger and better than ever in this completely updated and expanded fourth edition!

For busy, successful people who want to live well, care about quality, and prefer not to cut back on the luxuries they enjoy right now, here is the book that offers hundreds of ways you can do what you do, eat what you eat, wear the clothes you want to wear, and live the way you always have—but for less money than you're spending now.

PENNY PINCHING

Lee and Barbara Simmons

BANTAM BOOKS

NEW YORK · TORONTO · LONDON · SYDNEY · AUCKLAND

PENNY PINCHING
A Bantam Book

PUBLISHING HISTORY
Bantam edition published September 1991
Bantam revised edition / February 1993
Bantam third edition / February 1995
Bantam fourth edition / February 1997

ISBN 0-553-57366-7

Published simultaneously in the United States and Canada

Bantam Books are published by Bantam Books, a division of Bantam Doubleday Dell Publishing Group, Inc. Its trademark, consisting of the words "Bantam Books" and the portrayal of a rooster, is Registered in U.S. Patent and Trademark Office and in other countries. Marca Registrada. Bantam Books, 1540 Broadway, New York, NY 10036.

PRINTED IN THE UNITED STATES OF AMERICA

OPM   0 9 8 7 6 5 4 3 2 1

CONTENTS

§ Introduction: § No Pain, Much Gain

This is the fourth expanded, completely updated edition of a book first published in September 1991.

It is filled with dozens of completely new tips and many more that have been extensively revised because of changes in the consumer environment. It includes many new sources, telephone numbers, and—for the first time—on-line and Internet addresses that will be invaluable to any penny pincher with access to a computer and a modem.

We had no idea when we started working on the first edition back in 1990 that it would soon be followed by a flood of other books and newsletters filled with advice from self-proclaimed tightwads, skinflints, cheapskates, and other promoters of frugal living. But the reason why so many of these newsletters and books were successful is clear. In the 1990s, cutting costs became a necessity for millions of beleaguered middle-class American consumers.

For the husband-and-wife authors of this book, that wasn't bad news at all. Long before the recession of the early 1990s, when a change in jobs in 1988 sharply reduced our income, we began to learn, test, develop, and live with many of the penny-pinching strategies you will find in the following pages. Our goal: to reduce our expenses without lowering our standard of living. We didn't want to buy cheap substitutes for the kind of food and clothing we had always enjoyed. We didn't want to spend hours of extra time each week doing things like bartering cents-off coupons or washing and saving old aluminum foil.

We still don't. That's why *Penny Pinching* is different from most of the books on the subject that followed our first edition. This is *not* the book for you if you think you might want to save money by:

- identifying reusable food in Dumpsters.
- buying a goat to mow your lawn.
- rinsing coffee filters for reuse.
- baking your own dog biscuits.
- cutting wide rubber bands in half lengthwise so you'll have two for the price of one.

We watch with both amazement and amusement as rival frugality newsletters try to outdo each other with advice like the above—all actual examples. But we have no intention of trying to compete.

As we told Oprah Winfrey when we appeared on her show to discuss defensive shopping in supermarkets, we are serious about saving money and reducing waste, but we aren't crazed coupon-clippers or anti–brand-name fanatics. We will continue to revise and update this book for people who agree with us that life is too short to devote it entirely to pinching every last penny.

"Penny pinching" is, after all, a term that has been passed down from a time when a penny was actually worth something. It's still a useful description of a worthwhile discipline, but we concentrate on pinching dollars, not cents. Of course, if it is easy to take advantage of a 25 cents-off coupon on a $1.00 purchase, we do it. If we can easily save a few cents by switching to a product of equal quality, we do that, too. Cents still add up to dollars. But the operative words are "easy" and "quality"; we insist on both. So this book is for busy, successful people who want to live well, care about quality, don't want to sacrifice a lot of precious leisure time, and prefer not to cut back on the luxuries they enjoy right now. What they need are ways to do what they do, eat what they eat, wear the clothes they want to wear, and live the way they always have—but for less money than it is costing them now.

How can you cut your weekly grocery bill by 10 to 15 percent without changing your family's eating habits? What are the no-pain ways to cut heating expenses? How do you buy the cheapest airline ticket possible? How can virtually anyone save up to 10 percent on automobile insurance even without changing insurance companies?

This book has some answers. You'll find money-saving tips on everything from cabbages and lightbulbs to designer clothes and treasury bills. How much can they save you? Perhaps hundreds, perhaps even thousands of dollars a year. For most people, changing just a few habits can lead to very substantial savings. What's more, although effective penny pinching requires a more organized approach than most people take to managing their money, many penny-pinching strategies will in the end actually save you time as well as money.

IT'S YOU AGAINST THEM

There's no question that the American consumer is protected by a number of local, state, and federal laws, Better Business Bureaus, and regulations imposed by various industries. The question is, what do they really protect you from?

Usually there are safeguards in place against out-and-out fraud, theft, and outrageously obvious deception. But America is still very much a free-enterprise society, still the country that invented most of the marketing techniques that have created consumer-driven economies around the world. So *caveat emptor*—let the buyer beware—is as useful a reminder in the late 1990s as it was back in the days when our great-grandfathers were buying cure-all elixirs off the backs of horse-drawn carts.

To be a successful penny pincher, you must understand that you live in a society dominated by marketers who have devised countless sophisticated techniques to sell you what they want you to buy, when they want you to buy it, at the prices they want you to pay. They have created powerful brand images that persuade people to pay $1.50 for Soap A, which is identical except for packaging to 50-cent Soap B. They advertise "enormous savings" when things are priced at a normal markup and don't advertise at all when the same things are really on sale. They invent products you don't need but soon want. They even create holidays to sell their products; Mother's Day now generates hundreds of millions of dollars in sales each year. And they bombard you every day with thousands of messages that say buy, buy, buy.

There's nothing wrong with any of this. Mother's Day has created thousands of new jobs. Selling, merchandising, advertising, and marketing are essential to a healthy national economy. But your own financial health depends on knowing when to turn off the sell messages and what tactics to employ when confronted with various purchase decisions.

Will anyone who reads this book want to or be able to use all of its strategies and tips? No. In fact, we've included quite a few ideas we can't or don't choose to use ourselves. Nevertheless, they have proved their usefulness with penny-pinching friends and readers who have shared them with us.

Are you already likely to be aware of some of the ideas it recommends? Certainly. We debated including some of them because they seem to turn up in every magazine article about saving money. But if everyone knows that a cheap, homemade window-washing mixture is just as effective as the expensive brand-name products, how come tens of millions of dollars' worth of those products are still sold year after year?

Even people who already are successfully pinching pennies are bound to find a couple of new ways to save money—at least enough to pay for the book a few times over.

THE PENNY PINCHER'S BEST FRIENDS

There are constant references throughout this book to libraries, 800 numbers, and Internet web sites. Pinching pennies would be far more difficult without them. That's because saving money is most often a matter of having the right information. Even the smallest public libraries have reference books and magazines that can help. A lot of people are nervous about doing "research" in a library because they never learned how or have forgotten what they learned in school. Don't let that stop you. Good librarians enjoy helping you get started. Tell them what your question is, and chances are they will immediately tell you where to find the answer.

The single most useful telephone number for a penny pincher is 1-800-555-1212. That's directory assistance for the toll-free 800-888 system. It doesn't cost a penny to call it in most areas of the country. Thousands of companies and organizations have set up 800 and 888 numbers because they want you to call for information or service. You can get free brochures and booklets, advice on how to fix just about anything, and competitive prices on virtually every product made. All without leaving home, all at no cost.

The information explosion on the Internet is making "http://www" at least as important a code beginning as 800 or 888. We never imagined, when we were working on the third edition of this book just two years ago, that Internet World Wide Web sites would become so powerful a penny-pinching resource in so short a period of time. If you don't have access to a computer and a modem, this book will still be as helpful as it has ever been. If you do, you'll find a few suggestions about Internet sites to visit that will make penny pinching easier than ever before.

KEEPING SCORE

Whatever you save by using the tips in this book, it will be difficult to tell how much unless you know how you are spending your money right now. That means—uh-oh, here comes the b-word. . . .

Yes, a *budget*. You don't absolutely need a budget to save money on what you eat, buy, invest, and do. You can still use the tips in this book. It will make your paycheck go further. No matter how much you save, though, you will still probably end up wondering where it all goes.

If you already have a family budget, or are willing to start one, you have made a very wise decision. Financial planners trade stories about perfectly intelligent clients who, after years of never examining where their money went, begin keeping score and are shocked to discover how much they actually spend on certain things.

One Chicago stockbroker, for example, had fallen into the habit of buying seven different magazines on a regular basis from the newsstand in his office building. By subscribing to the same magazines and paying annual instead of single-issue rates, he saved $435 a year. He cut his annual car expenses by nearly $2,500 a year by trading in his luxury convertible after three years instead of two. He adopted a simple new strategy for buying birthday and Christmas gifts and saved at least $1,000 a year.

You are nearly certain to be surprised by some of your own expenses in certain categories. And once you start a budget, you will probably set some different spending priorities. Even if you don't, experience has shown that people who keep budget records nearly always save money simply because they become far more aware of their spending habits.

Anyone with a computer can now buy one of the personal-finance software programs—most likely *Quicken* or *Microsoft Money*—for less than $40. Once you have such a program, you can use it for years to set up a family budget more quickly and easily than was ever before possible.

Even without a computer, there are some tried-and-true methods that work as well as ever. Your library probably has a number of books that will help you set up a family budget.

Whether you are working on a computer or with a few sheets of notebook paper, the hardest part of the process comes in the very beginning, when you have to pull together a lot of information and make decisions about priorities. Don't get discouraged. No matter what your family income, a good budget plan can put an end to those sleepless nights worrying about overdue bills. Most important, it can help you achieve your long-term financial goals.

If you don't have a budget right now, spend some time with this book before you start one. The whole idea of budgeting may be more appealing after you discover some specific ways to cut expenses in just about every budget category. Want to know how to spot the worst rip-offs in your supermarket? Where to buy name-brand hosiery at a 50 percent discount? How to get more miles to the gallon no matter what kind of car you drive? Where to buy houseplants for a fraction of their usual cost? The best way to invest in mutual funds?

Whether they save you hundreds or thousands of dollars a year, we hope you'll find enough penny-pinching tips and strategies in these pages to help you live the good life for a lot less money.

THANKS TO FELLOW PENNY PINCHERS

who have amended and added to our tips and strategies since the first edition of *Penny Pinching* was published, especially Paul DeLuca, President of Telecom Consultants of Greenvale, New York, who continues to share with us his sound strategies for saving money on telephone and communications service and equipment

SHARE YOUR IDEAS WITH US

We will continue to expand and update *Penny Pinching* and invite you to send us any ideas you have. If we use them, you'll be acknowledged in future editions. Write to:

> Bantam Books
> Penny Pinching Editor
> 1540 Broadway
> New York, NY 10036

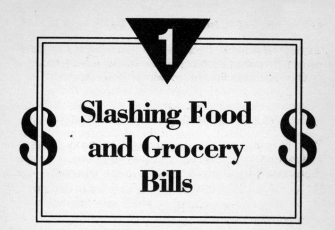

Slashing Food and Grocery Bills

Have you ever given much thought to how a modern supermarket is organized? Probably not. But the corporations that own the supermarkets sure have, and so have Procter & Gamble, RJR Nabisco, Coca-Cola, and the other giant package-goods companies that make and market what's on the shelves.

After hundreds of millions of dollars and hours spent on continuing research and consumer testing, they have learned to stack the supermarket deck to accomplish one basic goal: to separate you from as much of your money as possible every time you set foot in a store.

Every element of a supermarket's design and floor plan is carefully set up to encourage as much unplanned "impulse" buying as possible. That's why the staple items needed by most shoppers are strategically spread all over the store; you are forced to walk through as many aisles as possible to get to them. Does that enormous display of one product at the end of an aisle signal a great bargain? Sometimes, but more likely it is just a great promotion, usually paid for by the manufacturer.

The only way for you to win is to change the rules of the game so it is played your way, not theirs. The supermarket marketers want you to wander through their aisles making last-minute decisions about tonight's dinner. Don't do it. Some of the strategies and tips in this chapter help you cut your grocery bills by avoiding impulse shopping. If you adopt most of them, annual savings of 15 percent or even more are a realistic goal. What's more, by cutting down the number of extra trips you make to the supermarket, you'll save time and a lot of aggravation as well.

The highest profits made by the giant food companies and supermarkets are in products that cost more because they promise to save you time and effort. To achieve maximum savings in your weekly food bill, cut out convenience foods altogether.

That's easier said than done, of course. It is cheaper to make your own soups than to buy cans, to bake a cake from scratch than to buy one from a bakery, to prepare a homemade chicken pot pie than to buy a frozen one. But few people these days have either the time or the inclination to do such things very often. It is worth paying for convenience—in some food categories, some of the time.

What is not worth paying for is the marketing ingenuity that has extended the convenience-food concept to laughable extremes. Only a few of the more outrageous or pervasive examples are cited in the tips that follow. They will help you avoid some obvious rip-offs, but you can easily find hundreds more if you keep just a few rules of thumb in mind about shopping and paying for "convenience":

■ The more removed from the original basic ingredients and the effort needed to prepare them, the more expensive the convenience product. For instance, making pancakes from flour, milk, eggs, baking powder, salt, sugar, and cooking oil is cheaper than buying a package of pancake mix; which is cheaper than frozen, premixed pancake batter; which is cheaper than frozen pancakes; which are cheaper than (the most recent gimmick) frozen, *microwavable* pancakes. Estimated cost of quality ingredients to make one dozen 4-inch pancakes from scratch: 40 cents. Cost of the same number of frozen microwave pancakes: $2.59.

- In any blind taste test, which kind of pancakes do you think would win? The addition of convenience characteristics nearly always means some loss of freshness, taste, texture, etc.
- Avoid convenience that is only a matter of smart packaging. Example: a can of chow mein vegetables sold in the same box with a pouch of soy sauce. Buy them separately. This kind of packaging provides no meaningful added convenience, just higher prices.
- Convenience is most expensive in small packages. Food marketers know that, as a group, busy single people are most likely to want no-hassle ways to prepare a meal. They charge especially high prices for "individual servings."

Prices used in this chapter were actual store prices at the time this book was going to press. Although the prices you will see on many items will no doubt be different, the price ratios between competitive choices probably won't change much at all.

▶ SHOP ONCE A WEEK

If you remember that impulse buying is the enemy, it makes sense to limit the number of times you face temptation. Besides, think of all the time (and gasoline and shoe leather) you waste by running to the supermarket for three or four items at a time.

You have to break this rule when you eat fresh fish or other highly perishable foods. But the principle is still sound: Try to buy everything you can on a once-a-week basis, and head right to the fish counter, the fresh bread case, or the fruit-and-vegetable section when you have to make a special trip.

▶ SHOP ALONE

Watch the next time you see a couple doing their weekly shopping together. The odds are good that she's filling her shopping basket with exactly the items on her checklist. He's roaming the aisles, reading the labels on all sorts of exotic stuff, and idly slipping jars of gourmet mustard and salsa into the basket. Kids are just as big a problem, and harder to argue with when they simply must have the new super-sugared Technicolor cereal they just saw on TV.

▶ BEND AND STRETCH

Supermarkets tend to display the most popular, fastest-moving merchandise at eye level, encouraging impulse buying by making it easy. You may find better buys higher or lower on the shelves.

That bottom shelf may also hold items that cost less than they should. Clerks don't like bending over any more than you do and may not have repriced them.

▶ DON'T SHOP WHEN YOU'RE HUNGRY

You'll be far less likely to buy foods impulsively if you shop on a full stomach, not an empty one.

▶ USE UNIT PRICING

Most states now require "unit price" information to be displayed on supermarket shelves, along with the price of the item. Especially given the often deceptive packaging practices of some food companies, unit price information is extremely helpful to consumers who want to know exactly how much they are getting for their money.

Example: Package A, priced at $1.50, sits right next to a competing brand of the same product, Package B, priced at $1.60. They are in exactly the same size package. Is A a better buy? No, because A contains only 6 ounces and B 8 ounces. In a unit price state, the unit price per quart or pound as well as the price of the package must be displayed under each product: $4.00 a pound for A ($1.50 divided by 6 ounces = 25 cents per ounce, 25 cents × 16 = $4.00), and $3.20 a pound for B ($1.60 divided by 8 ounces = 20 cents per ounce; 20 cents × 16 = $3.20).

It isn't difficult to do your own unit pricing if your state doesn't mandate it. Use a pocket calculator. When you are deciding between competitive packages, read the small print that tells you how much is inside. It will take a couple of seconds to divide the price by its weight or volume, as we did in the paragraph above, to come up with a unit price.

▶ START WITH A LIST

There is no way to avoid making a few lists if you're serious about saving money. Grocery lists are probably the lists you'll use most often, and good ones can save you hundreds of dollars a year. The important impulse-avoiding rule is: *Never* shop without a grocery list in hand.

One way to have an efficient list each week is to first write down categories of food and groceries on a sheet or two of paper, *in the same order that your supermarket's aisles are laid out.* This is important; if you just jot down things you need in no particular order, you will spend a lot of extra time doubling back through aisles you have been in before, thus increasing the likelihood of impulse buying.

Leave space under each category to write down the items you may need each week, and photocopy this basic list. Keep a few dozen copies on hand.

Then, each week, before you go to the market, plan your menus and check your supplies, with preprinted basic list in hand. Write down the items you need in each category. Include brand names if you have strong preferences.

Many families keep a preprinted basic list on the refrigerator and make it each person's responsibility to note when, say, the eggs are running low or the last of the tuna fish cans has been used.

▶ BUY DRY STAPLES IN BULK

All you need is adequate storage space (someplace dry and cool) to save from 10 to 30 percent a year on items like toilet paper, paper towels, diapers, pasta, soap and detergents, toothpaste, and canned goods. Moving from your kitchen shelves and laundry to linen closets and bathrooms, make a list of items you are positive you use in case quantities.

Properly stored dry spaghetti, for example, lasts at least eighteen months. If you use twenty-four one-pound packages a year, it makes sense to buy a case at a time. Canned food is nearly always good for two years or so, but check the "best if used by" date before buying in bulk.

Some supermarkets quietly give regular customers a discount when they buy by the case. When you make up your first list, show it to the store manager and ask him what discounts he can offer. If necessary, you might politely suggest that you're prepared to go elsewhere for such discounts—and perhaps buy the rest of your groceries there, too. Since the list will probably represent quite a significant purchase, he'll want to keep you happy. Thereafter, when you may want to buy just a case at a time, remind him that he *always* gives you case discounts.

Whether or not you can get discounts on case purchases at your supermarket, if you have a warehouse club within driving distance, by all means check out prices there. It may be worth paying the annual membership fee most warehouse clubs charge and making a few special trips a year, if the discounts are better than your supermarket's. We saved 37 percent off the supermarket price of spaghetti recently by buying in bulk from our warehouse club.

Dividends: When you make special trips for bulk purchases, you'll be amazed at how much less you have to
carry home from your weekly supermarket trip. And
you will be far less likely to run out of the staple items
you store in quantity.

▶ BUY SEASONALLY

Modern agriculture, transportation, and storage methods have made it possible to buy just about anything at
any time of the year. But if you live in the Northeast, the
$4.00-a-pint strawberries in December don't taste any-
where near as good as the 89-cent pint that's available
in June. Anybody who eats corn on the cob except for
the few weeks a year when locally grown corn is available is paying far too much for a vastly inferior vegetable. Penny-pinching corn-on-the-cob lovers gorge on it
three or four times a week when it is at its best—and
cheapest.

▶ BUY SEASONALLY FOR YOUR FREEZER

When your favorite berries are in season and at their
cheapest and best, why not buy a few extra boxes and
freeze them? It's easy to do, and the frozen berries are
both cheaper and superior to the sugar-loaded commer-
cially frozen products you might otherwise buy. Simply
clean and dry the berries—blue, straw, black, or rasp-
berries—put them in a single layer on a cookie sheet,
and place that in the freezer. An hour or two later, move
them a bit to prevent them from sticking or settling.
When they are solidly frozen, pour them into a freezer
bag and seal. They will be good for months.

Sample saving: April price of Birds Eye frozen strawberries in sugar syrup, $2.19 for a 10-ounce package.
Since the price of a quart of fresh strawberries when
they are in season in our area is about the same amount,
we pay at least 50 percent less for berries that we think
are 500 percent better.

▶ SOME ADS WILL SAVE YOU MONEY

At least once a week, your local newspaper probably includes an advertising insert listing dozens of items on sale at your supermarket. It makes sense to use this ad when planning menus and making out your weekly grocery list. All supermarket chains make special quantity buys that allow them to price some items at genuinely lower prices than usual.

▶ GENERIC VERSUS BRAND-NAME PRODUCTS

The standard advice about saving money on food and groceries involves substituting store brands and/or generics for national brands. The problem is, you prefer the taste or the quality of certain brands and don't want to give them up.

If you have a strong brand preference, one that you are sure of, stay with it and save other ways. If you are not convinced about such a preference, though, experiment. Try the least expensive option first. If you like it, why not save money by using it thereafter? If you don't, move up in price until you find an acceptable choice.

In many cases, you'll be equally satisfied with two or three similarly priced brands. When one of them is on sale or you have cents-off coupons saved for it, stock up.

In the last few years, many supermarket chains have moved away from the idea of selling generics but have improved the quality and variety of foods offered under their store-brand names. If you haven't used them lately, you might want to try again. Many store-brand products are produced by major manufacturers whose own brands are made with the same ingredients in the same factories. The only differences are often just the labels and the prices.

▶ A FEW ALWAYS-BUY STORE BRANDS

We can't think of a single reason to buy brand-name packages of certain staples. Typical savings:

- Store-brand granulated sugar: 5 pounds, $2.29 cents (44 cents per pound). Domino brand: 5 pounds, $2.79 (55.8 cents per pound).
- Store-brand all-purpose, enriched, bleached flour: 5 pounds, $1.29 (25.8 cents per pound). Pillsbury brand: 5 pounds, $1.69 (31.8 cents per pound).
- Store-brand distilled white vinegar: 54.8 cents a quart. Heinz brand: $1.09.
- Store-brand ammonia: 67 cents a quart. Parsons brand: $1.25.
- Store-brand regular bleach: $1.19 for two quarts. Clorox brand: $1.39.
- Store-brand iodized salt: 30.2 cents a pound. Diamond Crystal brand: 40 cents. But the price of Morton's brand at our warehouse club was 79 cents for a four-pound box (19.8 cents per pound). If bought in bulk quantities, similar savings on all of the staples cited in this tip are available at our warehouse club.

▶ THE TRUTH ABOUT COUPONS

Some people brag about saving thousands of dollars a year in grocery bills by using coupons. But unless you join a "trader's club" (or trade on-line; see next tip) and spend hours a week searching for, clipping, organizing, and trading coupons, that kind of saving is unlikely. In fact, what some obsessive coupon-clippers are doing is "saving" money on a lot of products they otherwise wouldn't have bought and in many instances won't ever use.

Nevertheless, coupons are an important part of any grocery-shopping strategy. They may not save you thousands a year, but they can definitely save you hundreds. You don't have to be obsessive about them, but you do have to manage and organize them properly.

There are two major sources of coupons—the manufacturers and the stores themselves. Actually, the stores use promotional money provided by manufacturers for their own special offers. Although some manufacturers have recently announced plans to reduce their dependence on couponing and switch instead to an "everyday low-price strategy," we expect couponing will continue to play an important role in every major package-goods company's marketing plans. Study after study proves that they increase sales, despite the fact that fewer than 10 percent of the coupons issued by manufacturers are ever redeemed. In-store coupons are far more profitable for stores than simply lowering the shelf price of a product. That's because at least 4 out of 10 people buying a couponed product in the store won't bother to use the coupon and will pay full price.

So the first, obvious tip for any penny-pinching grocery shopper is to compare your shopping list with the store's special sales flyer before you start shopping. You may very well want to adjust your list to take advantage of a special. Also:

- Don't clip and use coupons for new products. You'll break this rule occasionally, but it is good advice ninety-nine times out of a hundred. All food manufacturers offer coupons to entice you to try their new products, but few new products—nearly always "convenience" foods—offer significant improvements over what's already available.

- Clip, save, and use coupons only for the brand names you normally buy or substitutes you know are acceptable. Do this on a regular weekly basis. It takes very little time to review the coupon advertising you receive when you look for and clip only the coupons for known, wanted brands. This way, you don't have to waste time reading the ads!

- Very often, when a brand-name product is being "couponed," coupons appear in more than one place in a very brief period. Clip and save every coupon you see for a product you know you use. If it is for a perishable product, check the coupon expiration dates and use as many as feasible. If the product isn't perishable, use all the coupons you can and stock up.

- Don't be in too great a hurry to redeem coupons. Supermarkets have been known to raise the prices of certain items the week after they are couponed. It is very possible that the same item will be "sale-priced" two weeks later, and your coupons will end up saving you even more.

- Stores in some areas accept double coupons on certain products; that is, they allow two coupons to be used toward the purchase of a single item. If so, it may be worthwhile to buy another copy of the newspaper in which the coupon appears.

- Stores in some areas sometimes honor a different kind of "double coupon" or even "triple coupon" by allowing a 25-cent coupon, for instance, to be redeemed for 50 or 75 cents.

- Keep all the coupons you clip in one envelope or in an old checkbook cover. If this becomes unmanageable, divide the coupons by category into a few more envelopes.

- It takes just a couple of seconds per coupon to mark the expiration date of each with a yellow grease pencil or felt-tip pen. Once you do, you'll spot that date whenever you look at the coupon. Missed a date? There are greater tragedies. Throw it away.

- Review your coupons quickly before you make out your weekly shopping list. Then put an *X* next to each item you plan to buy for which you have a coupon. As you select each of these products, pull the coupons out of their storage envelopes and paper-clip them together for easy retrieval at the checkout counter.

- Check the before-coupon price before you buy a product. Every once in a while, you may find that price minus the coupon value is still higher than the price of the uncouponed but acceptable substitute right next to it.

▶ TRADE COUPONS ON-LINE

Visit *Coupon Net* (http://www.couponnet.com) on the Internet and trade coupons with people nationwide. There is a big advantage to trading this way instead of locally in a "trader's club." Marketers tailor coupons to different regions of the country. One example: In some areas, where double couponing is rare or nonexistent, marketers may issue 50- or 75-cent coupons instead of the 25-cent coupons for the same product issued in areas where double couponing is common. If you live in the double-couponing area and can get a 75-cent coupon for the product, you may be able to save $1.50 instead of 50 cents.

▶ JOIN SUPERMARKET SHOPPER CLUBS—ALL OF THEM

In the past couple of years, many supermarkets have begun issuing free cards that regular customers present at the checkout counter. Some cards give you special discounts; some give you "points" that you can accumulate and turn in for a free gift. In most cases, the cards are also supposed to guarantee you all the coupon savings offered that day by the store itself—without the hassle of cutting out the coupons.

As long as they are free, why not get cards even for supermarkets you use infrequently? Keep in mind that the cards that give you automatic savings do so only on the store's own coupons, not on those issued by manufacturers. You still have to clip those. Double-check your register receipts to make sure you really have gotten all the discounts you know are coming to you. Computers don't make mistakes, but the people responsible for updating them often do.

▶ CASH IN ON REFUND OFFERS

Coupons you redeem in stores save you money. Manufacturers' refund offers give you cash. For some reason, many people who use coupons in stores never take advantage of refund offers. Yet it is really quite an easy way to pick up a few extra dollars a month without much effort—perhaps as much as a few hundred a year, if you want to devote some extra time and energy to it. We never have, but if you are interested, your library probably has a book or two about how to achieve maximum savings by using both coupon and refund offers. (Look for *Shop Like a Coupon Queen* by Michelle Easter, $3.99, Berkley Books.)

You'll find refund offers in the same places as coupons, as well as on forms attached to the product itself. Because it costs you a first-class stamp to mail the refund form (along with proof of purchase—normally a specific panel from the product's label), it would be silly to return one to get a 40-cent check. Most manufacturers' refund offers are therefore for at least $1.00. Exchanging 32 cents for a dollar or two makes perfectly good sense to us, even taking into account the typical eight-week delay until the manufacturer's check is sent to you.

▶ DON'T TRUST THE CHECKOUT SCANNER

Large supermarket chains typically make thousands of price changes every week. Mistakes are made by those who input the changes into the central computers as well as by those who don't update shelf price tags. One study of supermarkets using scanners at their checkout counters estimated that as many as 40 percent of customer bills contain some kind of error.

Not even a penny pincher wants to delay a checkout line interminably, and it is true that sometimes the mistakes are in your favor. More often (no surprise) the errors are significantly in the store's favor. Your best defense is to write down the prices of items on your shopping list as you put them in your cart. Then monitor and compare the prices that appear on the scanner at the checkout counter. If one of them is incorrect, speak up immediately. The people behind you will understand and some stores will give you the item free if their scanners are wrong.

▶ ON SALE NEAR THE CHECKOUT COUNTER? BEWARE

Among the highest-margin items in the store are those such as gum, candy, batteries, and magazines displayed by the checkout counter line. Don't succumb to impulse shopping at the end of your shopping trip. Buy your batteries elsewhere for a lot less money.

▶ JOIN A WAREHOUSE CLUB

The first warehouse club was opened by a man named Sol Price in San Diego in 1974. Offering a hodgepodge of merchandise—including brand-name food and groceries—at deeply discounted prices, the Price Club limited its customers to small-business owners and government employees and charged them an annual membership fee.

The concept was an immediate success, and by the end of the 1980s several rival companies were competing for business in virtually every part of the country. So fierce was the competition that by 1994 only Wal-Mart's *Sam's Club,* a merged *Price-Costco Club,* and the regional *B.J.'s Wholesale Club* had survived. Many huge individual stores do over $100 million in annual business, and warehouse clubs as a group do well over $30 billion annually. Typically, they charge a $25 membership fee, and although all have some restrictions on who can be a member, most people find a way to qualify for membership in one category or another.

Should you join a warehouse club? The best way to decide is to visit one first. Either call ahead to confirm that the club will allow you to look the place over before joining, or accompany a friend who is already a member. Before you make the trip, make a list of all of the staple grocery, food, drugstore, and hardware items you use in bulk or large quantities. Then go to your normal sources for these items, and price them. *Important:* Very often, warehouse clubs sell only larger packages that are not available in other retail stores, so make sure you note unit pricing of food and groceries (the cost per ounce, quart, or pound).

Have you also been considering buying a new small appliance of any kind? New tires? Sheets? Towels? Garden hose? A computer? You are likely to find just about anything for sale in a warehouse club, including major national brand names, but you won't find the variety of choices within product categories that you will in other stores. Knowing beforehand the competitive prices of anything you might purchase is important, because incredible buys are likely to sit right next to items that can be purchased elsewhere for even less.

In our experience, however, it isn't likely that a careful shopper will make a big mistake at a warehouse club. Nearly all of the food and grocery prices we have checked at our warehouse club are at least competitive, and we save from 20 percent to as much as 60 percent on some items.

Warehouse clubs are profit-making businesses, not consumer clubs. Don't get carried away, buying things in bulk that will ultimately spoil or will never get used. Also, be wary of two or three disparate items shrink-wrapped together and sold for one price (a cookbook with a Teflon fry pan, for instance). This kind of merchandising is how the clubs enhance "perceived value," but do you really want both items? If not, the combined price is certainly not a bargain.

▶ SOME WAREHOUSE CLUB RECOMMENDATIONS

It is stupid to buy in bulk anything that won't get used in that quantity or that will go bad before it is used. But there are a number of food items that will last a very long time, so buying in what may seem to be too-large quantities can make sense. Five years ago, tempted by our warehouse club's extremely low price, we bought a two-bottle package of Worcestershire sauce. Two huge, 15-ounce bottles, in fact. We laughed about having a lifetime supply; as it turned out, it was only a five-year supply. We just bought two more bottles.

This is an extreme example, and we are not recommending you buy five-year supplies of many things. We have plenty of good, dry storage space, though, so if the price is right we buy the giant, warehouse club bottles or packages of the following long-lived items:

- Spices, including bay leaves, whole black pepper, cayenne pepper, chili powder, cinnamon, cumin, nutmeg, paprika, and rosemary.
- Vinegars and oils, including balsamic vinegar, white vinegar, white and red wine vinegar, vegetable oil, and sesame oil.
- Flour, granulated sugar, brown sugar, baking powder, baking soda, unsweetened cocoa, cornstarch, and cornmeal.
- Ketchup, chili sauce, Dijon mustard, soy sauce, and Worcestershire sauce.
- Pasta and rice.

▶ KEEP TRACK OF PRICES

The rise of wholesale clubs was a direct challenge to all kinds of retail stores, especially supermarkets. The giant supermarket chains have fought back with a vengeance, and now sometimes offer bulk quantities of some items at prices below those at wholesale clubs. This competition is terrific news for penny-pinching consumers, but it has also made shopping for the best price far more confusing.

Unless you want to check prices daily at every conceivable outlet for every item on your shopping list, it is virtually impossible to make certain you always get the best price. We carry a small pocket notebook in which we jot down the prices of items we know are likely to be on sale at different places in which we shop. That way, when we visit our wholesale club—usually every four to six weeks—we can compare prices with those at our supermarket, discount drugstore, and discount hardware store.

Do we always succeed? Of course not. Recently, the day after buying a case of paper towels at our wholesale club, our supermarket had a "warehouse sale" on the same brand for 10 percent less than we had paid. Nevertheless, the system works well most of the time and we think we buy at the lowest prices 90 percent of the time.

▶ AVOID SUPERMARKETS FOR MOST NONFOOD ITEMS

As supermarkets grow larger and stock a wider variety of products, you can get in the habit of using them to buy products that are cheaper elsewhere. In our area, discount drugstores always have lower prices on toothpaste and aspirin, for instance. Lightbulbs are cheaper at Home Depot. Diapers are much cheaper at Toys "R" Us. Our wholesale club sells all of these things at lower prices than our supermarket. If we aren't able to buy in bulk there, we try to stock up on items sold in discount stores so we don't find ourselves "running out" and buying them one at a time from our supermarket.

▶ JOIN A FOOD CO-OP

There are more than 600 food cooperatives (retail stores owned by co-op members) and more than 3,500 cooperative buying clubs (groups formed to buy in bulk, then fill individual member orders) in the U.S. Many of them require members to donate a few hours a month in return for membership. Savings can be substantial—from 20 percent to 50 percent below normal supermarket prices—but in nearly all cases you will have to supplement what you can buy in a co-op with trips to a supermarket.

It is easy enough to check into what kind of co-ops are available in your area. The National Cooperative Business Association (800-636-6222) will give you a list of regional warehouses that supply co-ops. A warehouse in your area can then tell you what clubs it supplies.

▶ START YOUR OWN FOOD CO-OP

We don't belong to a food co-op, but we have developed an informal co-op with four neighbors, all of whom shop at the same warehouse club. First, if we are low on one item that we normally buy in bulk from a warehouse club, we might check to see which of our friends has a visit scheduled next and ask her to buy that item for us.

Because our club is ten miles away, a few phone calls a year save us all both time and the costs of gasoline.

Second, because many items in a warehouse club are sold only in quantities that none of us could individually justify buying, we agree to split up certain purchases. We get big savings this way, but nobody gets stuck with ten years' worth of pickles or pineapple chunks.

▶ USE PRODUCE DEPARTMENT SCALES

Don't use them just to weigh items sold by the pound. When lettuce is sold by the head, the weight difference among heads can amount to as much as 33 percent. "Five-pound" bags of potatoes or apples don't all weigh exactly five pounds; why not buy the one that weighs nearly six?

▶ COMPARE LOOSE VERSUS "BY-THE-BAG" PRODUCE PRICES

Kept in a cool, dry place, potatoes will keep for about a month. If you will use 10 pounds in that time, buying a 10-pound bag (as we recently did for $3.99) beats buying loose (99 cents a pound). The loose potatoes were larger, but we don't find it inconvenient (at a saving of 59 cents a pound) to use an extra couple from the bag when we are baking them.

Yellow onions, which will keep for up to a month, were 59 cents a pound loose, $3.59 for a 10-pound bag. Per pound difference: 23 cents.

▶ MAKE YOUR OWN BABY FOOD . . .

Few parents would want to give up the convenience of prepared baby foods altogether, but you can save a significant amount of money, particularly when fresh fruits and vegetables are in abundant supply, by making baby meals from the same foods you'll be eating. Just put them in a mini–food processor after cooking. Use fresh foods, and don't mix two or more together—babies prefer single flavors. (For some excellent recipes and advice on making and storing your own baby food, see *The Complete New Guide to Preparing Baby Foods* by Sue Castle, $4.99, Bantam Books.)

▶ ... AND CHECK OUT TOYS "R" US

Competitive pricing is always subject to change, but Toys "R" Us does sell baby food, and the last time we checked, its prices were 10 percent lower than our supermarket's for Gerber's brand prepared baby food and formula. Our wholesale club also often sells case quantities of baby food and formula at better-than-supermarket prices.

▶ SAVE WITH FRESH VERSUS CANNED OR FROZEN VEGETABLES

There's a reason to buy one can of mushrooms that will keep indefinitely and can be used at the last minute in an emergency. Otherwise, why not buy fresh? Price per pound: $2.49. Price for a 7-ounce jar (4 ounces drained) of Green Giant whole mushrooms, $1.49 ($5.96 a pound).

Not every example is as dramatic, and store-brand frozen green beans may not cost significantly more than fresh green beans at certain times of the year. But there's normally some kind of saving, and the extra time devoted to washing and cutting fresh beans always seems to us to pay off when they are served.

▶ CONVENIENCE RIP-OFFS: PRODUCE SECTION

- A 16-ounce cellophane package of chopped cabbage and a few bits of carrot labeled "Classic Cole Slaw." Price: $1.59. Three feet away: cabbages at 49 cents a pound. Estimated time to chop a pound of cabbage: 90 seconds. Hourly rate being charged: $44 for the convenience of prechopped greens that are usually dried out.
- A 10-ounce package of shredded carrots. Price: $1.29.

Two feet away: a bunch of carrots ($1^1/_2$ pounds).
Price: 79 cents. Weight after removal of tops and peel-
ing off outer skin: 18 ounces. Adjusted price for 10
ounces: 43.8 cents. Estimated time to remove tops,
peel, and shred 10 ounces of carrots: three minutes.
Hourly rate: $17.00.

■ A 16-ounce package of celery hearts. Price: $1.89. In
the adjacent bin, bunches of celery (weight from 24
to 32 ounces) for 99 cents. Since all that distinguishes
the two kinds of celery is a simple swipe of a chopping
knife (removing the leafy top part of the celery; estimated time: 5 seconds), the price of convenience was
at least $648 an hour.

▶ CONVENIENCE RIP-OFFS: SALAD AND FRUIT BARS

Salad and fruit bars charging a set price per pound or
ounce no matter what you put on your plate have become commonplace in supermarkets and many inexpensive restaurants, especially those catering to office
workers looking for a quick, take-back-to-the-desk
lunch. The price of convenience at all of them is very
high, but it may be unavoidable if you insist on 3 varie-
ties of lettuce and salad dressings, 4 different salad vegetables, and 5 different fruits—all on the same lunch
plate.

If, however, you simply want a plate of 3 different
fruits for a light lunch, you will probably save at least 80
percent by buying the individual fruits in the produce
section and slicing them yourself. If you have coworkers
who share your eating habits, you can multiply your
choices and still save hundreds of dollars a year.

▶ CONVENIENCE RIP-OFFS: BABY FOOD

This is a section of the supermarket where the price of
convenience and individual servings is particularly high.
If you don't want to make a lot of your own baby food

(and food processors, blenders, and food mills make it very simple with many foods), at least compare prices with what's offered in other sections. For instance, six 4-ounce jars of Gerber's apple juice cost $2.79 ($3.72 a quart). Store-brand apple juice was 79 cents a quart (made from concentrate) and 99 cents a quart (not made from concentrate).

▶ CONVENIENCE RIP-OFFS: RICE, PASTA, CEREAL

■ A 10-pound bag of Uncle Ben's converted rice cost $5.99 at a warehouse club ($7.49 at a supermarket). A 7-ounce package of the same rice in four "boil-in" bags cost $1.29. Per pound premium for the convenience of boil-in bags: $2.35 (versus warehouse club), $2.20 (versus supermarket).

■ Five pounds of macaroni cost $2.19 (44 cents a pound) at a warehouse club. The supermarket price of a 7¼-ounce package of Kraft's "Macaroni and Cheese" was 79 cents ($1.74 a pound). For the $1.30 per pound difference, you can buy a lot more and a lot better cheese than the salty stuff inside the pouch included in the convenience package.

■ Quaker Oats instant oatmeal comes in a box that includes 10 pouches of different "with fruit" flavors. Total weight: 13.7 ounces. Price: $3.59, or 35.9 cents per average serving of 1.37 ounces. Quick Quaker Oats are $3.49 for 42 ounces. Add your own fruit and save 24.5 cents a serving.

■ Any cereal with fruit in the box is invariably more expensive than the ingredients warrant, and the fruit is a pale imitation of the real thing. At least in our experience, the raisins in those cereal boxes are often hard and dry. We buy and add our own.

■ While on the subject of cereals, you should also check prices out at health-food stores. Very often, because they buy and sell bran and other cereals, grains, flours, beans, rice, pasta, and other staples generically and in bulk quantities, you'll find prices well below those in your supermarket.

▶ CONVENIENCE RIP-OFFS: FROZEN FOODS

The frozen-foods section of any supermarket is a virtual cornucopia of convenience rip-offs. Just a few:

- A 3.5-ounce "single serve" package of Ore-Ida microwave crinkle-cut french-fried potatoes. Price: 75 cents ($3.43 a pound). Price per pound of a 10-pound bag of russet potatoes: 25 cents. Price of one pound of potatoes (if you cook one for yourself, you can't often buy in large quantities), 49 cents.
- Gorton's Microwave Baked Scrod with Bread Crumbs: $3.19 for a 6-ounce package, or $8.51 a pound. But since the bread crumbs, by our measure, amounted to about 2 ounces of the weight, the price for the frozen scrod was actually $12.76 per pound. Fresh scrod was priced at $5.99 a pound.
- Like buttered vegetables? Add the butter yourself. A 9-ounce package of frozen small peas in a pouch with butter was $1.79, 40 cents more than the same size package of butterless peas.

▶ RETURN CANS AND BOTTLES

This tip appeared for the first time in the third edition because it never occurred to us before then that anyone didn't return bottles and cans for the deposit on them. The results of a survey back in 1994 astonished us: At least one out of four buyers of beer and soda routinely throws returnable cans and bottles away. Not only are these people wasting money; they are also contributing to a growing environmental crisis.

If, like us, you hate the slow machines supermarkets make you use to get your nickel deposits, collect cans and bottles in a big plastic bag until you have enough to make a trip to a large beverage dealer worthwhile. At least in our area, they still take returns the old-fashioned way.

▶ SAVE ON MEAT AND POULTRY

There aren't many bargains in the meat and poultry cases of supermarkets. Many people save by joining a service that makes home deliveries of frozen meats, buying in quantity for storage in home freezers. We tried such a service years ago, didn't like the quality of the frozen food we got, and found we always had the wrong quantities of the wrong things. Also, like many people, we have cut back on the amount of meat we eat these days, so buying in large quantities doesn't make sense for us.

If you have a large family, though, you might want to check into such a service. Look in your Yellow Pages under "Food Plans" or get recommendations from friends. You should be able to save between 10 and 20 percent by buying this way.

You can also take advantage of seasonal fluctuations in the price of different cuts of meat. Steaks and chopped beef are more expensive in the summer months because people are grilling outside. Roasts tend to be less expensive in the summer because many people think of them as "winter" fare. Either buy in quantity in the off-season and freeze, or plan menus around "out-of-season" cuts.

We try not to pay for the convenience of easy butchering. Our supermarket, for instance, was recently selling "pork kabobs"—chunks of pork loin—for $4.99 per pound. The pork loin itself sold for $3.99. There are many other examples of this kind of convenience packaging in the meat case, and you'll have to decide if the convenience is worth the price in each individual case.

▶ BUY LARGE WHOLE TURKEYS AND CHICKENS

There is more meat per pound on a large whole roast chicken than on a small one. Buy a larger one than you need and use the leftovers for inexpensive second and third meals. There are a lot of great ways to use cooked

chicken and turkey; see our cookbook recommendations later in this chapter.

▶ MARINATE LESS COSTLY CUTS OF MEAT

Substituting less expensive round steak for sirloin (just
one example) doesn't have to mean giving up tender-
ness or flavor. Experiment with recipes that call for marinating the meat, and extend the length of marinating
time called for in the recipe.

You can often cut down on the amount of liquid called
for in a marinade, and therefore its cost, if you marinate
in a self-closing plastic bag instead of an open, flat pan.
Less mess, too.

▶ MAKE YOUR OWN SALAD DRESSINGS

Homemade salad dressings, without chemicals and pre-
servatives, taste better than brand-name prepared salad
dressings. That's just an opinion, of course, but if you
share it you can save from 25 to 90 percent on salad
dressings without spending more than five extra minutes a week mixing your own. Try the recipes in any
good general cookbook. Here are three that we use constantly:

■ *Spicy sweet-and-sour dressing.* Mix 1 cup salad oil, $1/3$
cup red wine vinegar, $1/4$ cup chili sauce, $1/4$ cup may-
onnaise, 1 tablespoon sugar, 2 crushed garlic cloves,
pinches of salt and cayenne pepper to taste. Shake all
ingredients in a jar, chill well, and always shake before using. Will keep for a couple of weeks.

■ *Sort-of-French dressing.* Mix $1/2$ cup salad oil, $1/3$ cup
red wine vinegar, 1 teaspoon dry mustard, 1 teaspoon
sugar, 1 teaspoon dry basil or 2 teaspoons finely
minced fresh basil, $1/2$ teaspoon garlic powder, $1/2$ teaspoon freshly grated black pepper, $1/2$ teaspoon salt.
Chill and shake well before using. Will keep for a couple of weeks.

■ *Sort-of-Italian dressing.* Because it will keep for

months, we make this in larger quantities. Mix $1^1/_2$ cups salad oil, 1 cup white vinegar, $^1/_4$ cup sugar, $^1/_2$ cup finely minced onion, 3 teaspoons dry basil, 3 teaspoons oregano. Chill and shake well before using.

Storage: Use old glass jars and bottles that have clean lids that still close tightly. Sterilize them first by simmering (just below boiling temperature) jars and lids separately in a large pot for fifteen minutes.

▶ USE A FOOD PROCESSOR

Why buy bread crumbs when you can make them in seconds from frozen crusts of stale bread you would otherwise have thrown out? A lot of the prepared and processed foods you may be buying now at your supermarket can be made for a lot less money with a food processor. Many processors come with free recipe books that explain how to buy when foods are at their lowest prices, then process and freeze them for later use. Processors are also useful for converting leftovers into appetizing soups, sauces, and casseroles. A good blender will do practically the same job.

▶ START YOUR OWN CONTAINER GARDEN

Too many people think that vegetable gardening is an all-or-nothing proposition, that you can't have a garden unless you cultivate a large area and spend hours a week seeding, weeding, and spraying. Not so. Container gardening allows you to plant enough tomato plants in a half barrel to keep a family of four well supplied with delicious tomatoes for a few weeks—at one tenth the cost of store-bought. A container or windowsill herb garden is easy to tend and is a real money saver. And if you do not have the land available and can devote a couple of hours a week to a small vegetable garden, even 100 square feet is enough to save hundreds of dollars a year.

▶ DON'T TAKE OUT, COOK AHEAD

Anyone with a full-time job knows how tempting it is to stop by a take-out place on the way home from work, or to have dinner delivered. But these are expensive options. Instead, when you are in the mood to cook, prepare such things as casseroles and soups in quantity. Freeze them in portions just big enough for one meal, then bake or microwave a quick, no-fuss dinner whenever you don't feel like cooking.

▶ CHANGE OFFICE EATING HABITS

How much do you spend a year on morning coffee and doughnuts? How much on take-out sandwiches you eat at your desk? If you work in an office in a big city, the answer could easily be as much as $30 a week—$1,500 a year. You can save at least 75 percent by making your own coffee (share a $19.95 coffeemaker and cleanup chores with two or three other penny pinchers in your office) and bringing lunch from home.

▶ INVEST IN A GOOD BASIC COOKBOOK

Many people who have grown up with prepared convenience foods think that cooking is terribly complicated and time-consuming. If you are one of them, a big basic cookbook, one that explains everything, including how to boil water, is likely to persuade you otherwise.

Perhaps you'll go back to the convenience products, but with the step-by-step guidance in these books you can at least experiment. Especially with the labor-saving appliances now available, preparing and cooking foods is far less time-consuming now than it was a generation ago. And as convenience food marketers add gimmicks to their products, prices continue to escalate. A "back to the basics" approach will pay off in better tasting, more nutritious, additive-free meals, in less environment-threatening packaging waste, and in lower food costs.

The book we turn to first for advice is *The Doubleday*

Cookbook by Jean Anderson and Elaine Hanna (Double-day, $35 list price). It is the most expensive of the good basic books (*The Joy of Cooking* and *The Good House-keeping Cookbook* are other good choices), but it is also mammoth—984 pages long and truly comprehensive.

2

Holding Down Utility and House Expenses

Despite the progress we have made in the past quarter century, Americans remain the greatest wasters of energy in the world. Although we have seen energy costs soar since 1972, and have become far more aware of environmental costs as well, habits developed over generations of cheap and seemingly limitless energy have died hard.

If you own an average-size home and haven't yet focused on saving energy, you should find it easy to lop a few hundred dollars a year off your energy bill. The first thing you should know is what your energy dollar buys. Based on national averages, the Department of Energy estimates that 46 percent of it goes to heat and/or cool your house. An additional 15 percent is spent on heating water. Refrigerators and freezers use 15 percent. The remaining 24 percent goes into lighting, cooking, and running appliances.

This chapter is filled with tips that will help you cut

your costs in each one of these areas. It will also tell you where to go for more technical advice on major projects such as replacing heating equipment or installing solar energy. For tips about buying energy-saving appliances, see Chapter 5.

If you rent a home or apartment and pay utility bills, many of the energy-saving tips in this chapter will apply to you. If you don't pay for utilities, see what your landlord thinks about a serious effort on your part to cut costs. Especially if your apartment is separately metered, you might be able to work out a way to share his or her savings.

Other tips in this chapter can be categorized as general "household hints." There are a number of good books, including those by Mary Ellen and Heloise, that list an astonishing array of hints on everything from treating diaper rash to making bookends out of two upholstered bricks.

This book doesn't attempt to duplicate what's in the household-hints books. Our tips are limited to those we genuinely believe may save you dollars, not pennies, and don't involve a lot of extra time. Not that spending the time to do it yourself isn't the best as well as the most obvious way to save money when you own a house. If you always pay a plumber to fix a leaky faucet or a painter to put a new coat of paint on your bedroom walls, you are either very rich or very foolish. You most certainly are not a penny pincher.

Learning how to do a few basic repairs around the house is not that difficult, even if you've never held a hammer. Buy a good, well-illustrated, single-volume do-it-yourself reference and turn to it first when something needs fixing. (We depend on *Reader's Digest Complete Do-It-Yourself Manual.*)

Another resource you should cultivate and use is your local hardware store. We have carried leaky faucets into ours and gotten advice that saved us a $60 plumbing bill for the price of a 35-cent washer. We're grateful and still buy there. But in the past few years we have also come to rely on the giant Home Depot discount warehouse in our area. It has some knowledgeable salespeople, consistently low prices, and an enormous range of items in stock.

The few do-it-yourself-type tips in this chapter won't help you fix anything that needs major repair work. They may help, however, when something is so simple to fix that you would be seriously embarrassed had you called in a service person. Finally, you'll find tips that suggest cheap substitutes for expensive brand-name products everyone uses around the house.

▶ SAVE 20 PERCENT ON WATER HEATING

Hot water is usually the second most expensive item on your total annual energy bill, right after heating the house. Consider doing these simple things and save at least 20 percent a year:

- Buy and install a programmable water heater timer (about $100). How often do you need hot water at 3:00 A.M.?
- Buy and install an insulation blanket (about $25) to put on your water heater, especially if it feels very warm to the touch. All water heaters lose some heat through the walls of the tank. Depending on how well yours is insulated, a blanket could save up to 10 percent on your water-heating bills.
- Drain sediment and mineral deposits regularly—at least every three or four months—from the bottom of your water heater. If you haven't done this in years, though, have a plumber check it out first to reduce the risk of creating a serious leak.
- Lower your water-heater temperature from 140 degrees F to 125 degrees F. This is more than hot enough for bathing and washing clothes. Note: Check first to see if the lower temperature meets the specifications for your dishwasher. Some require the higher temperature.
- Wait until your dishwasher is full before turning it on.

One less load per week can save you as much as $50 a year.

- Fix any faucet drip, of course, but fix a hot-water-faucet drip immediately. It could easily add $25 a month to your fuel costs.

- Replace your showerhead with a low-flow head (about $20). This is simply a matter of unscrewing the old showerhead and installing a new one. Two people each showering five minutes a day will use over 18,000 gallons of hot water a year. With a low-flow head, you can cut that by as much as 8,000 gallons and pay for the new showerhead in less than three months.

- Take showers, not baths. A shower using a low-flow head produces a flow of about 3 gallons a minute, approximately 15 gallons for 5 minutes. It takes 30 gallons of water to fill the average tub. Assuming you use half-hot and half-cold water, the 5-minute shower saves $7^1/2$ gallons of hot water each time you substitute it for a bath. You can more than double that saving if you are spartan enough to use the next tip.

- Take a boat shower. Anyone who has lived on a small boat, where saving water is a necessity, knows the routine: Get wet quickly, turn the shower off immediately, lather up, turn the shower back on, and rinse off as quickly as possible. Yes, we know that a long hot shower is one of life's great pleasures for many people, but if you can change the habit, you'll save from $75 to $125 a year while helping to conserve a precious, dwindling resource.

- Try using a cold-water detergent and cold water for most laundry loads. We've found that only very dirty or greasy laundry needs hot water.

- Install aerators in bathroom and kitchen faucets. They cost a few dollars apiece and, by reducing the amount of hot water used, pay for themselves within a year.

- Insulate hot-water pipes. This will reduce the heat lost through the pipe walls as hot water flows from your water heater to the faucet. You will also save gallons of water by reducing the time needed to bring hot water to the faucet when you first turn the water on.

▶ CLEAN YOUR FURNACE AND FILTERS

If you have an oil burner, it pays to have the furnace cleaned and properly adjusted once a year. You can easily save 10 percent a year. At least once every two months during the heating season, clean the air filters on forced warm-air furnaces.

▶ LIGHT A CANDLE NEAR YOUR DOORS AND WINDOWS

The easiest way to check on whether your doors and windows need better weather stripping and/or caulking is to move a lighted candle around the frames. You'll know immediately if air is passing through.

▶ CAULK AND WEATHER-STRIP

Caulking and weather stripping two doors and a dozen windows should cost less than $50. Savings in annual energy costs could amount to 10 percent or more.

▶ SEAL ALL KINDS OF AIR LEAKS

Even in otherwise well-insulated houses, there may be drafts around electrical outlets and where plumbing and electrical wiring go through walls, floors, and doors. Check for drafts and seal with caulk and weather stripping.

▶ INSULATE FLOORS OVER UNHEATED SPACES

Even in newer homes, insulation during construction was sometimes skipped over unheated spaces such as garages and crawl spaces. Any do-it-yourself reference will show you how easy insulating is to do, and you'll cut energy bills significantly. One of the best short do-it-yourself guides is free from Owens-Corning Fiberglass. Call 800-438-7465 and ask for their *Homeowner's Guide to Insulation and Energy Savings.*

▶ SEAL THE BASE OF THE HOUSE

If the base of a house is exposed, as in the case of mobile homes, build an insulated "skirt" around it.

▶ BUY HEATING OIL IN THE SUMMER

You can nearly always save 10 to 20 percent by having your tank filled during the summer months, instead of waiting for a regular delivery in the fall.

▶ JOIN A FUEL-OIL-BUYING CO-OP

You can save a few cents a gallon, and perhaps more, by joining one of the local fuel-buying cooperatives that seem to be springing up all over the country. There is no national association to call, but check your Yellow Pages under "Oils-Fuel" or check with local consumer organizations.

▶ TAKE ADVANTAGE OF UTILITY OFF-PEAK USAGE DISCOUNTS

In some areas of the country, electric utilities offer residential customers cheaper rates at certain times of the day. If yours is one of them, it is easy to run your dishwasher, washer, and dryer at off-peak times and cut your electric bills by a few dollars a month.

▶ USE CEILING FANS

Ceiling fans use less than one tenth as much electricity as a room air conditioner. If it is too hot for a ceiling fan alone to keep a room comfortable, you will still save money by turning the fan on along with the air-conditioning. Because a good ceiling fan can make you feel from five to seven degrees cooler, you don't need to set the thermostat of your air conditioner as low.

▶ USE VENTILATING FANS SPARINGLY

One of those ventilating fans in the kitchen or bathroom is capable of blowing away a houseful of warmed or cooled air in just one hour. Turn them off quickly after they've done their jobs.

▶ OPEN A WINDOW NEAR YOUR FIREPLACE

It may seem strange, but if you open a window near the fireplace by about half an inch, air needed by the fire will be drawn from the outside instead of from the (expensive) heated air in the house.

▶ USE GLASS FIREPLACE DOORS

Those wonderful old-fashioned open-hearth fires create a draft that draws air heated by your furnace right up the chimney. They definitely remove more heat than they give off. If you use your fireplace often, a set of glass fireplace doors ($100 and up) will stop the draft that allows warm air to escape.

▶ CLOSE YOUR FIREPLACE DAMPER

Once the fire is completely out, close the damper immediately. It can let up to 8 percent of the heat in your house exit via the chimney.

Don't have a damper? Install one immediately. That 8 percent heating loss adds up to a lot of dollars going up the chimney every year.

▶ WEAR A SWEATER INSIDE

Most people discover they are just as comfortable wearing a sweater with the thermostat set at from 66 to 68 degrees F as they are without one with the thermostat set from 68 to 70. You will save about 2 percent of your heating bill for each degree you lower the thermostat.

▶ GET CREATIVE WITH YOUR THERMOSTAT

Turn it to its lowest setting when you'll be away for even a couple of days. Turn it down before a party—a crowd will generate heat. If you don't have a clock thermostat that you can preset for lower temperatures at night, or for during days when no one will be in the house, it is a good investment.

▶ USE A HUMIDIFIER

The thermostat can be set lower if there is sufficient humidity in the air.

▶ USE SHADES AND DRAPERIES

During cold weather, open them on sunny windows during the day and close them at night. During warm weather, do the opposite.

▶ AIM AIR-CONDITIONER VENTS UP

Hot air rises, cold air falls. Air circulation will be more efficient and energy costs less if you aim an air conditioner's vents up. Keep the unit away from drapes, furniture, doors—anything that might interfere with air circulation. Also make sure it isn't near appliances that heat up or in direct sunlight (the outside part of the unit as well as the inside).

▶ GET A FREE ENERGY AUDIT

There are a number of ways to save on energy costs involving such things as boiler efficiency, but it is best to get advice that can be applied to your own specific needs. In most areas, there is an easy way to do this. Call your local utility and ask if they will send a conservation expert to your house to do a complete energy review. Many utilities offer this service without charge; others charge a small fee. It is always a worthwhile expenditure. After the inspection, most will give you an individualized computer printout that will recommend various energy-saving measures. The printout will also tell you how much these measures are likely to cost and how much each one will save on your annual energy bill.

▶ GET PAID BY YOUR UTILITY

In some areas of the country, local utilities will pay part of the costs you incur to make your home more energy-efficient. It takes just a phone call to see if yours is one of them, and what it will pay for.

▶ GET BACK YOUR SECURITY DEPOSIT

Another quick call to your utility, if you paid a security deposit to them when you first moved into your home. After you establish a decent record of timely payments, you should get your security back plus interest. Ask for it.

▶ TURN OFF ELECTRIC STOVE BURNERS EARLY

Your stove is a major user of electric power, so get in the habit of turning off the burners a couple of minutes before the necessary cooking time is up. The heating element on an electric burner stays hot for about that long after it is turned off.

Do the same with either a gas or electric oven. If you don't open the door, an efficient oven will maintain its temperature for five to seven minutes after being turned off.

Have you been in the habit of leaving a pot of food on the burner or in the oven for minutes after turning them off? Now you know why you have been overcooking things.

▶ BOIL WATER IN A CLOSED POT OR KETTLE

It takes twice as long and costs twice as much if you bring water to a boil in an open pot. Don't boil any more water than you need, either. Why fill a teakettle half-full and spend seven minutes' worth of heating time when the ³/₄ cup you want will come to a boil in three minutes?

▶ USE SMALLER PANS

Use the smallest pans possible; they require less energy.

▶ MATCH THE PAN TO THE BURNER

If you put a 6-inch pan on an 8-inch burner, about 40 percent of the heat produced will be wasted.

▶ KEEP AN INSULATED CARAFE NEXT TO YOUR COFFEEMAKER

After the coffee is made, pour it into a thermos bottle or carafe and turn the electric coffeemaker off. You can save a few dollars a year by not using the coffeemaker's "keep warm" feature.

▶ BUY A SLOW COOKER

If you often cook foods that require long cooking times, such as casseroles, stews, and soups, using an inexpensive slow cooker like a Crock-Pot will soon pay for itself.

▶ USE TOASTER OVENS AND MICROWAVES

Use your regular oven only when necessary. Full-size regular ovens use four times as much electricity to accomplish the same cooking task as microwave ovens. Toaster ovens are more efficient, too. But don't use your microwave to boil water; a stovetop burner is more efficient for this task.

▶ SELF-CLEAN OVENS WHILE THEY'RE HOT

If you have a self-cleaning oven, the best time to turn it on is immediately after you've cooked a meal. The oven will still be hot and less energy will be required.

▶ USE A PRESSURE COOKER

Pressure cookers save energy by reducing cooking time by from 25 to 50 percent.

▶ KEEP YOUR FREEZER FULL

Because food retains cold more efficiently than air, a half-empty freezer actually costs more to operate than a full one. If you don't have anything else to put in a freezer, load it up with plastic containers of water.

▶ CLEAN THE CONDENSER COILS ON YOUR REFRIGERATOR

Unfortunately, they're not very conveniently located, so it's easy to forget about them. But you'll never ignore them again after you've watched a $75-a-visit service person get your refrigerator back in peak condition simply by vacuuming the condenser coils.

At least twice a year, pull your refrigerator away from the wall, unplug it, and vacuum or brush off the coils you'll see on the back of the machine. The dust and dirt that collect there seriously reduce its operating efficiency. If allowed to build up, in fact, the grime can totally block the heat transfer between the coils and the outside air and cause a breakdown of the refrigerator.

When you push the refrigerator back in, make sure that air can circulate freely around the condenser coils. There should be a minimum of $1^1/_4$ inches of space between the wall and the refrigerator.

▶ CHECK REFRIGERATOR DOORS

The easiest way to do this is to put a dollar bill in the door when you close it. If the seal on the door doesn't hold the bill firmly in place, it is not working properly. New seals for refrigerators and freezers are not cheap and should be installed by experienced repair people. Before doing so, consider whether you might not be better off buying a new, energy-efficient model (see Chapter 5).

► CHECK YOUR REFRIGERATOR'S TEMPERATURE

Don't depend on the settings inside your refrigerator and freezer. Check temperatures with an accurate thermometer every month or so. They should be between 38 and 40 degrees F in the refrigerator and within one degree of 0 F, either plus or minus, in the freezer. Keeping a freezer at minus 10 degrees can increase energy use by as much as 20 percent.

► INSTALL A GREENPLUG

If you have an older, energy-inefficient refrigerator, you can reduce its use of electricity by as much as 20 percent by plugging it into a device called a GreenPlug®, available for about $35 at some hardware stores and from *Ecological Innovations* (see tip below).

► COOL AND COVER FOODS BEFORE STORING

Let hot foods cool off before putting them in the refrigerator or freezer, and cover all foods, especially soups and other liquids, to avoid releasing moisture and raising the temperature.

► USE WAXED PAPER AND STORAGE CONTAINERS

Washing and saving old aluminum foil (recommended in all those household-hint books) seems to us to be taking penny pinching to extreme limits. Nor do we wash and reuse every plastic bag in which we have stored leftover food. But it is easy to save money by adopting two simple, environmentally friendly ways of storing and cooking food:

■ Use waxed paper. Plastic wrap (at least twice as expensive) is better for certain kinds of storage, but biodegradable waxed paper is just as good or even preferable for some food wrapping (sandwiches to be eaten within a couple of hours) and for microwave cooking.

■ Store leftovers in reusable glass or plastic containers. If they are sealed tightly, food will stay fresh longer and you'll cut way back on your use of expensive wraps and disposable bags.

▶ USE COLD WATER WITH YOUR GARBAGE DISPOSAL

Two reasons: Hot water costs extra money, and cold water solidifies grease so it can be ground up by the unit and efficiently washed away.

▶ USE A SPONGE

Too many people habitually use a paper towel every time they clean off a kitchen countertop. That can cost a few more dollars a year than using a sponge. Also, extend the life of a sponge by cleaning it the easy way— put it into your dishwasher.

▶ LET YOUR DISHES AIR-DRY

You can save up to 10 percent of the cost of using your dishwasher with the automatic air-dry switch available on new models. If your unit doesn't have such a switch, you can get the same saving simply by turning off the control knob after the final rinse. Prop the door open a little and the dishes will dry faster.

▶ PRESOAK HEAVILY SOILED CLOTHING

You'll avoid two washings and save energy.

▶ DRY CLOTHES IN CONSECUTIVE LOADS

Stop-and-start drying uses more energy because a lot goes into warming the dryer to the desired temperature each time you begin. Also separate drying loads into heavy and lightweight items; the dryer won't have to stay on as long for the lighter loads.

▶ CHECK FILTERS AND HOSES

It doesn't take much of a buildup of lint to reduce a dryer's efficiency and add extra dollars to your electric bill. Check hoses every couple of months and filters after every other use.

▶ REMEMBER THE OLD-FASHIONED CLOTHESLINE

A lot of people have forgotten the ultimate energy saver. As a bonus, clothes dried outside often seem fresher than they do when you use an electric or gas dryer.

▶ IRON WHILE YOU SHOWER

Hang clothes in the bathroom while you are showering. The steam will remove wrinkles, saving you both ironing time and energy costs.

▶ DO A LIGHTBULB AUDIT OF THE HOUSE

Most Americans overlight their homes. Room by room, analyze how much light is really needed. In many areas of a normal house, such as hallways, basements, and attics, replacing lightbulbs with bulbs of lower wattage is an easy way to cut electric bills.

▶ FINALLY! A USE FOR BURNED-OUT LIGHTBULBS

Many older houses are overlit and have fixtures that require two, three, or four bulbs. In nonworking space areas where light can be reduced, put one burned-out bulb in a multiple light fixture. It is safer to have a bulb in a live socket, but the burned-out bulb won't use any electricity.

▶ AVOID LONGLIFE BULBS

A longlife incandescent bulb in a hard-to-reach place can make sense, but they are less energy-efficient than normal bulbs, so shouldn't be used generally.

▶ SWITCH TO FLUORESCENT LIGHTS

State-of-the-art compact fluorescents are ecologically friendly and can save significant amounts of money despite their high initial cost. That's because they use about 75 percent less electricity to produce the same amount of light as incandescent bulbs. They also last about ten times as long.

Compact fluorescent lights have the same threaded base as incandescent bulbs and provide soft, warm light comparable to an ordinary bulb. Currently none of them provides light output quite as high as a 100-watt incandescent, however, so consider them only for replacing lower-wattage bulbs—40, 60, 75, and sometimes 100—that get a good deal of use or are in hard-to-reach fixtures.

An 18-watt compact fluorescent, used in place of a 75-watt bulb, will save about 600 kilowatt hours over an expected lifetime of 10,000 hours. If you pay 10 cents per kilowatt hour in your area, that's a saving of $60. The initial price of the fluorescent—about $25—is higher than the total price of the 10 to 15 incandescent bulbs (each with an expected life of 750 hours) it would replace. Nevertheless, you will still save close to 50 percent.

More and more lighting stores and home-improvement discounters such as Home Depot have begun carrying good selections of compact fluorescent lights. Or order from the *Ecological Innovations* catalog (see below).

A few utilities have a rebate program for each compact fluorescent bulb you install. Check to see if yours is one of them.

▶ CALL 800-876-0660 FOR A FREE CATALOG OF ENERGY SAVERS

You'll find many of the energy, water, and lighting products recommended in this chapter in the free catalog offered by *Ecological Innovations*. This mail-order supplier is an offshoot of the Energy Federation, Inc., a nonprofit organization that promotes conservation technologies and products. The prices are fair and the catalog also answers many commonly asked questions about energy and resource conservation.

▶ CALL 800-523-2929 WITH ANY ENERGY CONSERVATION QUESTION

This is the number of the Department of Energy's Conservation and Renewable Energy Inquiry and Referral Service (CAREIRS). Your taxes pay for it, but few people seem to realize that information on the full spectrum of renewable energy technologies and energy conservation is available free.

If CAREIRS itself can't answer your questions about such matters as active and passive solar energy, alcohol fuels, wind energy, and the like, they will refer you to appropriate trade or professional associations, federal agencies, or state and local groups.

▶ BUY A BATTERY CHARGER

A nickel-cadmium battery charger with six rechargeable batteries (2 each of 3 sizes) cost $12.99 at our warehouse club last year. Packages of two nonrechargeable batteries cost between $1.99 and $2.79 at our hardware store. We expect to save at least $25 to $40 a year. If you have children who play with lots of battery-operated toys, or if you or teenage children are heavy users of something like a portable cassette player, your savings could easily add up to $200 or more in a year.

▶ TURN OFF THAT SECOND REFRIGERATOR

Except for central air-conditioning, a refrigerator is the single largest devourer of electricity in most homes—responsible for from 10 to 15 percent of most monthly bills. So it makes sense to operate one large refrigerator/freezer rather than two small ones. The next time we buy a new one, we plan to take our own advice. In the meanwhile, we cram everything possible into the unit in our kitchen, and turn on the old unit in the cellar no more than two or three times a year, when we need the extra room before Christmas or a big party.

▶ DON'T PUT BRICKS IN YOUR TOILET TANK

This often-recommended technique for saving water in older, pre-low-flush toilets usually doesn't work. Chances are, you'll find you often have to flush twice instead of once—an annoyance as well as a waste of water. Better to experiment by lowering the water level an inch or so (just bend the float rod or make a screwdriver adjustment, depending on the type of assembly in the tank). If the toilet still operates efficiently, you'll save a significant amount of water. If not, unbend the float rod a bit until it does.

▶ CHANGE TOOTH-BRUSHING HABITS

Actually, change just one pointless habit shared by millions of people: allowing the water to run while brushing. Wet the brush, turn off the water, apply toothpaste, brush, then turn the water back on to rinse. Savings: In a family of four, each brushing two times a day, from 20,000 to 30,000 gallons of water a year (cost in our area: $25 to $35).

▶ SWITCH TO LOW-FLUSH TOILETS

Since about 1980, most new and remodeled bathrooms have been equipped with "water-conserving" toilets, which typically use about 3.5 gallons per flush instead of the 7 that was the standard for the preceding half a century. In the past few years, efficient "low-flush" toilets, which use only 1.6 gallons, have been widely introduced.

Over 35 percent of residential water use in this country is directly attributable to the flushing of toilets, so the environmental benefits of toilets that use less water are compelling. As far as saving money is concerned, especially if you live in an area where water is expensive, replacing a 7-gallon water-waster with a new low-flush toilet will probably pay for itself in from two to five years.

It's easy to work out your own math yourself. *Example:* six flushes a day times 5.4 gallons (7 gallons minus 1.6 gallons) times 350 days a year you are in the house equals 11,340 wasted gallons a year. If you pay $4 per thousand gallons of water (check your water bill for your actual cost), that's $45.36 wasted each year. A new toilet will cost $100 to $250 plus a plumber's installation charge.

▶ CHECK YOUR WATER METER

A year ago, after two quarterly water bills that seemed ridiculously high, we had our water company check the meter. The meter was fine, but they discovered a leak in the system. Now, a couple of times a year, we turn off the main valve, check the meter, wait an hour or two, and check the meter again. If there is ever any difference at all in the readings, however slight, we will call the water company right away.

▶ USE CHEAP BUT GOOD SUBSTITUTES: BAKING SODA

It is hard for many people to accept, but a lot of brand-name products are no better at certain tasks than some simple, cheap alternatives that our great-grandparents knew about. In many cases, the only active ingredient in the brand-name products is the alternative; what you pay dearly for are things like fragrances, fancy packages, and brand images.

This is not to say that because plain baking soda has a multitude of possible uses, it is as effective in all of them as any brand-name product. It isn't. Until the introduction of fluoride toothpaste, a good case could be made that baking soda was as effective a dentrifice as anything else. It no longer is.

What follows, then, is not a complete catalog of all the ways you might use baking soda. But we believe baking soda is still superior to, or at least equally as effective as, branded products for these uses:

- *As a carpet deodorizer.* Sprinkle it on a dry carpet, brush it in a bit, leave for at least an hour, then vacuum.
- *To remove odors from refrigerators and freezers.* Keep an open box in your refrigerator as a preventative.
- *To clean and deodorize thermos bottles, coffeepots, etc.* Use it just as you would any cleaning powder.
- *As a general scouring powder.* Baking soda is an effective cleaning agent for pots and pans, stovetops, etc. Good on porcelain because it is less abrasive than other scouring powders.
- *As a toilet-bowl cleaner.*
- *As an antacid.* If you are on a low-sodium diet or have other medical reasons to avoid sodium bicarbonate (baking soda), check with your doctor first. But sodium bicarbonate is the only active ingredient in many brand-name antacids sold for twenty or thirty times what it will cost you by the teaspoon out of a plain baking-soda box. Just add a teaspoon to a 6-ounce glass of water.
- *As a fire extinguisher.* Keep a box next to the stove to use in case of a small grease fire. Water won't work on a grease fire and will probably make it worse.

Want more? The Arm & Hammer Company (800-524-1328) will send you a free wheel guide to other uses of baking soda.

▶ USE CHEAP BUT GOOD SUBSTITUTES: WHITE VINEGAR

White vinegar is just as good or better than brand-name products for these uses:

- *To scour copper pans.* Mix $1/2$ tablespoon salt with $1/4$ cup of vinegar. Scrub on, remove with water, then wipe dry to shine.
- *To clean and shine chromium faucets.* Wipe on, wipe off with a paper towel.
- *To remove coffee oil residue.* Once a week, soak and then scrub the filter holder of your coffeemaker with vinegar diluted in an equal amount of water. You can also use a vinegar-water mix in your automatic coffeemaker, turning it on after you insert a clean filter. After all of the vinegar solution has come through, repeat the process using plain water to rinse.
- *To remove soap residue* from clothing, add a half cup of vinegar to your washer's last rinse cycle. This is safe for most fabrics and will also eliminate static cling.

▶ USE CHEAP BUT GOOD SUBSTITUTES: MINERAL OIL

- *Instead of baby oil.* Actually, baby oil is mineral oil plus a fragrance.
- *To remove eye makeup.* Read the ingredients on your current brand's package. Mineral oil is the only active ingredient.

▶ USE CHEAP BUT GOOD SUBSTITUTES: CORNSTARCH

- *Instead of talcum powder.* It is at least ten times as absorbent, and it is pure enough to use as a baby powder.
- *As a carpet cleaner.* Probably not as effective on hard-to-remove stains as some other products, but an effective absorbent powder for general use and safe on any

fabric. Brush it on, leave for at least an hour, then vacuum. Mix 1 cup of cornstarch with 2 tablespoons of ground cloves and 2 cups of baking soda to deodorize as well as clean carpets. Leave on overnight before vacuuming.

- *For grease stains.* Shake on, let dry, brush off.
- *After polishing furniture* with furniture oil, sprinkle on a little cornstarch and wipe off. It will absorb oil and help maintain a finger-proof surface.

▶ MAKE YOUR OWN WINDOW-CLEANING FLUID

There are a number of cheap alternatives to the expensive blue stuff inside that fancy brand-name spray bottle. Save the pump sprayer and the bottle, but when it is empty fill it instead with:

- 2 ounces household ammonia mixed with one quart of water. Good for most jobs. If you miss the color of the expensive stuff, add a drop of blue food coloring; it won't do any harm.
- 2 ounces household ammonia, 4 ounces rubbing alcohol, and half a teaspoon of dishwater detergent mixed with one quart of water. Helps keep windows frost-free.
- A mixture of white vinegar and warm water in equal parts is also effective, if you prefer not to use ammonia.
- 1 ounce of deodorized kerosene mixed with a quart of water is particularly effective on extremely dirty, greasy windows.

To avoid streaking, don't wash windows when they are in direct sunlight. All cleaners can damage painted surfaces; wash them off quickly with plain water and dry. Using old newspapers is cheap but messy; we prefer paper towels.

▶ ON-LINE HELP IN STAIN REMOVAL

You can get a fast answer to a sudden "how do I get that stain out?" question on the Internet. Use a search site such as Yahoo (http://www.yahoo.com) to locate sites sponsored by companies like Du Pont which have home pages that offer stain-removal advice about their own products. Cutting across product lines are two sites that offer advice on removing a wide variety of common household stains:

- *University of Illinois Cooperative Extension Services* (http://www.ag.uiuc.edu/~robsond/solutions/consumer/stain.html)
- *Mississippi State University Cooperative Extension Service* (http://www.ces.msstate.edu/pubs/pub1400.htm)

▶ FREEZE CANDLES BEFORE USING

Not only will they burn more slowly, saving money, candles will also burn more evenly and with minimal wax dripping if you put them in the freezer for a few hours before lighting.

▶ PLUMBING: QUICK AND EASY FIXES

- *For running toilets.* The odds are that all you need is a new flapper or tank ball. Turn off the water valve under the toilet, take the tank cover off, and unscrew the ball or (in newer assemblies) lift off the flapper. Buy a new one ($3 to $6), install (it will come with instructions, but essentially you are just reversing the procedure by which you removed the old one), and turn the water back on. If the toilet still runs, check out other possible solutions in a good do-it-yourself repair book.
- *For clogged drains.* Try a plunger first. It will usually work. You can avoid most clogged drains in kitchen sinks, usually the result of grease deposits, by pouring a half cup of baking soda and a half cup of vinegar down the drain once a month. Wait fifteen minutes, then flush with hot water.
- *For obstructed showerheads.* Unscrew, soak in a half-and-half solution of vinegar and water, then remove

sediment using a small brush. If this doesn't work, buy and install a new one.

■ *For leaky faucets.* Buy an inexpensive box of assorted washers at any hardware store or discounter. The next time a faucet leaks, just turn off the valve controlling its water supply, loosen the packing nut at the top of the handle with an adjustable wrench taped to prevent scratching, and remove the handle. Then remove the entire valve assembly, unscrew the old washer at the bottom of the unit, and replace it.

▶ APPLIANCES AND ELECTRIC CORDS: QUICK AND EASY FIXES

■ *For defective electric-stove burners.* Turn off the stove, pull up the burner, and unplug it from its outlet. Do the same thing with a working burner of the same size. Replace the defective burner with the working burner. Turn it on. If it works now, all you have to do is buy a replacement at an appliance store. If it doesn't, call the repair service.

■ *For clothes dryers that won't heat.* It is embarrassing to call in an expert to clean lint from the filter inside the dryer or the one you'll find in the venting pipe. That's often the only problem, though.

■ *For loose or damaged electric plugs.* Buy a snap-on plug for about $3. All you have to do is cut the old plug off the cord, push the cord into the new plug, and snap it shut. No involved knot-tying and handling of wires is necessary. Snap-on plugs work on the kind of flat cord used with most lamps and appliances.

▶ DOORS: QUICK AND EASY FIXES

■ *For stuck door locks.* Buy a tube of graphite at the hardware store and squirt it into the keyhole. Work it in by turning the key a few times.

■ *For doors that won't latch.* First check the hinges and tighten loose ones with a screwdriver. If that alone doesn't solve the problem, put some colored chalk on the latch bolt, close the door, and see how far from the hole in the strike plate it hits. Usually the difference is so slight that you can tap the top or bottom edge of the strike plate with a small hammer, enlarging the hole enough to allow the bolt to engage.

■ *For doors that won't slide.* Clean and wipe the tracks of the sliding door assembly. Then spray with a high-viscosity silicone product such as It or, in a pinch, rub the tracks down with a bar of soap.

▶ USE A MANUFACTURER'S HELP LINE

Many appliance manufacturers offer free technical assistance by telephone to help you resolve minor problems without calling an expensive repair person. Among them: *General Electric* (800-626-2000); *Maytag* (800-688-9900); and *Whirlpool* (800-253-1301). In addition to explaining the problem, you'll need to tell the technician you speak to your model number, serial number, and date of purchase.

Check Internet sites for all of the above companies as well. By the time you read this, they should be up and running and perhaps offering even more help than they can by telephone.

▶ RENTERS: GET INTEREST ON SECURITY DEPOSITS

It's the law in some states. Even where it isn't, tell your landlord you expect to be paid the going amount of interest on your security deposit. When you renew a lease, ask for your initial security deposit back—plus interest. If you have been an exemplary tenant, you might just get it back. Demand the interest in any case.

▶ GET THE LANDLORD TO PAY FOR DO-IT-YOURSELF PROJECTS

Many people who rent would love to build in some bookcases or make other significant improvements in their living space, but don't do so because a) they need the landlord's permission; and b) they don't want to spend money on improvements that eventually will just make the apartment more valuable for the landlord.

If you show your landlord what you want to do and he thinks it makes sense, he may be willing to pay for all of your materials. After all, he's getting your labor free and he'll benefit eventually from the improvement.

▶ SHARING A RENTAL IS CHEAPER

Renting a larger apartment but sharing the cost with a roommate or roommates is nearly always much cheaper than renting on your own.

▶ WATER YOUR GARDEN AND LAWN AT NIGHT

At noon on a sunny summer day, probably half the water a lawn sprinkler throws on your lawn evaporates before it does any good. If you water at night, you can cut back significantly on the amount used. Your grass, flowers, and shrubs won't know the difference.

▶ GET THE MOST FOR YOUR FERTILIZER DOLLAR

A 25-pound bag of fertilizer for $20 may not be a better buy than another at $25. The easiest way to judge is by nitrogen content; a higher count is worth more.

▶ MAKE YOUR OWN PESTICIDE

It won't work on every bug or pest, but most of them will avoid this environmentally friendly, homemade spray formula:

Put 2 heads of garlic, 3 onions, and 4 teaspoons of Tabasco (or any hot-pepper sauce) in a blender with a pint of water. Liquefy the garlic and onions. Thoroughly mix the result with a tablespoon of liquid soap and another pint of water.

▶ PLANT DECIDUOUS TREES TO THE SOUTH AND WEST

Trees and vines that lose their leaves in the winter can cut your costs of heating and cooling significantly. Plant them on the south and west sides of your house; they will provide shade in the summer but allow sunshine in during the winter.

▶ TRY A PUSH LAWN MOWER

Unless you live on a third of an acre or more, it won't take much more effort or time to use a nonpower push lawn mower instead of a smoky gas guzzler. Most people are surprised at how little effort is needed to push one of the well-made new models. You'll cut your annual mower maintenance bills by at least 300 percent (a bit of lubricating oil and an occasional blade sharpening will do it), save on gas, save at least 100 percent on the initial price of the mower, and reduce air pollution. And most of us can use the extra exercise.

▶ RELOCATE

The ultimate way to reduce housing costs may be to take advantage of the wide disparity in housing and living costs in different parts of the United States. Utility costs and taxes may be 75 percent less for similar houses in two different areas. A house with a market value of $250,000 in one area might be duplicated for less than $100,000 in another.

Places Rated Almanac by David Savageau and Richard Boyer (Prentice-Hall Press) is a good source of information on housing costs in 343 metropolitan areas in the United States. You'll find it in most libraries.

3

Spending Less on Computers, Phones, and the Information Revolution

The first three editions of this book avoided offering tips on buying and using personal computers for three reasons:

- In the early 1990s, only a small percentage of people were using PCs at home.
- Beyond software that helped with personal finance and tax preparation, there didn't seem to be much penny pinching involved in using a PC.
- Our own experience with buying and using PCs—during the past 10 years we have upgraded from an original IBM PC to a 286 to a 486 to a 486 with a Pentium overdrive chip—has made it painfully obvious that specific advice on buying anything was usually hopelessly outdated within six months after it was written. That also happens to be the time frame between our delivering this manuscript to the publisher and the finished book reaching bookstores.

The first two of these three reasons are no longer true. While the majority of homes still don't have a PC, most industry forecasters believe that will change before the year 2000. And the explosive growth of on-line services and the Internet's World Wide Web has opened up a new world of consumer-oriented services that are useful for anyone interested in saving money. Nearly every chapter of this fourth edition includes at least one or two penny-pinching tips that require using a PC and a modem.

The third reason previous editions hadn't included computer tips hasn't really changed. In fact, we don't believe anyone, including Bill Gates, could write a book in 1996 that told you with absolute certainty what computer equipment you will want to have in 1998. The experts who are predicting that the majority of homes will have some kind of computer capability by the year 2000 hedge their bets when it comes to what form that capability will take. Some believe that the PC as we now know it won't even exist in a few years. It will be replaced by some kind of hybrid machine that will combine the capabilities of television, computers, telephones, and who knows what else.

We don't, and you certainly aren't reading this book to get our predictions. There are at least a few tips about computers we can pass along, however, that will probably be useful no matter what revolutionary changes occur in the next couple of years.

Back in 1984, the breakup of AT&T was a momentous event in terms of revolutionizing how we all buy telephone equipment and services. By 1996, most of us had become accustomed to choosing from what once seemed to be a bewildering array of equipment, services, competing long-distance carriers, and billing options.

If you think you were bewildered then, "you ain't seen nothing yet." The passage of the Telecommunications Bill of 1996 means a vast increase in the choices you will be able to make over the next few years. After nearly a century as a monopoly, your regional telephone company now must compete for your business with cable companies, companies like AT&T and MCI that had previously been limited to long-distance service, and anyone else who wants to enter your market. In turn, the regional companies can now offer long-distance service. And all the phone companies can enter the cable television business, breaking up yet another monopoly.

If this sounds like a free-for-all, that is exactly what we expect. Telephone, computer, cable television, cellular, and other companies, including large entertainment and media conglomerates, are going to be competing with each other in so many areas that the distinctions between those businesses are going to become increasingly blurred. That's why we have thrown our tips about telephones into this new chapter about "the information revolution."

We freely admit that by 1998, this chapter may be far less useful than many others in the book. That's how rapidly we expect things to change. But will all of our tips about telephone service be outdated by the end of 1997? Probably not. Not every local telephone market will be invaded immediately by aggressive competitors. Some people, especially in rural areas, may never have a choice of more than one local telephone service provider.

Whatever changes do come to your area, any new competition should result in lower prices, especially during the wild-and-woolly period when giant companies are trying to establish a beachhead in new markets. This may not be true everywhere; because the new legislation also removed federal rate caps for telephone and cable service, there is a chance that in areas where competition doesn't develop, prices may go up.

Even if you live within a market affected by fierce competition, in order to get lower prices you are going to have to make some effort to keep up on developments in a rapidly changing telecommunications environment. Our best guess now is that by our scheduled 1999 edition, we will have some tips about choosing a combined telephone–Internet–cable-television–wireless-dig-

ital-communication service and how to take advantage
of discounts for multiple services provided.

In the meanwhile, you still want to save some money
on the information and communication devices and service available in 1997 and 1998. We hope some of these
tips help.

▶ LEARN COMPUTER BASICS, THEN KNOW YOURSELF

If you are an absolute novice, don't know a hard drive
from a floppy disk, and just have a general feeling that
you ought to own a computer, perhaps because you are
afraid of being left behind, don't go near a computer
store. You are not ready.

First, learn what a computer can do and, just as important, what it can't do. The best way to do that is to take
a quick course in computer basics. Many school districts have excellent, inexpensive adult education
courses. If you don't want to take a course, visit a patient
friend who is seated before a computer that he has been
using for at least a couple of years. Look. Ask. Play with
the mouse. Go on his on-line service and see what's
there. Visit a few Internet web sites. Don't worry about
the technical stuff.

While you are sitting there, ask your friend whether
you should buy an Apple or an IBM-compatible machine. Invariably, he will tell you to get what he uses.
Apples used to be easier to use; that advantage is now
arguable. The great advantages of IBM-compatible PCs
are that a lot more software is being written for them,
many more people use them, and they are cheaper. So
opt for the IBM-compatible unless you have a compelling reason to do otherwise.

When you leave your friend's house, go to your library or buy a copy of the most basic book you can find.
The best one we know is *PCs for Dummies* by Dan Goo-
kin and Andy Rathbone ($16.95, IDG Books). The only
thing we don't like about this book is the title, but the
publisher of the wildly popular *Dummy* series could care

less. Just remember you are not a dummy. You are simply new to a lot of dumb techno-babble that the old-time computer nerds love to use to keep their club exclusive.

The last thing you want to do is learn much of that stuff. But you should know some basics—the difference between hardware and software, for example, and what hard drives, memory, CD-ROMs, and modems do. Any basic book will explain all of these things. Then go back to your patient friend with even more questions. You are never going to know how to write a computer program or how a microprocessor works, but you don't know how to tune your own automobile engine either. You know enough to proceed to the next step:

Second, decide what you want a computer to do for you and other members of your family. Do you just want to write a few letters and be able to send and receive E-mail? Do you want to play games? Do your own taxes and improve your family budget? Load the machine up with all kinds of memory-hungry software programs?

Of course you won't be absolutely sure how you will ultimately want to use your computer, but if you walk into a store without some sense of what kind of machine you need to accomplish what you want to do, you will encounter a salesperson eager to sell you the most expensive machine possible. You don't need a Porsche to go to the supermarket and back, and you don't need a top-of-the-line computer for 99 percent of most in-home use.

We won't make any specific recommendations, given how rapidly the technology changes, except for these few sure-to-be-still-relevant tips:

- Blazing speed in a microprocessor (how many megahertz or MHz it runs on) is wonderful if you are crunching huge spreadsheets of numbers or doing major-league computer graphics work, but most of us can settle for more modest speed for less money. If you plan on playing a lot of games, however, you may want to pay extra for a speedier machine.
- You don't need a huge hard drive, but you will need

more hard-disk storage than you originally estimate.
Buy something in the mid-range.

- Spend the extra money for more than whatever the
  current "minimum" random access memory (RAM)
  recommendation is. Recommendations about minimum memory requirements from some software programs are inaccurate. To run well, they need more
  memory. Whatever you buy, make sure that the RAM
  you buy is expandable.

- Buy the fastest modem you can possibly afford if you
  plan on using on-line services and accessing the Internet. You'll quickly save the extra cost in lower access charges and reduced frustration. If you plan on
  heavy use of the Internet, look into ISDN (Integrated
  Services Digital Network) high-speed telephone service. Installation costs at the time of this writing were
  still high for home use, but they were falling rapidly.

- Big monitors are much more expensive than smaller
  ones. Unless you make a living as a graphic artist,
  you are better off putting your money into extra memory and a fast modem.

- If you are buying a first computer, you will want all
  the hand-holding advice and technical backup possible during your first few months of use. Pay for that
  up front, probably at a retail store. Check out exactly
  what support is offered as part of your purchase price
  in different stores; this is as important a part of your
  purchase decision as the machine itself. Yes, you can
  save money by buying from one of the large mail-
  order vendors, but don't believe a word they say
  about how easy it will be to get their help by telephone or modem.

▶ BUY YOUR *SECOND* COMPUTER BY MAIL

Your library has the latest copies of computer magazines full of ads from mail-order vendors. When you
know what you are shopping for, and are confident
enough to take a chance on their technical support sys-

tems, you can nearly always get a better price on computer hardware from a mail-order source rather than a retail store. *Caveat:* Before buying from any mail-order vendor, visit its web site or on-line forum. Expect to find a reasonable number of forum messages from disgruntled buyers complaining about malfunctioning equipment and slow technical support. But if there aren't also a number of thank-you notes as well as positive comments about decent service and products, think twice before buying from this source.

▶ BUY SECONDHAND

Here is a true penny pincher's way of looking at the purchase of a computer. Whatever I buy is going to be obsolete in a year, so why not buy a machine that has already been obsolete for a year—at a fraction of the price of the new one? Is saving 80 percent and being just one year behind all that terrible?

Not for most people. Check your Yellow Pages under "Computer Sales, Used." Or check out the classified ads for used equipment in a magazine called *Computer Shopper.* You can also call the Boston Computer Exchange (800-262-6399) or NACOMEX (212-614-0700). They will usually be able to give you a price over the phone, whether you are a buyer or a seller of equipment.

Unless your needs are truly minimal, don't even consider buying anything below a 486 PC. You'll have a terrible time finding new software for anything older.

▶ DONATE YOUR OLD COMPUTER

Buying secondhand is attractive because there is a glut of old computers on the market. Selling into that glut may be far less attractive. By all means establish a price you might get for your old computer (see above resources), but then consider donating it to a school, church, synagogue, or some other nonprofit organization. The tax deduction may be your best bet. The National Christina Foundation (800-274-7846) accepts used computers and will give you a written receipt of its value. Gifts in Kind America (703-836-2121) will give you the names of organizations in your area that may need your equipment.

► BUY DURING THE EARLY SUMMER MONTHS

There has been a consistent price-cycle pattern in computer sales during the past few years. It will probably continue. Vendors introduce new systems at the big Comdex trade show in late spring. Inevitably, retailers then lower prices on existing inventory.

► CHECK COLLEGE CAMPUS-STORE PRICES

Computer and software vendors have given special discounts to colleges for years, no doubt on the theory that the college years are a good time to establish relationships with new customers. If your college-bound son or daughter doesn't yet have a PC, you might want to wait and buy at the campus store. That store will also know what equipment and software is in general use on campus, so you can be sure what you buy will be compatible with the college's system.

► IS A FAX CHEAPER THAN A LETTER?

You don't need an expensive stand-alone fax machine to send a letter by fax. Most modems now include fax capabilities, so you can send a letter directly from your word-processing program to any fax number. Especially if it is a local call or you send the fax during off-hours, the price of a one-minute call may be less than the price of a first-class stamp. It is also far faster.

► E-MAIL IS ALWAYS CHEAPER

If you have friends and family you want to keep in touch with anywhere in the country, electronic mail—a message from one person to another across the Internet—is the single best penny-pinching resource to come out of the information revolution. In order to send and receive E-mail, you will have to pay someone a monthly fee—an on-line service such as American Online or Compu-Serve, a telephone company such as MCI or AT&T, or one of the many Internet service providers—to establish access and an E-mail address. Prices and discount plans are changing too rapidly for us to make specific recommendations. Talk to friends who already use E-mail and check out their recommendations first.

▶ CALL ON THE INTERNET

The most popular web browsers now include software that allow you to use the Internet to establish voice contact with a similarly equipped computer user anywhere in the world. All you need, in addition to the software and an Internet access provider, is a computer equipped with a sound card, speakers, and a microphone. You can call only people who are on-line when you make the call and have compatible software. And the sound quality is not always dependable. Nevertheless, if you talk often to the same person thousands of miles away, using the Internet instead of a telephone line can literally cut your costs from hundreds of dollars a year to zero.

We expect some exciting new developments in this technology in the next couple of years, including the possibilities of a single software standard, improved voice quality, and even some ability to place a call to a standard telephone via the Internet.

▶ DON'T RENT YOUR TELEPHONE

There are still nearly five million people in this country who rent their phones, more than 13 years after the breakup of AT&T. A basic Touch-Tone phone probably costs less than one year's rental, and any well-made telephone should give you years of trouble-free service. Since on-site repairs or rented phones are not free anymore, there really is *no* advantage to renting.

If you are still renting, look at your bill. You'll find the number to call to cancel the service and get information about buying your telephone and converting it, if necessary, to a modular instrument (the only kind you want). Check that price against the prices of telephones sold by an electronics discounter (see Chapter 5 for mail-order sources). For guidance on what to look for when you buy, see the next tip.

▶ INSTALL YOUR OWN PHONE

Repair or install new wiring. Pinpoint problems when you have trouble getting a dial tone, the phone doesn't ring, or sound quality is bad. Too difficult? Absolutely not. In fact, modern telephone equipment is easy for even a habitually klutzy do-it-yourselfer to work with.

The single best source of easy-to-understand-and-follow instructions is no farther away than your local library, which should still have *The Phone Book,* a Consumer Reports Book by Carl Oppendahl that was unfortunately declared out-of-print (no longer available in bookstores) in 1996. We hope it soon comes back in a new edition, because this book clearly explains how to choose, fix, and install equipment. Although some of its information is a bit dated, it is also still a good source of information on getting the best service at the lowest cost.

▶ READ THE WHITE PAGES OF YOUR TELEPHONE DIRECTORY

Prices and options in telephone service vary greatly in different areas. Different people use their telephones in different ways. So it is impossible to spell out exactly the best penny-pinching strategy for you to use with your local telephone company. But you may very well discover quick and easy ways to save money simply by spending a few minutes reading the first few pages of your telephone directory.

Every detail about different charges, rate time periods, calling plans, etc. must by law be set forth in this directory. Match various plans against the usage detailed in your last few telephone bills. For guidance on how to do this, use *The Phone Book* (see previous tip).

If a competitor to your local company has appeared in your area, factor its plans into your calculations.

▶ STOP PAYING FOR TELEPHONE "WIRE MAINTENANCE"

Pull out your last telephone bill. If you see a charge for wire maintenance (usually from $1.50 to $2 a month), call your phone company's business office and cancel this "service." Why? Because you are paying a high premium to ensure yourself against an unlikely event.

The phone company is already responsible for maintenance of wires that lead up to your house. The charge on your bill also makes the company responsible for fixing the wires that lead from that point to your telephones. Since problems with inside wires are rare, you are better off taking your chances and paying an electrician (or fixing them yourself; see previous tips) in the unlikely event that something goes wrong.

▶ BUY LONG-DISTANCE SERVICE THAT FITS YOUR USER PROFILE

Fierce competition among long-distance telephone companies has resulted in a competitive standoff in terms of most regular rates for most users. All the companies offer discount plans for different kinds of usage, however, and it is possible to cut your bills substantially using one of them.

Which plan? Which company? Those aren't the right first questions. The single best penny-pincher strategy is first to analyze how you and your family actually use long-distance service and only then look into different discount plans. If you make just a few short calls a month, a discount plan offering a flat rate for the first one hour of service may not make sense. If you make most of your calls to a single area code or to the same numbers, there are discount plans that will make these call patterns cheaper. If you access the Internet, you can sign up for a plan that packages free hours with other long-distance services. If your local telephone company has begun offering long-distance service, or special rates for regional long-distance service, you must factor their prices and plans into your decision as well.

As confusing as this may sound, one thing is certain as we write this: If you are among the majority of long-distance customers who haven't switched to a discount plan, you are paying more than you should for long-distance service. There is definitely a discount plan that will save you money.

One common mistake is to buy a plan that offers steep discounts with a minimum fee for late-night use, based on a vow to change your habits by talking to your sister on the other coast only after 10:00 P.M. After an initial period of compliance, you will probably fall back into old routines and end up paying a fee for an unused service.

It's a good idea to look into competitive plans whenever your long-distance calling habits change—when a child goes away to college, for instance, or when a close friend moves. Don't sign a long-term contract (more than six months) with any long-distance company, no matter what promotional advantages are offered. And don't sign up with any carrier because they promise rebates stretching into the far future. Reason: None of them will guarantee their rates won't change, and the rebates—or the terms of your long-term contract—may not look so attractive in a few months. You have a legal right to switch long-distance carriers whenever you like, so keep them competing for your business.

The long-distance companies don't want you to know it, but quite a few penny pinchers have switched back and forth between competing long-distance carriers, month after month or as soon as the initial contract period is over, taken big up-front cash rebates when they switched, and ended up with free service plus a few dollars more!

When you do decide to switch, make sure to ask your

new long-distance carrier to credit you for the switching fee (currently $5 in our area) charged by your local telephone company. Also, watch your bills carefully during the following ninety days; your old carrier may conveniently neglect to drop you and still bill you some kind of monthly fee.

Four numbers to call for up-to-date information on available discount plans: *AT&T* (800-222-0300); *MCI* (800-444-3333); *Sprint* (800-877-4646); *Frontier* (800-631-4000). Or, if you prefer a single source that gives you comprehensive listings and comparisons of various long-distance plans currently available, from these companies and others, send $2 with SASE to TRAC *(Telecommunications Research & Action Center)*, Box 12038, Washington, D.C. 20005.

▶ AVOID YOUR HOTEL'S LONG-DISTANCE LINE

If you don't yet have one, get your own long-distance charge card from AT&T, Sprint, MCI, or other carrier, and place your calls through its operator. Whether it is a great luxury hotel in a major city or a budget motel out in the sticks, long-distance calls by guests are often looked upon as a source of incremental profits. Surcharges of 100 percent or more are common.

If you are traveling abroad, things are even worse. But MCI, Sprint, and AT&T have toll-free access numbers you can reach in most countries that connect you with an operator in the United States. Not only will you save money; you'll also avoid non-English-speaking operators.

▶ BEWARE OF PAY PHONES

One of the best reasons to carry a telephone card from one of the major long-distance companies is to use the access number on it when you are at a pay phone. When you dial this access number, you'll be connected to your carrier's operator and will pay its rates for calling-card or collect calls. Otherwise, if you are unlucky enough to be calling from a pay phone owned by a company that pays a commission to the owners of the facility in which the phone is placed, you risk paying up to five times as much for your call.

▶ GET THE BEST DEAL IN A CALLING CARD

Calling-card rates are invariably higher than the rates you pay when you call from your home phone. But long-distance companies usually offer special discounts on calls made with calling cards issued to home subscribers ("primary users" to the carriers). If you make frequent calls with a card, factor this into your decision about a long-distance carrier. Some calling cards tack on an extra charge for the first minute of the call, others don't. As we write, there are cards available that charge as low as 25 cents a minute with no additional first-minute charge. You can get an up-to-date calling card comparison chart, with the latest prices from five different providers, by sending a SASE to Tele-Consumer Hotline, 1331 H Street NW, Washington, D.C. 20005.

▶ USE A PREPAID CARD

Using a prepaid phone card may be as cheap as using a calling card. You'll find them for sale just about everywhere these days, including gas stations and supermarkets. One of the best deals in a prepaid card as we write is offered by 7-Eleven—as low as 25 cents per minute when you buy the most expensive card. You simply buy a card in denominations usually ranging from $5 to $50 and get a preset number of telephone minutes for calls anywhere in the United States. When you make a call, you dial the access number printed on it and press in an identification number. Before you dial your party, you will be told how many minutes of use you have remaining. However many minutes you use will be deducted. When all of your minutes are used up, you just toss the card away.

▶ GET YOUR OWN 800 OR 888 NUMBER

This could make sense if someone in the family travels a great deal, you have kids away at college, or there are other reasons why you pay for hours of long-distance calls made each month to your home number. Some companies charge a small monthly fee (typically $5) plus the cost of calls. Others charge no monthly fee but charge more per call minute. Either way, using an 800 or 888 number is cheaper than calling-card rates from most distances. You don't need any new equipment and don't even have to pay a connection fee; calls come in on your present line. You also have complete control over who knows about the 800 or 888 number.

For information and current rates, call the numbers listed in the previous tip about buying long-distance service. Ask for details about a personal 800 or 888 number.

▶ USE THE PHONE BOOK

Telephone companies have turned their directory-assistance operations into major profit centers. In our area, it costs 48 cents to get an in-state number from an operator. How much longer does it take to look a number up yourself?

Even if you've lost Aunt Tilly's phone number and she lives 2,000 miles away, a phone book is probably available. Our local library has a CD-ROM with every telephone number in the United States on it. On the Internet, we use *Switchboard* (http://www.switchboard.com).

▶ BUT CALL 800-555-1212 WHENEVER YOU LIKE

The 800/888 directory-assistance line is free—*in most areas.* If you are unsure about this, check with your local telephone company. Once you ascertain that the line is free, the next time you are about to make a regular long-distance call to a company or organization, call 800-555-1212 first. Very often, you'll find the company has an 800 or 888 number you can call toll-free. You can also access AT&T's directory of customers who lease 800 or 888 numbers from it on the Internet (http://www.tollfree.att.net/). Also check out Switchboard (previous tip).

▶ HOLD DOWN FAX OR MODEM EXPENSES

If you plan to buy a dedicated fax machine, get one with an answering machine built in. You can then use the same line for both fax and voice calls. Even when you are away, the machine will be able to recognize a fax call and accept it as well as take voice messages.

If you have a fax or modem that you use only occasionally and want to avoid the expense of an additional line, look into the "distinctive ringing" plans that most telephone companies offer. You can get two or three different telephone numbers that share the same line for a lot less a month than the extra lines would cost you.

▶ HOLD DOWN CELLULAR-PHONE EXPENSES

Unless you absolutely have to have one, the best penny-pinching advice is to avoid using a cellular phone. The average cellular-phone user spends between $60 and $70 a month in addition to regular phone bills. During peak hours, a call can cost up to 80 cents a minute. At those prices, we prefer to stop at a pay-phone booth.

If you do decide you need a cellular phone, think first about how you plan to use it. If you will use it infrequently, perhaps only in case of an emergency, look for a plan that offers a low monthly access fee, usually including a few free minutes of use, combined with high usage charges. If you will use the phone constantly, look for a plan with the lowest usage charges, especially during the hours when you will make the most calls.

Until proven otherwise, don't concern yourself with claims from any carrier about superior quality or service; in most areas there's not much difference. Once you have chosen a phone that has the features you want, buy the cheapest package available. The phone itself may cost you little or nothing if you sign up for a certain plan. You will nearly always be given some free minutes of use during your first three months. Shop around and add up all the elements of the package.

When you do have a phone, it may pay you to switch carriers after your initial contract period is up. If you can get a lot of free minutes, a front-end rebate (often of up to $100), a lower monthly access fee, or cheaper time rates, why not? Just make sure that either the new company will waive its activation fee or that the deal is so good that it makes sense even with that fee included.

In the next couple of years, a new wireless technology—Digital PCS (Personal Communications Services)—will be introduced in many parts of the country. Promising better reception than cellular, it will initially be more expensive as well. Cellular carriers will no doubt try to head off this new competition with price cuts, so when you hear that a PCS system is coming to your area, shop for better cellular prices right away.

▶ HOLD DOWN ON-LINE EXPENSES

Two months before this book went to press, we got our first telephone bill based on a single charge for unlimited local calls. We switched to this discount plan the day it was announced by our local telephone company, not because we talk that much on the telephone, but because we have become heavy users of both our on-line service and the Internet, both of which we access on a local number.

Once you begin to spend a lot of time on-line, this kind of discount plan—increasingly available around the country as the competition to supply local service heats up—is a must.

Reducing Insurance Premiums and Taxes

Twenty-five years before he uttered the immortal phrase "Nothing is certain but death and taxes," Benjamin Franklin started America's first insurance company. Obviously he still had no idea how inevitable a part of our lives insurance premiums would become.

That very inevitability leads some people to treat their insurance bills, along with taxes, as fixed and unalterable. They wince when they get their semiannual automobile insurance premium bill and see that the premium has gone up once again. But they decide it is easier to pay the bill than to open up that boring file filled with a few years' worth of unexamined policies, policy changes, and premium notices.

It's easy for these people to make two basic mistakes about insurance. They pay more than they should for the insurance they have, often because they don't really need all of it. And they don't insure or grossly underinsure themselves against some very real risks.

Insurance of any kind is simply a way for a large group of people (the policyholders of an insurance company) to *share risk*. There's only a small risk of your house being one of the few thousand in the country that will burn to the ground in the next year, but if that did happen, it would be a financial catastrophe for you. So you pay a small amount each year to protect yourself against that loss. You *want* what you pay for insurance premiums to be "a waste of money."

Cheap is not always the best penny-pinching idea when it comes to insurance. Although there may be some governmental or industry safety nets in place to protect you in case your insurance company goes bankrupt, you certainly don't want to test them. Deal only with insurance companies rated A+ or above for financial stability in *Best's Insurance Reports,* published by the A.M. Best Company and available in most libraries.

Only after you have established that the companies you are considering are financially sound should you begin comparison shopping among them. Price now becomes a compelling factor, but so is service; talk to people who have dealt with the company when a claim was necessary. Don't avoid paying a bit more if it will give you access to a knowledgeable agent who is willing to tailor a program that is right for your individual needs.

Finally, keep in mind that too many insurance agents love customers whose eyes glaze over because all the details are confusing and the whole subject is, well, *dull.* You can't afford to feel that way about your money and your family's security.

As for taxes, Ben Franklin has yet to be proven wrong. But simply because taxes are inevitable doesn't mean you shouldn't do everything legally possible to minimize them.

This book is not an income-tax guide. But many readers of tax preparation guides who are concentrating on line-by-line instructions for their returns are likely to miss the penny-pinching strategies included in this chapter. These strategies may also require you to analyze your tax situation well before the end of a calendar year. If you wait until next April, it is often too late to activate some very easy ways to reduce this year's—or next year's—taxes.

▶ BUY THE HIGHEST POSSIBLE DEDUCTIBLES

Whether you are buying automobile, home, or medical insurance, the purpose of insurance is to protect against sudden, unforeseen expenses that you could not afford yourself. If a leaky pipe were to cause $300 worth of damage to a ceiling, for instance, spending that sum might be frustrating, even painful. But if you can afford it, you shouldn't insure yourself against it by paying for a homeowner's policy with a $100 deductible.

Such a policy would pay for $200 of the damages in this case. But the premium paid for a policy with that low a deductible will be much more expensive than one with a $500 deductible. The lower your deductibles (the amount over which your insurance company has to pay the damages), the higher your insurance premiums. The difference in premium cost between a $500 and a $100 deductible for your home or car can be 30 percent or even more.

There's another practical reason to buy the highest possible deductibles for auto and home insurance. Many insurance companies punish people who file too many claims by raising their premiums. In fact, just a couple of small claims may be too many for some companies. If you are therefore going to limit your claims to large amounts of money, it would be extra foolish to pay for low deductibles at the same time.

▶ BUT DON'T UNDERINSURE

The big risks are the ones you are worried about. If you have a car that's less than three or four years old, don't try to save on auto insurance by skipping collision coverage. If your family would need $200,000 to live decently and you could no longer provide for them, don't try to get away with a smaller life insurance policy. If you live in a house that would cost $150,000 to replace if it burned to the ground, don't settle for anything less than a homeowner's policy that guarantees full replacement cost.

Pinching pennies doesn't mean being pound foolish; the worst way to save money is by risking future financial catastrophe.

▶ KNOW HOW MUCH LIFE INSURANCE YOU NEED

How much you need is more important than what kind you buy. So you must calculate what your family would need to replace you—financially—if you died tomorrow.

There are a bewildering number of different kinds of life insurance policies. But the first basic choice you must make is between term insurance, which pays off only if you die, and one of the many forms of permanent insurance, which also pays the amount of the policy in case you die but in addition is worth something while you are alive. As the agents say, it has both insurance and investment components.

You'll pay less for term insurance. Many parents use a combination of term and permanent insurance during the years before their children are self-sufficient, then drop the term insurance. You'll have to spend some time in your library and with life insurance agents before you decide what's best for you. Just one word of advice: Take with a grain of salt the arguments of both the "buy only term and invest the rest" crowd and the "term is a waste of money" school. There is no answer that fits everyone, and many people are best off with a combination of both.

Back to the big question: How much will you need? Start with the worksheet on page 75; it will be a big help if you fill it out before reading books and talking to agents. Actually, this is a simplified version of the capital-needs-analysis form a good agent will use.

Because it is easier to use such a worksheet if you can see how it applies in a real-life example, we've included a

How Much Life Insurance Do You Need?

To Cover:	What they'll need		Example
1. Funeral			$ 3,000
2. Other miscellaneous final expenses	+	+	$ 1,000
3. Estate taxes	+	+	0
4. Pay off mortgage	+	+	$120,000
5. Pay off other debts	+	+	$ 1,000
6. College fund	+	+	$ 44,000
7. Other needs	+	+	$ 5,000
8. Total	=		$174,000
Living expenses:			
Current living expenses			$ 45,000
× 80%			$ 36,000
− Spouse's take-home pay	−		$ 12,000
− Social Security survivor benefit	−		$ 16,000
= Annual need	=		$ 7,200
× number of years needed			20
9. Total living expenses	=		$144,000
10. Total assets needed (add 8 + 9)			$318,000
11. Group insurance proceeds	−		$100,000
12. Income-producing assets	−		$ 10,000
13. Your insurance need (10 − 11 − 12)			$208,000

column with numbers filled in. Our example is a man of thirty, married, with an income of $50,000 a year. His wife works part-time, making $12,000 a year, and they have a two-year-old child. The man has a $100,000 group life insurance policy through his job. They have just moved into a $150,000 house, using all but $10,000 of their total joint savings for a down payment of $30,000.

The example covers this man's life insurance needs only; his wife's should be calculated separately. Note that he needs assets of $318,000 to pay off the mortgage on the house and other debts, send his child to college, and cover twenty years of living expenses for his wife and child. In this case, he and his wife decided that she and the child could both be self-supporting after the child graduates from college. Since he already has a $100,000 group policy and $10,000 in assets that could provide income, his insurance need comes to $208,000.

Not many thirty-year-olds making $50,000 a year will be able to afford that much permanent life insurance, so some combination of term and permanent is likely.

The worksheet doesn't take inflation into account, although investing the insurance proceeds wisely should keep pace with inflation. There are no taxes on estates of less than $600,000. Your family might not choose to pay off your mortgage and other debt, but doing so simplifies the necessary calculations.

Adjust up or down our estimate of 80 percent of current living expenses as the amount your family could live on. *Don't* use the Social Security Survivor Benefit number in the example. Call the Social Security Administration (800-772-1213) and ask for a Request for Earnings and Benefits Estimate Statement; you'll eventually get an estimate of your own current survivor's benefits. And by all means, adapt or add to this basic worksheet in any way necessary to fit your individual needs.

▶ SHOP FOR TERM INSURANCE BY TELEPHONE

It's an easy way to check out rates and compare them with what your own agent or bank has offered. There is no fee involved; just call all four of the quote services below and tell them how much coverage you want. They'll ask your age, what the general state of your health is, and other pertinent questions that may or may not qualify you for preferred rates. A few days later you'll receive a free computer printout from each of them, listing prices from several companies.

These services can also give you advice on what you need, but you will be better off figuring that out yourself beforehand. They get commissions on sales from the insurance companies they represent, and have a vested interest in selling you as large a policy as possible.

Before you buy, check the company out in *Best's* (see page 72) and make sure you understand all the terms of the contract. Companies to call:

- *Select Quote,* 800-343-1985.
- *Term Quote,* 800-444-8376.
- *MasterQuote,* 800-337-5433.
- *Quotesmith, 800-431-1147;* also on the Internet: http://insure.com/Quotesmith.

▶ OPT FOR ANNUAL RENEWABLE TERM

Until 1996, level-term policies (premiums start out higher but remain unchanged for a set period, usually 10 or 15 years) were often just as attractive as annual renewable policies (premiums rise each year) for people who needed the insurance for only that set period. However, most states have recently changed regulations that affect how much money insurance companies must keep in reserve to settle claims. The bottom line for consumers is a much higher price for level-term policies and a shorter guarantee period, now often just five years. If your health deteriorates, you might not be able to renew. Most annual renewable policies guarantee you have the right to renew up to a certain age regardless of your health.

▶ STOP SMOKING AND REDUCE PREMIUMS

If you were a smoker when you took out your life insurance policy, you are paying higher premiums than a nonsmoker. If you have been off cigarettes for a year, call your insurer and ask for nonsmoker's rates.

▶ SKIP LIFE INSURANCE FOR CHILDREN

Your kids won't need life insurance until they have dependents. Insurance cushions you only against financial losses, not emotional ones.

▶ CONSIDERING AN ANNUITY? IT ISN'T INSURANCE

Annuities are sold by insurance companies, but they aren't really insurance. They are investment vehicles, often tax-advantaged. See Chapter 10.

▶ GROUP RATES AREN'T ALWAYS BETTER

Many companies pay the premiums on employee life insurance policies. Obviously, this is a great deal. Many also allow you to buy additional life insurance at group rates. This *isn't* always a good deal. First, because you may not have the right to convert to an individual policy if you leave the company. Second, because "group rates" for this kind of insurance aren't necessarily less expensive than a term policy you could buy on your own. Comparison-shop before you sign up.

Exception: If you are in poor health, you should probably grab any group-rate policy you can get, since you won't have to take a medical exam to get the insurance.

▶ SAVE ON DISABILITY INSURANCE

Don't save by skimping on it. Disability insurance, which provides ongoing monthly income if you are physically unable to work due to accident or illness, is essential if you have to work to maintain your lifestyle. That includes most of the nonretired population, but too many people believe Social Security and workmen's compensation laws provide adequate protection. They don't. Since one of every seven workers in the United

States will suffer a five-year or longer period of disability before age sixty-five, a good disability policy is just as important as a good life insurance program.

Most people are covered by group disability insurance where they work. More and more often, they must choose from among different features within flexible benefit plans. If you aren't covered by a group plan, you will have to pay higher individual rates. In either case, the best way to save on premiums without skimping on necessary coverage is to choose a longer waiting period. A thirty-day waiting period—the time between the onset of a disability and when benefits start—is often 20 percent more expensive than a ninety-day waiting period. If you have a reasonable emergency fund, you won't absolutely need the money within the first ninety days and you'll save a significant amount in premiums.

You definitely want a policy that can't be canceled and offers some written rate-hike protection. Finally, although you can save on premiums if you buy an "any occupation" policy, pay extra for the "own occupation" policy. With this policy, the insurance company has to pay benefits if you are unable to perform your own job.

▶ HAVE FLEXIBLE BENEFITS? PAY YOUR OWN DISABILITY PREMIUM

More companies each year are offering flexible benefit plans, allowing employees to choose from a smorgasbord of health, life, and disability plans but limiting the company's total contribution to premium payments. It makes sense to have the company pay the nondisability premiums first. If there's none of their money left over, buy your own disability insurance through the company's low group rate. Why? If the company pays disability premiums, and someday you need to collect benefits, payments would be taxable to you as ordinary income. If you pay the premiums, payments would be tax-free.

▶ THE PENNY PINCHER'S DOWNFALL: MEDICAL INSURANCE

Even if the cost of group health benefits through your employer has doubled or tripled in the past few years, count yourself lucky. More than 40 million Americans have no medical insurance at all, and people who have no choice but to buy individual policies are paying as much as $18,000 a year in premiums.

Unless new laws make significant changes, there aren't many penny-pinching ways to cut those costs and still retain the benefits most people want and need. You simply have to give up something to reduce premiums. If you have, and want to maintain, a traditional major-medical fee-for-service policy, higher deductibles are the best first step. Right now your policy may pay 80 percent of your medical bills after you pay the first $250 each year, and 100 percent after those bills total $5,000. If everyone in your family is in good health and you seldom visit a doctor or take medicines or drugs, you might want to raise your annual deductible from $250 to $1,000 or even $2,500. If a policy like that is available, you would still have insurance against a medical catastrophe, and your premium costs would be significantly lower.

If you have a traditional policy through your employer and also have a flexible benefits plan, by all means choose to put pretax dollars into the plan every year to pay for out-of-pocket medical expenses. If you are in the 28 percent tax bracket, that automatically makes out-of-pocket medical expenses 28 percent cheaper. Don't put in more than you are sure will be spent, however; you won't get any refund if the funds aren't used up by the end of the year.

Health Maintenance Organizations (HMOs) and/or Preferred Provider Organizations (PPOs) offer less expensive alternatives. If your employer offers a choice between an HMO, a PPO, and a traditional policy, you can probably cut medical expenses by at least 50 percent with the HMO, somewhat less with the PPO. Many employers now offer only HMO plans. The good ones provide excellent medical care at a lower cost than traditional medical providers, but you will be limited to doctors and hospitals within the HMO organization.

If you must buy your own policy, your state insurance department (phone number in your telephone book or via Internet; see later tip in this chapter) should be able to give you a list of companies that sell individual policies in your state.

Quotesmith (800-431-1147) maintains an up-to-date data bank on health insurance policies offered by more than 150 companies for individuals and small businesses. They will provide a free printout describing all the policies available in your area that meet your specifications.

▶ CHECK HMO RATINGS

Call the National Committee for Quality Assurance (NCQA) at 202-955-3515 and ask for its free Accreditation Status List. Some badly run HMOs avoid NCQA review, and some HMOs with good reputations simply don't want to pay the fee NCQA charges for an evaluation. But just about all of the larger HMOs are now getting these evaluations. If you are making a choice, the information you will get—on everything from the qualifications of the HMO's physicians to how appropriately they respond to patients' needs—will be invaluable.

▶ SELF-EMPLOYED? HIRE YOUR SPOUSE AND DEDUCT MEDICAL EXPENSES

If you are the only employee of your company, there is a compelling reason to hire one more person: your spouse. As long as he or she performs actual services for you and receives a nominal salary, this will allow your company to deduct 100 percent of your family's annual medical expenses—not just insurance premiums, but every other out-of-pocket expense as well. You must set up an employee medical-reimbursement plan to do this, and you will need some help from a good accountant with the initial paperwork required.

▶ SHOP FOR AUTO INSURANCE BY TELEPHONE

The next time you get the premium bill for your auto insurance, take a few minutes to do some comparison shopping. It really isn't much trouble when you do it by telephone, and the results may surprise you. If nothing else, you can satisfy yourself that the rates you are paying are competitive. Ask friends who they use and how satisfied they have been; among the companies you might try are USAA, State Farm, GEICO, and Allstate.

Most insurance companies will quote prices by telephone. Even those who at first say they won't, may change their minds when you tell them it's the only way you'll do business. Enter the information they'll need from you along with the prices from your current policy in the worksheet on pages 84–85. Don't volunteer any information they don't need, but be honest about mileage, moving violations, etc.

Establish all of your current deductibles and get prices based on those. If you want to explore different deductibles, make sure you get a quote from your current company as well as the competition.

It's possible other companies may offer discounts your present company doesn't. Ask.

▶ CHECK ON ALL POSSIBLE DISCOUNTS

The checklist on page 85 includes the most common discounts on automobile insurance: for air bags/automatic belts, antitheft devices, safe-driver education courses, and senior drivers. There may be others (some insurers give discounts if you have antilock brakes, or if the car is driven only a certain number of miles a year, for instance), so ask. If you belong to a credit union or an auto club, check with them to see if they have any arrangement for group rates.

▶ DROP COLLISION INSURANCE ON OLDER CARS

Especially if you follow our penny-pinching advice on buying high deductibles, it doesn't make sense to pay for collision insurance on a car that is worth less than $2,500. If you have a $500 deductible, the most you could collect would be $2,000. Your collision premium for that maximum coverage could be from $100 to $200 a year—5 to 10 percent of your highest possible claim. That's far too high a price to pay for the risk involved.

▶ SHOP AROUND FOR YOUR TEENAGER'S CAR INSURANCE

Depending on where you live and how your insurance company handles the issue, adding one newly licensed teenager to your own policy could double your premium cost overnight. Before this happens, make a few telephone calls, first to your present insurer and then to some competitors, to check on different coverage. Some companies offer discounts to teenagers who have completed driver's-ed courses, are "good students," or qualify as occasional drivers.

A couple of years later, if your teenager heads off to a college more than 120 miles or so away from home, call your insurer and ask for a rate reduction. The teenager is no longer residing in your house full-time.

▶ SAVE ON HOMEOWNER'S INSURANCE

Homeowner's insurance is easier to buy than some other types because the industry has a standard coding system (the HO number) that identifies different types of policies.

Many policies also label themselves as "comprehensive" or "all-risk," but these are meaningless terms. The HO number tells you what you are buying.

Comparing Automobile Insurance: A Worksheet

A. List cars you plan to insure:
    Car A: Year, model, vehicle i.d. number ....
        Miles driven per year ....
        Percentage used for commuting ....
    Car B: Year, model, vehicle i.d. number ....
        Miles driven per year ....
        Percentage used for commuting ....

B. List members of family who use the cars:
    Include name, age, driver's license number,
    convictions for moving violations and dates,
    accident records, percentage of use on each car

C. Comparing premiums:	CURRENT POLICY			CO.			CO.			CO.
	Car 1	Car 2		Car 1	Car 2		Car 1	Car 2		Car 1	Car 2
1. Bodily injury liability:											
$_____ per person											
$_____ per occurrence											
2. Property damage liability:											
$_____ per occurrence											
3. Medical payments:											
$_____											
(Note terms/deductibles, etc.)											

4. No-fault personal injury protection:
$_____

5. Uninsured motorists:
$_____ / _____ bodily injury person/occurrence

6. Auto medical payments:
$_____ each person

7. Collision:
$_____ deductible
$_____ deductible
$_____ deductible

8. Comprehensive:
$_____ deductible
$_____ deductible
$_____ deductible

9. Discounts:
_____ % of _____ for air bags/automatic belts
_____ % of _____ for antitheft devices
_____ % of _____ for safe-driver education
_____ % of _____ for senior drivers
_____ % of _____ for _____
_____ % of _____ for _____

TOTAL COSTS (total using deductibles selected less applicable discounts):

HO-1, HO-2, HO-3, and HO-5 policies are for house owners. An HO-6 policy is for owners of condominiums or co-ops. An HO-4 policy is for renters who need coverage for the contents of their houses or apartments as well as the same kind of personal liability insurance (in case someone is injured on the premises) homeowner policies provide.

If you are a homeowner, avoid the HO-1 and HO-2 policies, which are too limited to provide adequate protection, and price out HO-3 ("open peril") and HO-5 ("comprehensive, all-risk") policies. The HO-5 is more expensive because, although it has the same coverage as the HO-3 on the structure, it offers broader coverage on contents. Most people find the extra coverage isn't worth the increase in premium payments.

Perhaps the most important feature you should insist on (and pay extra for) in an HO-3 policy is guaranteed replacement. This means that if you insure your house for 100 percent of its value as determined by the insurance company, they will rebuild it no matter what that costs, even if the cost exceeds the amount of the policy.

Among the ways to save on homeowner's insurance:

- Install smoke alarms.
- Consider some form of antitheft system, but don't install an expensive system just to save on insurance premiums. Depending on where you live, the savings may not be very large.
- Get nonsmoker's discounts if you qualify.
- Use the same company for your automobile policy, and get a combination-policy discount.
- Shop around. For most people, automobile insurance is more expensive than homeowner's insurance, so you may want to price that out first. But look at the total costs of both from different companies. Most of the companies mentioned in the tip about auto insurance also sell homeowner's, and you should also talk to at least one independent agent in your area.

▶ BUY A RENTER'S INSURANCE POLICY

If you rent an apartment or house, it is foolish not to buy a renter's (HO-4) policy that covers the contents of your premises in case of fire or theft. It also protects against liability suits if someone has an accident in your home or you cause an accident outside it.

In most parts of the country, such policies are less than $200 a year. If you live in a metropolitan area with higher-than-average burglary statistics, you'll pay more. In any case, get estimates from a number of different insurers, compare exactly what is covered in each policy, and weigh the premium costs of different levels of deductibles.

▶ BUY AN UMBRELLA POLICY

Personal umbrella liability policies pick up where home owner's and automobile policies leave off. You need one if you have assets that amount to more than the liability coverage in those policies. An umbrella policy will provide overall protection against a variety of claims—such as being sued for a million dollars because of an automobile accident or because someone slips on your sidewalk. Most companies that sell home and auto insurance also sell umbrella policies, and a million-dollar policy is relatively inexpensive.

▶ AVOID CREDIT INSURANCE

Most credit-granting organizations (banks, auto dealers, etc.) will attempt to sell credit life and/or disability insurance to you in connection with the loans they make. It is hardly ever a good idea. If you need more life insurance, a separate term policy sold by the bank or an insurance agent will always be cheaper. What's more, if you buy credit insurance, the beneficiary is not your family, but the lender. That's not who you want to protect in case of your death or disability.

▶ ONE FAIL-SAFE WAY TO SAVE ON CAR INSURANCE

Most states now mandate a certain percentage discount in car insurance premiums for anyone who has recently taken a defensive-driving course. Admittedly, there's a trade-off of time here—the courses typically run six to eight hours in two evening sessions—but the savings can be major (as much as $150 a year), recurring (for three to five years), and you get an important dividend: You may just learn something that could help you avoid an accident.

▶ SKIP CREDIT-CARD INSURANCE

Selling credit-card insurance is profitable for issuers, but you simply don't need it. If your cards are lost or stolen and you notify the issuers right away, you aren't liable for their misuse. Even if you never notify the issuers, your maximum liability, mandated by federal law, is $50 per card.

▶ SKIP AIR-TRAVEL INSURANCE

Don't buy it at the airport, and don't buy it from the credit-card company that makes it "so easy," after you allow them automatically to add a "small" charge for $100,000 worth of insurance whenever you use the card to buy your tickets.

That "small" charge is actually a ridiculously high insurance premium, given the statistics on airline fatalities. If your dependents need protection, they need it whether you die in an airplane crash or from a heart attack. For the same reason, and because premiums are similarly overpriced, never buy illness-specific life insurance either.

▶ SKIP CAR-RENTAL INSURANCE

You can't unless you are already covered, of course, but most people are. Most personal automobile insurance policies cover you for damage to a rental car. Many credit-card companies also now offer free car-rental insurance as a way to persuade you to use their card. If the credit-card companies can afford to give it away free, think how profitable selling the insurance must be for the rental-car companies.

▶ SKIP STUDENT-ACCIDENT INSURANCE

If you have family health insurance coverage, you don't need this coverage, which is offered by many school districts. They like selling these policies because the district is less likely to be sued by a purchaser in case of an accident.

▶ REVIEW LIFE INSURANCE NEEDS AS YOU GET OLDER

When you have been paying life insurance premiums regularly for a number of years, it is easy to lose sight of just why you bought the insurance in the first place. Most people do so to protect their families in case of loss of income. As you get older, put kids through college, and, hopefully, build a good retirement fund and substantial other assets, you may not need life insurance at all.

Certainly, once you have retired, your family doesn't need protection from loss of your income. In fact, your spouse's expenses would be reduced if you die. Paying larger and larger premiums for renewable term insurance makes no sense at all for many older people.

▶ CHECK WITH YOUR STATE INSURANCE DEPARTMENT ON THE INTERNET

Insurance departments in most states have now set up home pages on the World Wide Web. They provide basic consumer information about all kinds of insurance as well as an easy way to get a fast complaint about any insurer to the proper state authorities. Check in with the National Association of Insurance Commissioners (http://www.naic.org) to get to your state's home page.

▶ FIGHT FOR LOWER PROPERTY TAXES

Maybe you think your property is being assessed at too high a rate. Maybe you didn't think so until you got a computer-generated letter in the mail from a property-tax consultant telling you how much they can save you by challenging the assessment authority on your behalf.

Don't hire anyone to do this for you if they ask for an up-front fee. They should be willing to work for a percentage of your first year's tax reduction. Local real-estate agents may be able to recommend consultants who are reputable and have a good record of success in your area.

▶ PREPARE YOUR OWN TAX RETURNS

Given the starting point of 2 percent of adjusted gross income for all miscellaneous deductions, most of us can no longer deduct the cost of an outside tax preparer on our income-tax returns. Fortunately, especially if you have access to a personal computer, you can now safely dispense with outside experts unless you are in the tiny minority of people who have extraordinarily complicated tax problems.

TurboTax ($39.95; Intuit) and *Personal Tax Edge* ($18.95; Parsons) are the best tax-preparation software programs we have seen. Both do all the math calculations and offer step-by-step instructions on completing your form, asking you every conceivable question along the way to ensure the return will be correct. *TurboTax* is designed to work seamlessly with *Quicken,* the most popular personal-finance software program. If you enter all of your budget and investing activities correctly in *Quicken,* you don't have to do it all over again in *TurboTax.* Otherwise, the Parsons program is cheaper and just as good for most people.

If you don't have a personal computer, there are a number of annual income-tax guides such as *J. K. Lasser's Your Income Tax Guide* ($14.95, Macmillan) and *The Ernst & Young Tax Guide* ($14.95, John Wiley) that are reliable if somewhat more difficult and time-consuming to use.

▶ BEGIN DECEMBER WITH A TAX-STRATEGY SESSION

Too many people put off thinking about income taxes until March or April, when the forms are due. By that time it is too late to take advantage of a few simple techniques that can transfer income and/or expenses from one year to another.

Suppose you are reading this in late 1997, and know roughly what your final income will be for that year. If you expect your income, tax rates, and/or tax brackets to be lower in 1998, you have got a good reason to 1) defer as much potential 1997 income as possible to 1998, and 2) move as many deductions as possible from 1998 to 1997.

If it looks like your 1998 taxes will be higher than 1997's, on the other hand, you will probably want to 1) move as much potential 1998 income into 1997 as possible, and 2) defer deductions from 1997 to 1998.

The next two tips tell you a few ways to do both.

▶ PAY LOWER TAXES THIS YEAR

It is December 1997 and you think your potential taxes will be lower for calendar year 1998 than for calendar year 1997. Consider the following:

- Look ahead at the charitable contributions you would normally make in 1998. Write those checks, and mail them, on the last day of 1997.
- Prepay real-estate taxes. If a property-tax bill is due in January, pay it instead in December.
- Prepay state and local income taxes. Even if they're not due until April, if you pay in December you can

deduct them on your 1997 federal return. Pay all outstanding estimated state taxes in December.

- Prepay your mortgage payment. Make your January payment on December 31 instead, and deduct that month's mortgage interest from your 1997 return.
- Look over medical expenses for the year. If your total medical expenses (including insurance premiums, doctors, dentists, hospitals, drugs, eyeglasses, contact lenses, hearing aids, and medically necessary travel) amount to 7.5 percent of your adjusted gross income (AGI), you can deduct expenses that exceed that threshold. This would make December 1997 a great time for any kind of elective medical or dental care you know you'll need sooner or later.
- Defer bonuses. This is a bit tricky, and you should get the advice of a tax expert, but if you have been getting a regular bonus at the end of December and can change that on a permanent basis to January, you should be able to defer your tax liability as well.
- Buy CDs and treasury bills that mature next year. You are not credited with the interest on either until they mature. Actually, if you are trying to reduce interest income for the year, doing this in December doesn't help much. If, however, back in July you had bought a six-month CD maturing in January 1998, you could have deferred quite a bit of interest income. Tax planning is really a year-round activity.
- If self-employed, bill clients in early January instead of late December.

▶ PAY LOWER TAXES NEXT YEAR

It is December 1997 and you think your potential taxes will be higher for calendar year 1998 than they have been for calendar year 1997. Consider doing the following:

- If you normally get a bonus in January, ask if you can instead get it on the last workday of 1997.
- If you normally make charitable contributions at the

end of the year, write the checks instead on January 2.

- Delay payment of medical and dental bills until 1998.
- Cash in CDs that would mature in 1998, or ask your bank to credit the interest on them by the end of 1997.
- Cash in savings bonds before the end of the year. Especially if your income in 1997 was considerably lower than you think it will be for the next few years, you have a good reason to cash in savings bonds that may have accumulated years of accrued interest income.

▶ DON'T BUY SHARES IN A STOCK MUTUAL FUND IN EARLY DECEMBER

Unless you have other good reasons to do so (dollar cost averaging being one of them), you are probably better off waiting until the very end of December or January 2 of the new year to buy shares in a stock mutual fund. The reason: These funds usually make their capital-gain as well as major income distributions for the year in mid-December. You incur a tax liability for that year on whatever amounts are distributed to you (even if you take the distributions in the form of more shares in the fund).

This is no reason to avoid a stock mutual fund you want to invest in for the long term, but toward the end of the year you should at least call the fund's customer-service department to check on when a distribution will be made.

▶ TAKE CAPITAL GAINS EARLY IN THE YEAR

Don't make any investment decisions based solely on tax consequences. All else being equal, though, the earlier in the year you take a capital gain, the longer a period of time you have to put that gain to work before paying taxes in April of next year. If you will pay a 28 percent tax on the gain but invest it for a full year in a mutual fund that gains 14 percent, the tax hurts 50 percent less.

▶ MAKE TAX-ADVANTAGED DONATIONS

You probably think only multimillionaire philanthropists can take advantage of the tax laws when making donations. But a lot of middle-class people give sizable sums of cash to a church, synagogue, alma mater, or charity. The question is: Why cash? Suppose you own 100 shares of a stock or mutual fund that you bought for $5 a share years ago. Now the price is $10. If you sell the shares for $1,000, you will have to pay a capital gains tax on a $500 gain. If you give the 100 shares to a charity, neither you nor the charity will owe a penny in taxes and you can deduct the full $1,000 contribution.

Still like the stock or fund? Buy 100 new shares with the $1,000 cash you would otherwise have given the charity. Advantage: Your basis is now $10 a share instead of $5. If the share is someday worth $20, you will pay tax on only a $1,000 capital gain instead of a $1,500 one.

Given transaction costs, this works better with no-load mutual-fund shares than with shares of an individual stock.

▶ TAKE ADVANTAGE OF THE CHILD-CARE TAX CREDIT

Only 5 percent of U.S. households now conform to the traditional ideal of a working father and a mother who stays at home full-time taking care of minor children. So there are a lot of people who can take advantage of the child- and dependent-care credit on their federal tax returns. Surprisingly, many don't.

Any good income-tax guide will explain the rules. Basically, if your work causes you to incur expenses for care of a dependent, you may be eligible. Potential savings: up to $4,800 a year if you have more than one qualifying dependent.

▶ SHIFT INCOME TO YOUR KIDS

A dependent child under fourteen can receive up to $600 unearned income (dividends and interest) and pay no income tax on it. On the next $600 in income, the tax is 15 percent. After that, the child is taxed at your rate.

You can give a child up to $10,000 a year ($20,000 with your spouse) without paying any gift tax. So it is easy to shift income-producing assets to your child and save on taxes overall. If your rate is 28 percent, you would pay $280 in taxes on $1,000 in dividends or interest. Your child would pay only $60 (0 percent of $600 plus 15 percent of $400). Savings: $220 a year.

After age fourteen, all income, earned or unearned, of less than $22,100 is taxed at 15 percent.

▶ TRANSFER CAPITAL GAINS TO YOUR KIDS

Suppose you want to sell a stock or a mutual fund you bought years ago, your basis price (what you bought it for) is $2,500, and it is now worth $12,500 (a very pleasant "suppose" indeed). If you pay the top capital-gains tax of 28 percent, you would pay $2,800 in taxes on your $10,000 gain. Since you and your spouse can give up to $20,000 a year to a child without paying a gift tax, you could instead make a gift of the stock to a child over fourteen, who would pay only $1,500 in taxes on the sale.

One reason you might want to do this is because the stock represents money you had put away for college expenses anyway, so making the gift and having your child pay a tuition bill is a simple way of picking up an extra $1,300. Unfortunately, there's a catch-22 to transferring assets if your child will be applying for financial aid to attend college; see page 250.

▶ PUT KIDS ON THE PAYROLL

A child's *earned* income (distinct from unearned income; see previous tip) is taxed at that child's tax rate.

If you own a business, you can pay a child a salary for work performed, thus shifting some family income into a lower tax bracket. What's more, the child can take the full standard deduction against earned income, so a lot of the salary won't be taxed. There are other considerations, of course, and what you pay the child must bear some relationship to the value of the services performed.

▶ CONSIDER FILING SEPARATE TAX RETURNS

If you are a two-income family and either you or your spouse has high medical or business expenses, you may be able to reduce your tax bill by filing separate returns. If one of you had $3,750 in medical expenses and your joint adjusted gross income (AGI) was $50,000, for instance, you couldn't deduct any portion of your medical expenses because they are not more than 7.5 percent of AGI. If you filed separately, and your AGI was $25,000, you could deduct $1,875.

▶ BIG TAX REFUND EVERY YEAR? BIG MISTAKE

Some people seem to feel a tax refund check is a kind of gift from Uncle Sam. In fact, the gift has been from them to the IRS. By overwithholding taxes from your salary check, you are losing the interest income you could have earned on that money all year long.

If you usually get a refund check, review the number of deductions you have been claiming and consider adding to it.

▶ GET HELP ON THE INTERNET

- The IRS home page (http://www.irs.ustreas.gov) is, surprisingly, both easy to navigate and useful. You can get free downloads of any IRS form you are likely to need as well as advice on how to fill them out. For anyone who ever waited for hours to connect by tele-

phone to the IRS information service, this is a giant leap forward.
- *Net Taxes* (http://www.ypn.com/taxes/) offers tips from CPAs, organized line by line for a 1040 form.

5

Shopping Smart for Appliances, Furniture, Housewares, and Gifts

§ §

When they buy cars, most people are very aware of the miles-per-gallon numbers and realize that an 18-mile-a-gallon gas guzzler is going to cost a lot more over the long run than a car that gets 30 miles to the gallon. Yet as conscious as most people have become about the costs of energy, not many estimate the long-term costs before they buy a new appliance. In some areas of the country, the cost of the electricity to run a refrigerator during its working life will be five times the amount paid for it. Given a worst-case energy scenario and a refrigerator that lasts for twenty years, even that estimate could prove to be extremely conservative.

What this means is that the initial price of an appliance is only one factor—in many cases, the least important factor—in deciding how much that appliance will actually cost over its lifetime.

The same basic point (that initial cost is only one factor shoppers must evaluate) is also true when you make purchase decisions about furniture and housewares you hope to use for years to come. You will usually save money by paying more for quality goods and taking good care of them.

Having said that, there is no reason to pay more than is necessary for those quality goods. Tips in this chapter suggest both strategies and specific sources for value-conscious shoppers. One simple thing to keep in mind if you tend to be a bit shy or just don't like to negotiate: If you ask for a lower price, the answer may be no. But you haven't lost a thing. *If you never ask for a lower price, you will never get one.*

▶ IS IT A STORE OR A BAZAAR?

The sign on the television set says: "Retail price $899. Our price $599." But the $599 is crossed out and "Special sale! $549" is written next to it. You are in a chain discount-appliance store. What's your next step?

Quietly ask the salesclerk, out of hearing range of other customers, for the store's *best* price on the set. Often, without any further conversation, he'll call up the item on his computer terminal and come back with an even lower price than the supposed "special." At that point, you can either accept that price or make an even lower offer. Depending on all sorts of factors you can never know—including inventory levels, the chain's cash-flow situation, and deals offered to the chain by that manufacturer—your offer may be accepted (although probably only after an act involving the clerk and a "manager") or rejected.

Many people are surprised by how many American retailers really do operate these days as open bazaars where quoted prices are only a starting point. But it is foolish not to attempt to negotiate a price on most high-ticket items. If you have decided on a specific brand and model, first call three or four stores to get their "best price." If one store's price is higher than another's, tell them so. You'll get a sense of how much maneuvering room there is on the price of that model.

Caution: The oldest trick of the bazaar operator is to quote you an extremely low price, whether by telephone or on the selling floor, then return from the stockroom apologizing for suddenly being out of that model but ready to give you a terrific deal on an even better one. Tell the clerk you won't deal with a "bait and switch" operation and walk away. Slowly, of course. There just might be one left of the model you want after all.

▶ HAGGLE WITH OWNERS AND MANAGERS

In many stores, it is useless to ask clerks for discounts off ticketed prices. They aren't authorized to make special deals. But the owner or store manager definitely can. If you figure the store is working on a 40 percent markup and you ask for a 25 percent discount, an owner can quickly decide that a 15 percent profit is better than no sale at all. Remember to do your haggling quietly, out of hearing of other customers.

▶ "THROW IN" SOME ACCESSORIES

Even if you can't get a reduced price on a big-ticket appliance, you may be able to get the store to "throw in" with your purchase some kind of accessory to it that you would have to buy anyway.

▶ WILL IT BE ON SALE SOON?

This is often a much better question to ask a store clerk or owner than "will you reduce the price for me?" Once you are told that the item will probably be on sale, say, next month, simply ask if you could save another trip and get the sales price right now.

▶ SHOP AT THE END OF THE MONTH

Stores that have not met their monthly sales quotas may be more anxious to sell at reduced prices.

▶ SKIP EXTENDED WARRANTIES

See Chapter 4 for a discussion of the purpose of insurance, which is what an extended (beyond the time limit offered by the manufacturer) warranty on an appliance or an electronic product really is. In the case of the extended warranties offered (and usually aggressively sold) by retailers, the cost of the premium (the price of the warranty) is far higher than it should be, given the risk it protects you against.

The salesperson you deal with probably gets a very healthy commission on sales of extended warranties. And the stores can afford the commissions, because many of them make as much or even more on the sale of the warranty as they do on the sale of the product itself.

A better idea: When you buy a new appliance, put half the money an extended warranty would have cost into a repair fund. Unless you have bought an inferior product or are very unlucky, you should cover necessary repairs and save a lot of money.

And check your credit card. You can automatically extend the manufacturer's warranty on an appliance or electronic product, usually for an extra year, if you use the right credit card to buy it (American Express and some Visa and MasterCards; check to see if yours is one of them). Unless you can get a cash discount, this is an extra reason to use your card. See Chapter 9 for more on penny-pinching credit cards.

▶ OFFER TO PAY CASH

If you offer to save a small store the commission it pays when you use a credit card to make your purchases, it may be more willing to negotiate.

▶ ASK ABOUT CORPORATE DISCOUNTS

If you own your own company, many stores offer corporate discounts. For instance, if you are incorporated, even the august Tiffany & Company will give you a 10 percent discount. Actually, if you have even a part-time business on the side, all you may need in some places is a business card, and perhaps a separate bank account.

▶ CHECK IT OUT FIRST IN *CONSUMER REPORTS*

Consumer Reports is published by the nonprofit Consumers Union, which independently tests different products and services and rates them in terms of safety, relative quality, and, sometimes, price competitiveness. This is the best single source of advice on buying just about anything from a VCR to a new convertible. The writing is straightforward, humorless, and for our tastes too often a bit self-righteous. We wouldn't buy a major appliance without knowing how *CR* rates different brands and models, but we skip its monthly report on readers' movie preferences and often disagree with taste panels that rate various foods and beverages. You may also sometimes be unable to find a model of a product highly rated by *CR,* because that model is no longer available.

If you are at a point in your life, perhaps just moving into a first house, where you are making a lot of major purchase decisions, a subscription to *Consumer Reports* could be an especially wise investment. Or do what we do:

Make a few notes about some upcoming purchasing decisions, then visit your local library to check them out with *CR*. You can also access *Consumer Reports* via America Online, CompuServe, or Prodigy.

▶ CALL AHEAD

When you are shopping for an unusual item or a specific model, telephone ahead to see if the store has it. A simple idea, but it can save a lot of time and cut down on travel expenses.

▶ BUY IN OFF-SEASONS

Air-conditioner sales peak in the summer months. The best time to buy them is in September, when stores want to unload excess inventory, and in January and February, when just about all big-ticket appliances—including ranges, refrigerators, washers, and dryers—are discounted most heavily.

The same principle applies in just about every product category. Lawn furniture, outdoor grills, garden tools, and golf and tennis equipment are much better buys in August and September than in May and June, the beginning of the season when people are planning outdoor living activities. Those are the months to buy utensils for indoor cooking and appliances like humidifiers and portable heaters.

Beware of calendars that purport to tell you exactly the best month to buy everything. They are no longer dependable. In fact, because "everybody knows" the best time to buy china and silver is in February, manufacturers and retailers target that month for widely promoted "sales" in which prices may not be as low as they are later in the year.

▶ AVOID DISPOSABLES

In the long run, reusable cameras, dishes, razors, and a host of other products are nearly always significantly cheaper than their disposable counterparts. The American obsession for "convenient" disposable products has a terrible environmental cost as well. Does it really make sense to add hundreds of millions of disposable plastic razors to our landfills just to save the few seconds it takes to change a razor blade?

▶ SAVE RECEIPTS, WARRANTIES, AND MANUALS

Get a receipt for everything you buy, and save every receipt for a major purchase—appliances, furniture, cars, and household repairs and improvements. To be super-safe, put these in a safe-deposit box; you'll have proof of ownership for the insurance company if the purchase is destroyed in a fire or other catastrophe.

More likely, you'll need the receipt and the warranty

when something goes wrong. If you keep owners' manuals and warranties in one place, you can try to fix something yourself before going to the trouble of asking for a warranty repair.

Periodically throw away warranties no longer in force and receipts for appliances that have been replaced, but keep a permanent file of all receipts for home improvements. You'll use them to lower your tax bill when you sell your house and want to establish the highest possible cost basis for it.

▶ USE THE ENERGYGUIDE LABELS ON APPLIANCES

Federal laws mandate the display of EnergyGuide labels on most home appliances. The efficiency ratings claimed on these labels are based on standardized tests and they are generally reliable. The ratings are expressed in one of two ways. Energy Efficiency Ratings (EERs) measure the efficiency of one product in relation to similar products. With EERs, the higher the rating, the more efficient the product. For instance, a central-air-conditioner unit rated 10 would use 50 percent more energy than one rated 15.

The second, more common, way appliance labels measure energy use is in terms of dollars. The dollar figures on an energy label represent the estimated annual cost of operating that specific appliance. The lower the dollar amount, the more efficient the product.

The problem is, most people don't do much more than glance at the big dollar number in the middle of the label under the arrow. Let's say that on refrigerator Model A, the number is $80 (the annual cost of energy to run this model in an average home). On Model B, it is $110. You prefer Model B and decide that the extra $30 a year isn't too great a price to pay for the features you like.

You are making a hasty decision. Before you shop for any major appliance, make sure you check your latest utility bills to see how much you are paying per kilowatt hour for electricity. We, for instance, live in an area with particularly high energy costs. The $80 and $110 annual costs given on the two refrigerators in question are probably based on a national average cost of 8.25 cents per kilowatt hour. But our cost per kilowatt hour is 14.44 cents.

If you divide $80 by 8.25 cents, you know that Model A is expected to consume 975.61 kilowatt hours in an average home. Model B is expected to consume 1,333.33 kilowatt hours in that same average home. But our costs would be $141 annually for Model A (975.61 × 14.44 cents) and $192 (1,333.33 × 14.44 cents) for Model B. That makes the difference between the two models not $30 but $51 a year.

That annual difference of $51 adds up to $1,020 in twenty years, the life span of an average refrigerator. So we have a major incentive to buy the most energy-efficient refrigerator we can find, even if its initial cost is hundreds of dollars more.

Actually, of course, the initial cost of energy-efficient refrigerators is nearly always less, not more, than less efficient models, which are equipped with devices such as automatic icemakers and through-door dispensers.

▶ BUY A GAS RANGE WITH AN ELECTRONIC IGNITION SYSTEM

If you cook with gas, avoid ranges that use pilot lights. An automatic ignition system will cut down your gas use by at least one third.

▶ CHECK UTILITY REBATES FOR EFFICIENT APPLIANCES

Many utilities now offer rebates to customers who buy energy-efficient air conditioners, refrigerators, freezers, heat pumps, water heaters, and other appliances. Before you buy a new major appliance, call the conservation office of your utility company and see what rebates are offered.

▶ CHECK OUT SECONDHAND STORES

There are some things we wouldn't consider buying secondhand, but there are many more where the idea doesn't bother us at all. We must have a lot of company, because there has been a definite growth trend in specialized secondhand retailers in the past few years. One company, *Grow-Biz International,* has more than 1,400 outlets nationwide, each specializing in one of five areas: sports, computers, products for children, musical instruments, and compact disks. If you want to check one out, call 800-433-2540 for the location of a store near you.

▶ BUY FROM MAIL-ORDER DISCOUNTERS

It's a lot easier to find deep discounts on appliances, furniture, and other items if you are looking for them and comparison shopping in a large metropolitan area, where strong competition holds prices down. If you live in a less populated area, your best sources of bargains may be discount catalogs that you can order from by mail or telephone.

You can save on just about anything by mail, and often the prices are better than at any retail store in the country—large metropolitan area or not. If you are especially serious about finding the best mail-order bargains, hundreds of sources are described within different categories by *The Wholesale-By-Mail Catalog* by The Print Project ($17.00, HarperCollins).

The next few tips list mail-order sources for various kinds of merchandise that we, and our network of sources, have found particularly noteworthy for price, dependability, and service.

▶ AUDIO/APPLIANCES/VIDEO/ ELECTRONICS BY MAIL

All of the discount operations listed below will give price quotes by phone but require manufacturers' model numbers. None of them sell "gray market" merchandise (products intended for sale in other countries; their manufacturers may not warranty them if sold to U.S. customers). Make sure you know exact shipping charges and return policies before ordering and use a credit card if you do.

- *LVT Price Quote Hotline,* 516-234-8884. Major appliances, vacuum cleaners, video, and electronics. Free catalog.
- *Dial-a-Brand,* 800-237-3220. Large and small appliances, video, air conditioners.
- *Crutchfield,* 800-955-9009. Video, computers, phone equipment, and home and car audio. The free catalog is especially informative.

► CAMERAS AND PHOTOGRAPHIC SUPPLIES BY MAIL

- *Porter's Camera Store,* 319-268-0104. A free catalog any camera enthusiast should receive regularly, with a wide range of heavily discounted merchandise.
- *Mystic Color Lab,* 800-367-6061. A good film-processing service at terrific prices. Call for price quotes and free film mailers.

► FURNITURE BY MAIL

- *Quality Furniture Market of Lenoir,* 704-728-2946. Deeply discounted prices quoted by phone or mail on furniture and bedding from hundreds of different manufacturers.
- *Blackwelder's Industries,* 800-438-0201. In NC: 704-872-8922. Various catalogs available for nominal costs, refundable with purchase, on high-quality furniture, clocks, pianos, rugs, carpeting, and home accessories.
- *Cherry Hill Furniture,* 800-888-0933. In NC: 919-882-0933. Home and office furniture, rugs, and carpeting. Free brochure and price quotes by phone.
- *Ephraim Marsh,* 704-782-0814. Made-to-order traditional furniture. The catalog ($5, refundable) is worth

having just for its descriptions of quality points in each group of furniture. Will use your fabric.

▶ BETTER THAN MAIL: GO TO NORTH CAROLINA

It is no accident that all of the furniture discounters mentioned above are located in North Carolina. The state produces at least 60 percent of the furniture sold in the United States and hundreds of deep-discount retail furniture operations are now located in and around the cities of High Point and Hickory. If you are planning to buy enough high-ticket items, making a special trip to the area is a good idea. A few manufacturers who want to protect their traditional retail customers in the other forty-nine states have put pressure on the North Carolina mail-order operations to stop discounting their products out of state. But if you shop right there, you'll find furniture from all manufacturers at consistently lower prices than anywhere else in the country.

Although they are deep discounters, many of the furniture retailers in the area operate handsome, spacious showrooms and offer professional interior-design assistance.

Before you go, call the Convention and Visitor's Bureaus in Hickory (800-849-5093) and High Point (910-884-5255). Each will send you big packets of maps, brochures, and special deals on motel accommodations.

▶ LIGHTING BY MAIL

■ *Golden Valley Lighting,* 800-735-3377, sells table and floor lamps as well as lighting fixtures from most major manufacturers at discounts that range from 25 to 50 percent off retail prices. Make sure you have the exact model number and other necessary specifications when you call for a price quote. A catalog ($5, refundable) is also available.

▶ COOKWARE BY MAIL

■ *Broadway Panhandler,* 212-966-3434, sells cookware for both home and professional use at discounts up to

40 percent. Check out the lowest prices you can find for names like Calaphon, Sabatier, and Braun, then call here with exact model numbers.

- *Fivenson Equipment,* 616-946-7761. Actually a distributor to the restaurant industry, but its catalog ($3, refundable) offers up to 50 percent discounts on ovens, mixers, microwaves, china, and other products that can be used in a home kitchen. Price quotes by phone.

▶ WALLPAPER BY MAIL

The companies listed below offer big discounts off the retail prices of virtually all wallpapers. Call with the name of the sample book and page number of the wallpaper you want to buy, and you will normally get an immediate price quote, usually 40 to 50 percent less than the suggested retail price and often 20 percent less than retail-store discounters offer. Delivery is usually quick and efficient as well.

We have felt a bit guilty about using our local store's sample books to choose wallpaper and then giving our order to a lower-overhead competitor. So we were glad to hear from Trudy Myers, a reader from Nanty-Glo, Pennsylvania. She wrote to tell us that when she quotes the best price she gets from a mail-order supplier, her local wallpaper store will match it. We'll try the same strategy next time; as Trudy points out, all the store can say is no.

- *Bennington's,* 800-252-5060
- *Peerless,* 800-999-0898
- *Wallpaper Outlet,* 800-488-9255

▶ CHINA, CRYSTAL, AND FLATWARE BY MAIL

Once we know patterns, these are the places we check first when buying wedding presents. We have learned that prices vary greatly. One source may have much deeper discounts on one china pattern than another, but the reverse can be true on yet another pattern. Check as many as you can before buying.

- *Barrons,* 800-538-6340, sells only by mail and will quote discounts of from 25 to 50 percent off the list prices of tableware and gifts. Free catalog.
- *The China Warehouse,* 800-321-3212, will also quote discount prices off Waterford, Lenox, Royal Doulton, Towle, and other makers of china, crystal, and flatware. Free catalog.
- *Thurber's,* 800-848-7237, had some of the best prices during our most recent shop-by-phone experience.

Also: *Michael Fina* (800-BUY-FINA; in NY: 718-937-8484); *Ross-Simon* (800-556-7376); *Fortunoff's* (800-283-2234; in NY: 516-294-3300). These large retailers of jewelry, gifts, and tableware all have good catalogs and will quote prices by phone.

▶ STUFF FOR BABIES BY MAIL

- *One Step Ahead,* 800-274-8440, guarantees to match any other catalog's prices on the products it sells—feeding and safety equipment, travel accessories, furniture, toys, clothing, etc.
- *The Right Start Catalog,* 800-548-8531, has good prices on a wide range of merchandise and a friendly, helpful staff.

These two specialized catalogs are hardly the only good sources of discount baby products. Among general merchandisers, *JCPenney* (800-222-6161) has especially good catalogs and prices devoted to children's products. Given the fact that the average cost of a baby is over $5,000 in the first year alone, consider calling 800-888-0385 and ordering a copy of *Baby Bargains* ($11.95 plus shipping) direct from the authors, Denise and Alan Fields. It is filled with money-saving tips, sources, and name-brand reviews. It is also available in bookstores (distributed by Publisher's Group West).

▶ **SHEETS AND TOWELS BY MAIL**

■ *Fieldcrest Cannon Factory Outlet Store* (for Fieldcrest products: 800-841-3336; for Cannon products: 800-237-3209) sells sheets, towels, blankets, bath rugs, and comforters at savings of 40 to 60 percent. Friends who can afford the best buy Fieldcrest Charisma sheets and towels this way, saving 60 percent on the most expensive mass-produced linens made in the United States. The telephone representatives are especially helpful.

▶ **CONSIDER SECONDS IN SHEETS AND TOWELS**

Now that everyone knows about January white sales and many, if not most, people wait for them, buying in January no longer guarantees you the best bargains in sheets and towels. In fact, manufacturers and department stores now target January as a key sales month even for new merchandise. "On sale" and "marked down" don't necessarily mean a thing.

The real bargains in sheets and towels are often found in stores and factory outlets selling discontinued patterns and/or "seconds" of brand-name merchandise. Most often, particularly with sheets and towels, it is very difficult to tell why a second is a second—a skipped stitch that won't affect wearability, or perhaps a slight variation in color that will be completely unnoticeable after one or two washings. Yet 50 to 75 percent discounts off list prices are common.

▶ **STOP BUYING GIFTS ON A DEADLINE**

Most people make the same mistake over and over again, year after year, when they buy gifts. A week before Aunt Betty's birthday, and only then, they begin to think about what to get her. Then they rush out and buy something often not quite the right color or model. They also make a panicked whirlwind tour of stores two weeks before Christmas to buy for everyone on their list.

These are the kind of gift shoppers that swell retailer profits, but they are wasting their own time and money.

The alternative is simple and guaranteed effective. Except for unpredictable events like weddings, you know exactly who you will buy gifts for annually. Get a small, pocket-size notebook and make a list—every birthday and anniversary as well as everyone on your Christmas list. Update the list once a year to add graduations, bar mitzvahs, and other predictable special occasions.

Take this notebook with you whenever you think there is even a remote chance you will be shopping. Every time you enter a store of any kind, take ten seconds to review the list. Aunt Betty lives in Vermont and loves sweaters of all kinds. You are on vacation in Mexico in April and see two different sweaters in her size that would cost at least twice as much at home. Too bad her birthday was a month ago, right?

Wrong. Buy both. For the next two years, you won't have to spend frustrating hours shopping specifically for her. And you've bought two years' worth of birthday presents for the price of one.

Obviously, there are limits to your attic space. Ten years from now, Aunt Betty might be two sizes larger. Styles may change. But the principle is an important one. The right gift, at the right price, simply doesn't appear as if by magic just because someone's birthday is a week away. The same sweater will nearly *always* cost much more on December 1 than it will in April. Different categories of merchandise are invariably cheaper during certain times of the year.

Remember to make notations of what you have bought in your notebook, or you are likely to forget what's up in the attic. Check items off as they are given. For safety's sake, because your notebook will become increasingly invaluable as a record of what you have given and what you've got stored, photocopy its pages from time to time and keep the copy in a safe place.

The only hard part of this is getting in the notebook habit. Once you have, you'll save hours of frustration and a lot of money—easily 30 percent or more.

▶ BEWARE THE $50 ROLEX

Of course you know you'll never find a real Rolex or Cartier watch for the price of the illegal counterfeit you may encounter for sale at a flea market or on the street. Some people are tempted, though—it may look so "real."

The sad fact is that when compared directly with the original, the counterfeit invariably looks shoddy. Save yourself the embarrassment of being discovered.

▶ SHOP OUTLET STORES

If you are unfamiliar with the outlet-store phenomenon, read the tips in Chapter 8 about shopping for clothing in factory outlets.

There are many outlet stores that sell merchandise other than clothing, of course. Among the many companies that sell seconds and irregulars, first-quality goods, or both through factory outlets are Bose (audio equipment), Corning Revere (Corningware, Pyrex, Corelle, and Revereware brand cookware and dinnerware), Dansk (Scandinavian-design cookware, flatware, gifts), Emerson Radio (Emerson and Scott electronic equipment), Hamilton Watches, Lenox (china), Oneida Silver (stainless and silver-plated flatware), Royal Doulton (china), Samsonite (luggage), and Wamsutta/Springmaid (sheets, towels, linens).

Outlet stores are unquestionably sources of great bargains, but see Chapter 8 for shopping strategies to use.

▶ SHOP ON THE INTERNET? MAYBE

To date, we haven't seen any compelling evidence that a lot of great bargains can be found on-line. We have found some competitive prices and quite a few interesting, even unique, retail sites on the Internet, however. By next week, if we had the time, we would probably find dozens more. And we are certain that a lot of bargains will soon be available, because sellers of goods should eventually realize great savings in overhead by selling from web sites. Here are three likely sites to check out—all of them selling a cornucopia of goods and services.

- *Cybershop* (http://www.nfic.com/Cybershop/Online)
- *The Gigaplex* (http://www.gigaplex.com)
- *Shopper's Advantage* (http://www.cuc.com) is a membership discount service with a $49 annual fee, but it offers a trial membership for just $1.

▶ SHOPPING ABROAD: AVOIDING THE VAT

Most European countries, Japan, Israel, and Canada add a hidden tax (usually called a Value Added Tax) onto the cost of merchandise sold domestically. To encourage tourism, however, most also allow foreigners to escape some or all of this tax (which in Europe can be as high as 20 percent of the displayed retail purchase price), especially on expensive items.

In some stores, such as Harrods in London, the clerks are so accustomed to selling to foreigners that all you have to do is tell them you are an American and they'll make sure all of your tax-avoiding paperwork is done. You may have to work a bit harder elsewhere.

It doesn't make sense to ask about the VAT on low-cost items, and most countries spare their merchants the bother by setting a minimum purchase amount for a VAT refund (ranging from less than $100 in England to about $500 in Italy). Most countries also limit VAT refunds to purchases of merchandise, not to services.

Here's what to do:

Before you buy a high-ticket item, ask if the store participates in the local VAT-reduction program, if your purchase qualifies, and how much your VAT refund will come to. Usually, the minimum amount necessary for a refund is not on a per item basis but on a per store basis—purchases listed on one form. This makes shopping in as few places as possible preferable.

Buy with a credit card if at all possible (it isn't everywhere) to get the best exchange rate on both the purchase and the refund.

When you leave the country, you show the customs official all the VAT refund forms you have received from stores. You either get a refund from customs then and there, or you mail validated forms back to the appropriate stores. They will either credit your account (if you paid by credit card) or eventually send you a refund check.

Many countries permit stores to deduct the VAT from the purchase price if you don't take possession of the item but instead have it mailed to your home address. If such shipments are limited each day to merchandise worth less than $50, you don't have to pay a customs duty tax on them. Otherwise, you will have to pay U.S. duty and clearance expenses.

There can be enough of a hassle involved in all of this to discourage even a dedicated penny pincher if only a few dollars are involved, but it is more than worthwhile if you buy an expensive piece of jewelry or an antique vase.

▶ BUY 364 DAYS EARLY

Don't you feel foolish, standing in a long line at the hardware store on December 24, waiting to pay for Christmas-tree lights you know will cost 50 percent less at the same place (with shorter lines) two days later?

Christmas-tree lights and ornaments, Christmas cards, holiday gift wrapping—all go on sale after December 25 for at least 50 percent off nearly everywhere. Even if you overestimate next year's needs, sooner or later everything you buy will be used.

The price of chocolates goes down right after Easter. Look for sales in wine and liquor stores right after New Year's Eve. And why not send a dozen roses to your valentine on February 15 (typically at a discount of at least 75 percent off February 14 prices) with a note declaring your ardor 364 days *ahead* of time? Now, *that's* romantic (just don't try it as a *substitute* for a gift the day before).

▶ SHOP CHARITY THRIFT SHOPS

Many churches, synagogues, hospitals, and charitable organizations operate thrift shops either year-round or on an occasional basis. Unless you are an inveterate shopper, forget 98 percent of them. The ones you are interested in are located in the most affluent sections of your metropolitan area. What gets donated to them is sometimes anything but thrift-shop junk. Especially if you are looking for crystal, china, cutlery, and high-quality cookware, try a couple of these first.

▶ CHOOSE THE MAILING LISTS YOU WANT TO BE ON

Why settle for what they want to send you? When you shop for the first time in a store you like, don't leave until you've asked to be put on its mailing list. Most retailers now have a mail-order capability, and many send advance notice to special customers when they are having a sale.

When you shop in a factory-outlet mall, ask to be put on its mailing list, too. You'll learn about mallwide sales in advance.

6

Minimizing Car Expenses

§ §

You should find some useful money-saving tips in this chapter no matter what kind of car you now own. But the first step in minimizing automobile expenses is to calculate what owning and operating a specific make and model will cost on an annual basis *before* you buy it.

One of the keys to this process is estimating the price you will be able to get for a car when you sell it or trade it in. Some new cars will still be worth 50 percent of their purchase price four years later. Others will lose 75 percent of their value. If you buy an $18,000 car and trade it in for $9,000 four years later, it has cost you $2,250 a year plus fuel, maintenance, insurance, etc. If you buy a $16,000 car and trade it in for $4,000 four years later, your cost is $3,000 a year.

Nobody knows for sure how much any car will be worth years from now, of course, but the annual (December) auto issue of *Kiplinger's Personal Finance Mag-*

azine uses historical data on different manufacturers and models to estimate the two- and four-year resale value of the next model year's cars. It's good information to have. Note especially how rapidly all new cars depreciate in value during their first two years. There is no more compelling argument for either buying a good used car or for hanging on to the car you own for a lot more than two years.

Whether you are buying a new or used car, you should also study the annual (April) auto issue of *Consumer Reports,* which is full of information about safety, repair records, prices, fuel economy, comfort and convenience, and handling on the road. Most libraries have both magazines.

Another expense to consider before you buy is what your insurance premiums will be. Similarly priced cars do not necessarily cost the same to insure. The difference, based on the car model's past and estimated future claims for theft and accidents, can be significant. Before you buy, talk to your insurance agent.

Working with an insurance agent, the magazines mentioned above, and prices negotiated with three different dealers in our area, we estimated annual costs on three similarly priced makes and models. The results are shown on page 120. The most expensive car in terms of initial price turned out to be well worth it.

When you next buy a car, use the same worksheet to establish estimated annual costs for each make and model you are considering. In fact, why not get your fingers together now and estimate what your present car is costing you?

Once you actually analyze how much you spend to own and operate a car on an annual basis, you may come to some surprising conclusions. We have city friends who figure they saved at least $3,000 a year by getting rid of their car and renting one when they went away on weekends or on a vacation trip. Many people decide that the convenience of a second car is not worth the price.

▶ SAVE MORE THAN 50 PERCENT ON OIL CHANGES AND LUBRICATION

The fact is, today's cars need less normal maintenance than the gas guzzlers of the 1960s and 70s, and this kind of maintenance is easier to perform than it ever was. The complicated stuff in modern cars—electronics— usually gets replaced, not repaired. But you'd never know that when you look at the bloated bills most new car dealers hand you after a normal periodic warranty checkup.

If something is wrong or you even suspect something might be wrong with your car, by all means take it to a good mechanic or back to the dealer. Otherwise, use one of the franchised quick-lube-and-oil-change outlets. Their employees are trained to check all the essentials—belts, tires, brakes, etc.—lubricate what's necessary, and change the oil and oil filter.

Most manufacturers insist you must use factory-authorized parts to keep your warranty in force. No problem. Stop by the dealer's service center, buy a factory-authorized oil filter, and give it to the quick-lube outlet when you drive in. They will deduct the price of an oil filter from a bill that is nearly always at least 50 percent less than the same service would have cost at a car dealer or a full-service garage.

▶ CHANGE MOTOR OIL MORE FREQUENTLY

Most cars in this country spend most of their lives being driven for relatively short distances in urban areas, with lots of stops and starts for traffic lights and traffic jams. These are exactly the conditions that age an engine prematurely, so it is important not to pinch pennies by stretching out the intervals between oil changes. Unless your car is driven under ideal conditions—long trips at a constant fifty-five miles per hour in temperate weather—don't go more than 3,000 miles or three months between oil and filter changes.

Annual Cost Worksheet for a New Car
(Sell/trade-in after 4 years and 60,000 miles)

		Car 1	Car 2	Car 3
A.	Estimated purchase price (including taxes)	$17,100	$16,500	$17,400
B.	Estimated resale value	6,000	4,800	7,830
C.	Subtract B from A	11,100	11,700	9,570
D.	Annual cost (C divided by 4 years)	2,775	2,925	2,393
E.	Estimated annual insurance costs	1,200	1,150	920
F.	Estimated cost of gas @ $1.20* a gallon, 15,000 miles a year (Divide 15,000 by estimated miles per gallon; multiply by $1.20)	857 (21 mpg)	720 (25 mpg)	643 (28 mpg)
G.	Estimated average yearly maintenance	200	240	130
H.	Estimated average yearly repairs/new parts	350	300	150
	TOTAL ANNUAL COST	$ 5,382	$ 5,335	$ 4,236

*Adjust to current conditions

▶ DON'T PAY FOR WORTHLESS HIGHER-OCTANE-RATED GAS

It is a waste of money ever to buy gasoline with a higher octane rating than is specified in your owner's manual (for most cars other than high-performance V-6s and V-8s, unleaded 87 octane). Some people think their car's engine needs a "super" gas treat now and then, that higher octane is somehow better for the engine. It isn't, despite the claims of the oil-company ads.

One note of caution: Modern engines do need high-detergent fuels with special additives. Stations selling no-name brands may offer cheaper gas with the octane rating you require, but poor-quality fuel can reduce efficiency and cause engine problems. Best to stick with the brands from the major oil companies.

▶ PAY CASH AND PUMP IT YOURSELF

Why pay cents a gallon extra to use a credit card at those stations that offer a discount for cash sales? And why pay cents extra to have someone else pump gas for you unless you are also getting some other useful service free? It's usually quicker, and requires hardly any more effort on your part, to use the self-service lane.

▶ BUY GAS EARLY IN THE MORNING

Especially in the hot summer months, you'll get more for your money—as much as 5 percent more—if you buy gas before the sun's heat has expanded the gas in the service station's fuel tank.

▶ DON'T TOP OFF YOUR FUEL TANK

Again, especially in hot weather, don't pump those few extra cents' worth in your tank after the automatic cutoff for a full tank. Heat will make the gas expand and overflow.

▶ USE YOUR CAR'S AIR CONDITIONER

Most new cars (utility vehicles less so) have become highly efficient in terms of aerodynamic design. Especially at higher speeds over long distances, you will waste more fuel in hot weather by opening windows and creating drag than you will by turning on the air conditioner.

There are still good reasons to turn the air conditioner off and open the windows, of course. When you are driving short distances at low speeds, leave the air conditioner off. Always turn it off when you are caught in a traffic jam and your car is hardly moving at all. Any engine idling with the air conditioner on in hot weather is working too hard for its own good.

▶ BABY PASSENGER? SAVE WITH A SAFETY SEAT LOANER

Some insurance companies and some communities have "loaner" programs that drastically cut the cost of a child safety seat. Check with your auto insurance agency, or send a stamped, self-addressed envelope along with a request for information on loaner programs in your area to the National Highway Traffic Safety Administration, Washington, D.C. 20590.

▶ CHECK TIRE PRESSURES REGULARLY

With the days of full-service-with-a-smile long gone at gas stations, most people put off checking tire pressures for months at a time. Yet you will lose about 2 percent fuel economy for every pound of pressure under the recommended pounds per square inch. Buy your own gauge (less than $5) and check tire pressures according to the manufacturer's recommendations at least once a month. You'll also save by prolonging the life of your tires.

Also check your wheel alignment whenever the car gets routine service. Even if wheels are only slightly out of line, they can affect gas mileage as well as shorten the life of tires.

▶ STEEL-BELTED RADIALS ARE WORTH THE EXTRA MONEY

They are safer, last twice as long as bias-ply tires, and will give you at least a couple of extra miles per gallon.

▶ REMOVE YOUR ROOF RACK

If you're not using it regularly, take it off to reduce both drag and the car's total weight. Clean out the trunk, too. Extra weight reduces gas mileage.

▶ CHECK YOUR AIR FILTER

A dirty filter will lower gas mileage.

▶ DON'T IDLE A COLD ENGINE

Letting a car idle for two or three minutes to warm up a cold engine was once a recommended procedure. That's no longer true. Modern cars need only a few seconds of idling time; any longer and you are just wasting gas. In fact, you reduce engine wear when you move the car after a fifteen-second warm-up, holding the speedometer down to under thirty for a couple of miles, then increasing your speed as you see the engine temperature begin to rise.

▶ WAIT TO USE HEATERS AND AIR CONDITIONERS

In cold weather, save gas by waiting until the engine begins to warm up before turning on the heater. In hot weather, save gas by waiting until after you start the car to turn on the air conditioner.

▶ NEED AN ODD CAR PART? CALL CAR TREK

There is nothing wrong with your ten-year-old car except for one part that must be replaced. Unfortunately, finding that part in any one geographical area can be time-consuming, difficult, or even impossible. *Car Trek* (800–728–3240 or on the Internet: http://www.car-trek.com) puts people who need hard-to-find parts together with suppliers who stock them. The fee is $25 to conduct six searches a month by phone or an unlimited number on-line.

▶ CHANGE A FEW DRIVING HABITS

If you can break a few bad driving habits, you can add at least 10 percent to your car's fuel efficiency.

- Minimize braking. Anticipate speed changes. When you see a red light ahead, take your foot off the accelerator and coast to it.
- Accelerate smoothly. Unless you are trying to fight your way onto a crowded freeway, there's no reason to jam your foot down on the pedal. Once you have reached your desired speed, keep a steady pressure on the accelerator, just enough to maintain speed.
- 55 saves money. The average car will use 17 percent less fuel when driven at 55 mph rather than 65 mph.
- Turn off the engine. It takes less gas to restart the car than it takes to let it idle for more than a minute.

▶ REDUCE THE COSTS OF BRIDGE TOLLS

Most bridge and tunnel authorities offer discounts if tickets or tokens are purchased in certain quantities. No doubt you buy this way if you commute over the same bridge most days. But even if you use a bridge only once a month, it is still probably worth your while to take advantage of reduced-fare discounts, especially since there is no time limit on when the tokens have to be used.

▶ TRADE IN YOUR CAR JUST ONE YEAR LATER

The quality of all makes of cars has improved dramatically in the past fifteen years. If you have been in the habit of trading a car in every three or four years, stretch that to four or five—or even seven to ten.

After it is three years old, the annual cost of owning a car drops dramatically. You'll probably spend more on repairs and replacement parts, but the years of big depreciation (the amount by which the car's value decreases simply because of age) are over, and insurance costs are lower. If you take proper care of your car and it remains rust-free, there is no reason not to get well over 100,000 miles of dependable service from it.

▶ BEFORE BUYING ANY CAR, CALL 800-424-9393

This is the toll-free number of the National Highway Traffic Safety Administration's Auto Safety Hotline. Call it to check on any safety recalls of the make, model, and year of any used car you are considering. You can also get information about how any new car model stacks up in the government's car-crash tests.

▶ MAXIMIZE GAS MILEAGE ON ANY CAR YOU BUY

All new car specification sheets tell you how many miles per gallon the car supposedly will deliver in both city and highway driving conditions. All make clear you'll get better mileage with a manual transmission than with an automatic. No matter what make, model, or type of transmission you buy, if you want to get the best possible gas mileage, you should also know:

■ A car with a sunroof, even when it is closed, will get slightly worse gas mileage than the same car without one. An open sun roof can cost you a mile or more per gallon.
■ A light-colored car reflects the sun, keeping the car cooler in hot weather. The less your air conditioner has to work, the better your fuel efficiency.
■ Cruise control is a worthwhile option. It will help you

get better mileage when you are driving on a relatively uncrowded, flat highway.

■ In most of today's cars, overdrive is standard equipment. If it isn't in the car you choose, buy it as an option. At higher speeds, it can cut your gas consumption by 20 percent. In a manual-shift car, a fifth gear is essentially the overdrive gear.

▶ BEFORE BUYING, KNOW WHAT YOU WANT

Don't start negotiating for any car before you have narrowed your choices to two or three models. The best way to do this is to first spend some time in your library with *Consumer Reports* and other publications, then visit a few dealers and test-drive a few cars. With a computer and a modem, you can visit the Internet sites of GM, Ford, and all of the other major manufacturers. These sites are becoming increasingly sophisticated and useful.

Buying a car can be a confusing process, and dealers love a customer who will accept their explanations. Start shopping after your research is done, not while you are doing it.

▶ SKIP FOUR-WHEEL DRIVE

Four-wheel-drive vehicles have become extremely popular, but unless you really need it, it is an expensive option. It not only adds to the purchase price, it also guarantees you will spend more for gas and insurance.

▶ KNOW THE DEALER'S COST BEFOREHAND

This is absolutely essential information to have before you begin negotiating the purchase price on any car. *Consumer Reports* Auto Price Service (800–933–5555; $12 for one report, $10 for each additional one) is a good source for up-to-date computer printouts that compare the manufacturer's suggested retail price (MSRP) with the dealer's invoice price, not only for the car you are considering but for the options you want on it. The print-out will also include current information on any factory-to-consumer or factory-to-dealer rebates, a depreciation rating, and tips on how to deal with the dealer.

You can also access *AutoNet* on CompuServe. They will provide similar (but not quite as detailed or complete) information on-line, ready to be downloaded, for $1.50 a report.

To make it even more complicated, most dealers actually pay less than their invoice price for the car. They get what is called a "holdback" from the manufacturer, usually 2 to 3 percent of the MSRP. Even if the dealer were to sell you a car with a MSRP of $20,000 for the dealer's invoice price of $17,000—"the price he paid for it"—he would make $600 if his holdback was 3 percent. That's unlikely to happen. But knowing the invoice price and the range of manufacturer's dealer allowances gives you a lot of room to negotiate.

Tell the salesperson you deal with that you want to negotiate the price based on the dealer's invoice, not on MSRP, normally about 15 percent higher. That way, your conversation will be about how much profit he'll make on the car, not on what a great deal he is giving you.

Don't expect to buy a car at invoice price; the dealer must make a profit of some kind beyond his holdback. If you want a car that is wildly popular at the time and in short supply, you may have to pay close to the MSRP. Normally, though, you should be able to negotiate a deal at 2 to 6 percent above dealer's invoice.

▶ CHECK THE "DAY'S SUPPLY" NUMBERS

Will the dealer be willing to negotiate a favorable deal for you on the make and model you want? You can get a very good idea beforehand of how strong your bargaining position will be by checking the "day's supply" statistics published once a month in *Automotive News*, available in some libraries. The statistics are also published in the financial pages of some newspapers. If the number of cars sitting on dealers' lots is equivalent to a hundred days' supply at the current rate of sale, you are far more likely to get a terrific deal than if there is only a twenty days' supply. The higher the days' supply, the more likely the dealer will be under pressure to move cars.

▶ CHECK ON MANUFACTURER'S INCENTIVES

Automotive News has another useful feature, a weekly column called "Incentive Watch" that lists all the rebate and financing deals currently offered by domestic and foreign manufacturers. It provides details—the amount of the rebates and expiration dates—not only for consumer deals, but also for the incentives available to dealers to sell certain makes and models. Deduct the dealer's rebate from the car's invoice price to know the true current wholesale price of the car.

▶ WHILE NEGOTIATING, DON'T TELL THE DEALER HOW YOU'LL PAY

No matter how many times the salesperson asks (and ask they all will), don't talk about how you'll pay until you have a reached a definite, final agreement on how much. And if asked about a trade-in during the negotiating process, tell them you won't be trading in your old car. You can always change your mind after you have established the price of the new one.

Why the secrecy? You don't spend your life negotiating car deals; they do. It is in your interest to keep the discussion as simple as possible. Once financing and trade-ins become part of the picture, the deal will get so complicated you'll never know just how much your new car actually cost. Also, if the dealer knows you intend to pay cash or have arranged financing elsewhere, the price may go up. Dealers make money on financing.

▶ PAY CASH IF YOU CAN

Sorry, but it's always a better penny-pinching strategy than any kind of loan. (See Chapter 9 about different kinds of loans.)

▶ ASK FOR MANUFACTURER'S REBATES UP FRONT

If the manufacturer is advertising rebates, tell the dealer you want the rebate deducted from the final negotiated price of the car, not in a check mailed later on from the manufacturer. You'll save on sales tax this way.

▶ FIRM BUT PLEASANT WORKS BEST

It's easy to forget a lot of good advice on how to buy a car once you are negotiating with a skillful salesperson. You'll be subjected to sales techniques and psychological tricks that have worked in millions of negotiations. If you've done your homework, though, you'll know a lot about how strong your bargaining position is. Smile, stay with it, and be prepared to walk away. There are always other dealers.

▶ JOIN AUTOVANTAGE

AutoVantage (800–843–7777; $49 annual fee; introductory offer of three months for $1) offers a number of services and discounts. Among them:

■ Prenegotiated discounts on most new cars. You call AutoVantage with the make, model, and options you want. They tell you the dealer's invoice price and the amount you should add to that for dealer profit. They fax that information to a participating new car dealer near you, where you can then buy the car at that pre-established discounted price. No fuss, no bother. When we checked this service out, we found the price higher than what we got when we negotiated on our own, but not by a great deal. If you are a bit shy or just hate negotiating with car salesmen, this is a useful service.

■ If you prefer to lease, AutoVantage also offer prenegotiated deals.

■ New car summaries. Dealer costs, operating expenses, resale projections, standard equipment, and options on most makes of new cars. A good way to comparison-shop at home.

■ Discounts (typically 10 percent) at places like AAMCO, Goodyear, Kmart Auto Centers, Sears, Jiffy Lube, Firestone, Meineke, etc.

AutoVantage is available on-line via CompuServe and America Online.

▶ GO ON-LINE WITH AUTO-BY-TEL

Auto-By-Tel (on the Internet: http://www.autobytel. com/) will take your request for a specific new car and the options you want, then give that information to one of the 1,300 dealers with whom it has a contract. The dealer will contact you with a discounted price. Since the service is free, why not get a price this way? But do it after you have shopped around, because the price you get from an Auto-By-Tel dealer may be contingent on a fast response.

▶ MORE PRENEGOTIATED PRICES ON A NEW CAR

AutoVantage and Auto-By-Tel (previous tips) aren't the only ways to avoid the hassle of haggling with car salespeople. You might also want to look into *CarBargains* (800-475-7283; fee: $150), which is run by the Center for the Study of Services, a nonprofit consumer group in Washington, D.C. You tell CarBargains the make, model, and options you want. They then get bids from at least five dealers in your area and submit all these bids to you, along with complete information on dealer invoice costs. The fee is stiff, but solid bids from five dealers are well worth having. Also, CarBargains will follow up if a dealer reneges on a bid.

Auto brokers—independent sales organizations that work for dealers, not for you—are another way to get discounted prices on a new car. You'll see their ads in classified sections of newspapers, and calls to a couple of them are an easy way to establish a price that you may or may not be able to get on your own.

Competition among services offering prenegotiated prices on new cars is increasing. Both Price/Costco and Sam's Club (see Chapter 1 on joining a wholesale club) now refer members to dealers who have agreed to sell vehicles at a fixed amount over their invoice cost.

▶ SHOP AT THE END OF THE MONTH

Dealers all have monthly sales quotas to fill. If you catch one who is desperate to fill such a quota, you may get a much better price than you would have at the beginning of the month.

▶ SAME CAR, DIFFERENT LABEL?

As automobile manufacturers struggle to cut costs and remain competitive, there are more and more cases of the same basic car being priced differently by two or more divisions of the same company or by two companies who have cooperated on its design and production.

The dealer price of a 1996 Chevrolet Geo Prizm, for instance, was about $1,000 less than the Toyota Corolla that was essentially the same car, built in the same factory.

The 1996 Ford Probe SE shares many parts with its same-factory-mate, the Mazda MX-6, but is nearly $6,000 cheaper.

In the near-luxury class, the 1996 Toyota Camry XLE V-6 has exactly the same engine and shares many of the same body specifications with the Lexus ES 300. Comparably equipped, except for minor items, it was about $7,000 cheaper.

There will be more such clones and near clones in the

1997 model year and beyond. One of the best sources of information about them is *Consumer Reports*. Check its report on the car you are thinking of buying, and it will invariably mention any clone or near-clone available.

▶ BUY FROM A NO-HAGGLE DEALER? MAYBE

GM's Saturn started the trend, selling cars through its dealers only at one posted price. The success of the Saturn led some dealers for other makes of cars to establish no-haggle, nonnegotiable prices. Typically, these dealers post their discounted set prices next to the manufacturer's sticker price on car windows.

It is a pleasant way to shop for a car. Most no-haggle dealers post fairly low prices and many of them also offer other attractive customer-friendly services (free cab rides to work when your car is being serviced, for instance). But a tough, informed buyer can nearly always negotiate a better price for the same car (except a Saturn) at a competing traditional dealer. Even if you can't, you can always go back.

▶ CHECK LOAN RATES BEFORE YOU SHOP

If you must borrow money to buy a car, talk to your bank (and check loan rates in other banks) before you negotiate with the dealer. Particularly in these days of dealers' either/or choices between rebates and low manufacturer financing, it is difficult to evaluate different deals. Are you better off taking a $1,000 rebate and financing with your bank? Or should you skip the rebate and pay the lower interest rate offered by the manufacturer? You'll have to work the numbers out yourself (or ask a friendly accountant to do it), but generally the more you have to borrow, the more likely it is that the low financing is a better choice. (See Chapter 9 for more on auto loans.)

▶ AVOID DEALERS' LOANS

A low interest rate offered as a special deal by the manufacturer is different from a normal dealer loan on an automobile. It is rarely a good idea to borrow from a dealer. See Chapter 9 for details.

▶ NEVER SHOP FOR A MONTHLY PAYMENT AMOUNT

The worst possible mistake you can make when negotiating with a car dealer is to tell him how much you can pay for a car on a monthly basis. If he knows that's your primary concern, he'll tailor a loan to fit that amount, adding more monthly payments, higher interest rates, and a far higher total price. *Always* negotiate for a car as if you are going to be a cash buyer.

▶ SKIP THE DEALER'S RUSTPROOFING OPTION

It is not only useless, it may actually be damaging. All new cars today are rustproofed at the factory and all manufacturers provide a long-term anticorrosion warranty. The compounds and drilling involved in additional rustproofing can disturb what was done at the factory. Dealer rustproofing has survived for only one reason: It is highly profitable for dealers.

▶ SKIP THE DEALER'S EXTENDED WARRANTY

See Chapter 5 on extended warranties. Same scam. Instead, buy a car with a good frequency-of-repair history (see *Consumer Reports,* April issue). If you want to keep track of the results of this advice, put the money you would have spent on an extended warranty into a special savings account, to be used *only* for repairs that would have been covered by the warranty. Nine out of ten people will have money left over in the account.

▶ IN FACT, SKIP ALL THE DEALER'S "EXTRAS"

You've negotiated a terrific deal, so good that you wonder how the dealer can afford to take so little profit. There are smiles and handshakes all around. Now the dealer is writing out the order.

Be careful. Rustproofing and extended warranties are only two of the extra services dealers can add on, and often these add-ons are the source of most of their profit. The easiest way to handle this is to remember that you have bought a car, period. Nothing else. Maybe there are exceptions to the rule at some dealers, but we've never encountered any. If you want a dealer extra, you can find it somewhere else better and cheaper.

Among the extras you may be offered, or even told you have to buy as part of a dealer "pak":

- *Fabric protection.* Buy your own can of Scotchguard.
- *Paint sealants.* Unnecessary.
- *Glaze protection.* An extra coat of wax. Buy it at a car wash for much less.
- *A car alarm.* Many cars now come with factory-installed security devices. If so, the dealer's add-on alarm is a complete waste of money. If you car doesn't come with an alarm and you really want one, it will be cheaper to have it installed by one of the many car-alarm retailers.
- *Any kind of insurance.* See Chapter 4, but you absolutely don't want to buy accident, health, disability, or credit life insurance from your dealer.
- *Preparation charges.* The factory price of the car includes dealer preparation charges. Don't pay any extra charges. Inspect the car when you receive it, and don't accept it if it isn't clean inside and out.
- *Processing fees.* There may even be a preprinted "processing fee" of $50 or $100 in the dealer's sales agreement. Processing what? This is simply a way for the dealer to get back $50 or $100 of the money you have saved by hanging tough in your negotiations about

price. Hang tough again. Cross it out. If the dealer objects, tell him you're willing to buy the car elsewhere rather than get taken by as obvious a scam as this. By now he should be taking you very seriously.

▶ LEASING IS *STILL* NOT FOR PENNY PINCHERS

We have had some spirited correspondence with readers who took issue with our previous editions' blanket dismissal of car leasing. Overall, we still believe that buying is nearly always more cost-efficient in the long run *if you intend to keep the car for more than three years*. Any penny pincher who buys a new car should definitely plan to keep it longer than that.

However, if you insist on driving a new car every two or three years, we agree that leasing has recently become a more attractive option, mainly because car manufacturers are subsidizing leases in order to encourage drivers to switch cars more often. The best leasing deals tend to be those that are widely advertised by the *manufacturers*. The catch is that these deals are prepackaged with locked-in features. Change any of those, and you won't get the advertised price.

Whatever our opinions, leasing now accounts for more than 30 percent of all new car sales, and the percentage is going up.

When you lease a car instead of buying it, you pay a monthly fee for the term of the lease. At the end of that time, you normally have an option to buy the car. Most leases include down payments and/or security deposits. Some monthly fees include insurance and maintenance, some don't. People who lease like the lower down payments and lower monthly payments, but at the end of the lease period they don't own anything.

Car leases are complicated, and it is often difficult to choose the best alternatives from among different leases or in a lease-versus-buy decision. New gimmicks and add-ons are constantly being introduced, so, before you start shopping, read the latest advice you can get on leasing, starting with the last annual automobile issues of *Consumer Reports* and *Kiplinger's Personal Finance Magazine*. Here are some basic tips:

- Don't lease for more than three years. After that, the warranty will probably be up and fees leasors charge for "excess wear and tear" may get especially stiff. In any case, know exactly how the dealer defines "excess wear and tear."

- Don't accept an "open-ended" lease. That means you will be responsible if the actual value at the end of the lease is lower than the target set in your lease contract. You want a "closed end" lease guaranteeing that value.

- Bargain with dealers about lease rates the same way you would bargain with them about a purchase price. The best way to do this is to negotiate—starting from the dealer's invoice price—the price of the car as if you were going to buy it. Once this is established, ask the dealer to work out a lease deal based on that price.

- Make sure you aren't responsible for future payments if the car is stolen or in a major accident before the term of your lease is up, but don't pay an exorbitant extra fee for this.

- If you plan on driving more than the preset number of miles per year allowed on the lease (usually 15,000), negotiate how much those miles will cost you before you sign the lease.

- Don't lease unless you are sure you'll want the car for the full term of the lease. Termination costs are often excessive.

- Is the security deposit refundable when the lease ends? It should be. Is there a lease-termination fee even if you don't return the car until the lease agreement ends? If so, how much?

▶ **BEFORE BUYING OR SELLING A USED CAR, CALL 900-446-0500**

At $1.75 a minute, charged to your phone bill, this call to *Consumer Reports Used Car Price Service* is not a bargain—the typical calls lasts five minutes. But you will get the up-to-the-minute market value for any used car up to seven years old—adjusted for your geographical area, mileage, condition, and the major options it has (air-conditioning, automatic transmission, etc.).

You can also find out how *Consumer Reports* rates the model in terms of its frequency-of-repair record (also available in the April issue of the magazine, which you can find at nearly any public library).

▶ USE THE NADA BLUE BOOK

Every month, the National Automobile Dealers Association (NADA) publishes its *Official Used Car Guide* in eight regional editions. Available at most libraries, the NADA guide is generally referred to as "the blue book," although it isn't blue. While we think the *Consumer Reports* used-car valuation (previous tip) may be worth the extra money, you should also know what the current blue book says about any used car you are seriously considering.

The most important information in the blue book is the current average trade-in price of the car when it is in good condition. You will also find "average retail" prices, "average loan" values (what a bank would lend you on the car), current values of various optional equipment, and mileage tables that tell you whether to add or subtract from the average price.

Your goal when negotiating price is to pay as little as possible over the NADA trade-in-price—certainly nothing like the "retail" price also listed in the guide. How much more? That depends on the usual supply-and-demand factors as well as on whom you are buying it from; you might get a better deal from an owner selling direct than from a dealer.

▶ A QUICK USED-CAR INSPECTION CHECKLIST

Bill McFaul, a penny-pinching Scot reader from Manhasset, New York, says he has bought in the past twenty years literally dozens of cars for himself, friends, and family—usually direct from their owners. He has developed a checklist of quick ways to decide *not* to make a bid. If a car passes these tests and you think you can get it at a good price, Bill recommends you then make an offer contingent on a mechanic's inspection.

- Inspect the brake and gas pedals. Maybe the odometer says the car has only 50,000 miles on it. A car with abraded, torn-up pedals may have a lot more (it is illegal to tamper with an odometer, but it has been known to happen). Or those 50,000 miles have been in tough, stop-and-go traffic. Pass.
- Check the tires. Not for wear, although you certainly should factor in the price of new tires if they need replacing, but to see if the four tires match. Owners who maintain their cars well usually replace all four tires, or at least a pair of tires, at the same time. If one tire is a different size or make from the others, it is a good sign the owners skimped on other things, too. Pass.
- Press down hard with both hands on both front fenders. The car should come back up just once and stop. If it shakes at all, the shocks are shot.
- Look at the front of the car. There is "good mileage" on any used car—mileage resulting from long trips in light traffic at interstate speeds—and "bad mileage"—mileage resulting from a lot of stop-and-start trip in heavy traffic. Naturally, the owner will tell you that all of the miles on this 70,000-mile beauty are good. If they are, the front of the hood will be pitted by all the insects and small debris that are an inevitable consequence of driving at high speeds on open highways. If the hood is relatively clean, it has probably seen much more city driving. Pass.
- Never buy a car at night. There is a reason those used-car lots have Christmas-tree lights all over. Dents show up as highlights.
- People who maintain their cars well usually maintain good files on when and why the car has been ser-

viced. Look them over. If they are "lost," be suspicious.

- Be wary if the car has been warmed up before your test drive. It might not act well from a cold start. When you drive it, put it in first gear ("low" for automatics) and accelerate for 30 mph. Then take your foot off the pedal, allow the car to decelerate, and check the rearview mirror for smoke and fumes. Finally, with your hands off the wheel, put on the brakes. The car should stop straight ahead.

▶ SELL YOUR OLD CAR YOURSELF? MAYBE

Although you will nearly always get more by selling your old car yourself rather than trading it in, think twice before doing it, because it can be a frustrating experience. It may also take longer (adding to insurance and upkeep costs) and require more advertising (more extra costs) than you initially plan on. Especially if you live in a high-sales-tax area, factor that into your decision. If you buy a new car for $20,000, sales tax at 6 percent is $1,200. If, as part of that deal, you trade in a car for $10,000, your sales tax is reduced by $600 (you pay only 6 percent of the $10,000 difference). That means you will have to get $10,600 for the car elsewhere to match the dealer's $10,000 offer.

▶ BUT ESTABLISH THE TRUE TRADE-IN PRICE BEFOREHAND

Whatever *Consumer Reports* and the NADA blue book tell you about prices, car salespeople will give you a dozen reasons why they don't pertain to your car. The acid test comes when you actually try to sell it.

It will take a couple of hours, but shop the car around to at least three dealers in your area who buy used cars. Simply tell them you are definitely selling the car, you are getting prices at four or five different places, and you will be back the same day to sell it to whoever gives you the best price.

The highest price you establish this way is what you should tell your new car salesperson you'll accept as a trade-in price. In fact, tell him who gave you that price. Chances, are, he'll factor in the sales-tax differential (see previous tip), but make sure he doesn't also use this as an opportunity to go back and renegotiate the deal you've already made on the new car.

▶ BUY A "NEARLY NEW" CAR

There are fewer "nearly new" low-mileage cars on dealers' lots now than there were a few years ago, mainly because too many people became aware of the bargains that resulted from manufacturer "buyback" arrangements with car-rental companies. In some cases, cars only three months old—many with fewer than 10,000 miles on their odometers—were bought back and then auctioned to dealers who resold them for 20 to 30 percent less than similarly equipped new models.

After cries of outrage from new car dealers who had to compete with "nearly new" sales, manufacturers have now generally extended buyback agreements to six months or longer. Even with a few more miles on them, though, these cars (and other highly desirable "nearly news" generally traded in by people in the automotive industry) can still be very attractive buys. The warranty coverage is usually transferable (don't buy unless it is), although there may be a small fee involved.

As with most "terrific deals," especially those involving the automobile industry, you've got to be careful before you sign a sales agreement. Here are a few absolute rules to follow:

- Know the price of a comparably equipped new model of the car. Go to another dealer and negotiate a price on one. If the nearly new doesn't save you at least 20 percent, think long and hard before buying it. The dealer probably got it for at least a 30 percent discount off the retail price of the new model.
- Don't even consider buying a nearly new unless the dealer will show you the title to the car before you

sign a purchase agreement. The title will tell you who owned it last. Was it Kamikaze Auto Rental or a vice-president of an auto company? The latter's car is probably a better buy. The title will also give you the odometer reading at the time of ownership transferal. Make sure what's on the car's odometer agrees.

- The dealer should be able to show you a mandatory written inspection record done on the car right after it was bought at auction. If an inspection wasn't done within two weeks after the auction, the manufacturer might not honor the warranty if something goes wrong.

▶ BUY A "PRE-OWNED" CAR

It is just a euphemism for a used car, of course, but the term "pre-owned" is now often used by dealers specifically to denote cars they have put through rigorous tests and sell with full manufacturer's warranty protection, always one year or 12,000 miles and sometimes longer. This has become a big business, particularly for dealers selling more expensive or luxury cars. The reason: In 1997 alone, more than 2,500,000 cars, most two years old, will come "off lease."

We have a friend who figured out years ago what a bargain these cars were. There is nothing new about the critical numbers: Depending on the make and model, most cars depreciate in value from 40 to 50 percent in their first two years. After that, depreciation slows down considerably.

So our friend buys a two-year-old luxury car every four years. He says he pays extra for a very clean, obviously well-cared-for car, and always has a mechanic inspect it first. When he sells the car four years later (when it is six years old) he gets about 50 percent of what he originally paid for it. He figures his annual costs of driving a Mercedes for the past twenty years have been about the same as if he had traded in a new Ford every two years.

Let the non–penny pinchers of the world spend thousands of dollars extra in car expenses annually because they insist on driving a brand-new car every two years. A two-year-old car with a superior frequency-of-repair record and 24,000 or 30,000 miles on it can be one of the best deals around.

▶ CHECK INDEPENDENT LEASING COMPANIES

More and more independent car-leasing companies are selling used cars direct to the public, cutting out the dealer middlemen. Most of their cars are just coming off a two-year lease and will come with manufacturer's warranty protection.

▶ SHOP THE SUPERSTORES? MAYBE

CARmax (owned by the nationwide electronics superstore chain Circuit City), *Car Choice, Auto Nation USA,* and *Driver's Mart* are the first names in the newest way to buy a used car—at a nonnegotiable price from a huge "superstore" of used cars. Like "no-haggle" new car dealers, these new superstore chains offer a consumer-friendly atmosphere. They also offer a much wider selection than traditional used-car dealers. As far as we have been able to tell, their prices are seldom as low as what a determined negotiator could find elsewhere. If you hate to negotiate, however, you won't do badly at these places.

▶ CALL AUTOVANTAGE

In addition to its new car and discount services (see earlier tip in this chapter), AutoVantage ($49 annual membership) will search for a designated used car among dealers in your geographical area and provide you with asking prices and locations for cars meeting your specifications. They may also be able to tell you how long each car has been in stock and give you a discounted price available only to customers using the search service. This search service wasn't available on-line as of this writing; the number to call is 800-876-7787.

▶ **CARPOOL**

If your drive to and from work each day adds up to fifteen miles, you'll put over 3,500 miles a year on your car. Just cutting that in half—by finding one person to carpool with—will save you hundreds of dollars. If your car pool allows you to use a special rush-hour lane reserved for buses and cars with more than a certain number of people in them, you'll also save time.

Many companies have van pools. Look into joining one of them.

▶ **USE PUBLIC TRANSPORTATION**

Taking a bus or train is invariably cheaper than driving your own car, and by not subjecting your car to everyday bumper-to-bumper traffic jams to and from work, you'll extend its life by years.

▶ **BUY A BICYCLE**

Other than walking, there's no better, healthier way to minimize transportation expenses. Count up all those two-mile trips by car to the 7-Eleven and consider how much you could save in a year by substituting a bike equipped with a basket.

Because this book is about penny pinching, we don't always mention environmental benefits of certain strategies. But we do care about them. Carpooling and riding buses, trains, and bicycles are—like many other penny-pinching ideas—earth-friendly activities.

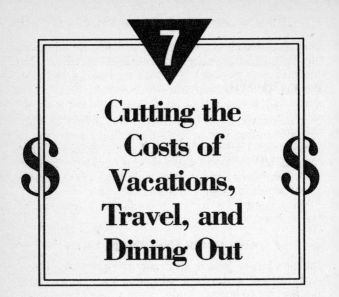

Cutting the Costs of Vacations, Travel, and Dining Out

Like fresh fish and bagels, the products of the travel industry are perishable—but even more so. A bagel maker may be able to sell his stale product for a reduced price a day later, but there is no way to sell either an empty seat after the airliner takes off or a vacant hotel room the morning after.

Car-rental companies, airlines, hotels, resorts, and cruise ships all have high fixed overhead costs. Their expensive buildings, cars, airplanes, and ships—along with the people it takes to operate them—must be paid for whether 50 percent or 100 percent of the rooms and seats are occupied. To make a profit, the number of unoccupied rooms and seats must be held to a minimum, even if that means reducing prices drastically.

The result is a bewildering system of ever-changing fare structures, hidden discounts, concealed wholesaler rates, and promotional deals. The tips in this chapter will help you cut through the confusion to get the best deals possible for your travel dollar. A few of them cover similar ground: If you join a last-minute travel club, for instance, you may get benefits that make a half-price coupon directory superfluous. Some of them make sense only if you travel a lot: If you would use only one or two coupons from a half-price coupon directory, don't buy one.

If you are young (usually 26 or younger, especially if you are a student) or old (50 or older, or even better, 62 or over), you have opportunities for discount travel denied those in the age groups in between. The travel industry is keenly aware that people over 50 are responsible for more than 80 percent of the total dollars spent on nonbusiness travel. Also, students and retired people are often flexible about scheduling, so they can fill airplane seats and hotel rooms that would otherwise remain vacant during nonpeak times. At the end of this chapter, there are some specific tips for these two groups.

Whichever tips you decide are right for you, here are three guidelines that are always operative:

- Comparison shopping is essential.
- Discounts are the norm, not the exception, throughout the travel industry. Look for them. Ask for them. Bashfulness is not a virtue among penny-pinching travelers.
- Especially if you don't have access to a computer with a modem, establishing a relationship with a savvy travel agent who is willing to work hard to save you money can be an enormous time-saver. The best way to do this is to make sure your agent gets commissions on your easy reservations as well as your more difficult ones. And the more work you can do yourself before you put your agent to work, the better your relationship will be. Clients who habitually change their minds and cancel reservations will not get first-rate service.

How do you know if you are working with a good travel agency? A penny pincher's agent won't always settle for the airline fares displayed on her computer screen. On many routes, unless you are buying coach excursion tickets, she will check at least one "consolidator" (see tip below) for a possible lower rate. She will also participate in a discount program for hotel reservations; if the only rates you can get from her are "rack" rates (see tip below), find another agent. A resourceful agent can save you enough to justify full agency commissions.

If you do the work yourself—and that is becoming easier every year, thanks to new resources such as the Internet—use an agency that rebates part of the commission.

Because rates and special offers change constantly, this book restricts itself to general tips and strategies for saving money on travel. If you travel a great deal, a subscription to a newsletter is a good way to keep up with trends and special deals. The best money-saving travel newsletter we have seen is the monthly *Consumer Reports Travel Letter* (800-234-1970; $39 a year). Check your library, too; ours subscribes for us.

▶ BECOME YOUR OWN TRAVEL AGENT

No travel agent could possibly take the time to investigate all the questions we have when we are planning a trip. Up until a couple of years ago, the best we could do was to write away for brochures and read books and magazines. This tip and the one that follows explain how our home computer and modem have completely changed the way we make travel plans.

The major on-line services, *CompuServe* (800-848-8199), *Prodigy* (800-776-3449), and *America Online* (800-827-6364), offer direct access to the *EasySabre* reservation system. Using EasySabre, which includes flight schedules and up-to-the-minute prices on commercial flights throughout the world, you can play "what if" scenarios as long as you like.

There are at least two big problems with EasySabre. First, it does not include schedules for "nonparticipating airlines," more than 300 worldwide and including many of the new small airlines in the United States that fly limited routes and aggressively cut prices. Second, you have to start your search with departure and return dates. You can then find out which of the participating airlines (all of the majors) offers the cheapest flights. You can't start a search asking first for the cheapest fares to your destination, then adapt your departure and return schedules accordingly.

Nevertheless, especially if you travel a great deal, access to EasySabre is a good reason to become a member of an on-line service (for moderate usage, the rates are between $10 and $15 a month). If you like, using EasySabre, you can actually book reservations, charge your ticket to your credit card, and receive tickets by mail. We prefer simply to shop by computer, pinning down the exact flight and fare we want. Unless we know of a small regional airline that flies where we are going (see tip below), we then call our travel agent to make those reservations. The travel agent is paid by the airline, not you, and in appreciation for getting such an easy commission, ours is willing to spend some extra time helping us in other ways.

EasySabre offers a hotel-reservation service, but you can do better elsewhere.

▶ EXPLORE THE WORLD WIDE WEB

Travel Weekly, the major trade magazine of the travel industry, has an incredibly useful home page on the Internet (http://www.traveler.net/) that is usually the first place we go to when we are even remotely thinking about a trip or a vacation. In addition to news clips from the magazine, *Travel Weekly* indexes and gives you immediate access to more than a thousand other travel-related Internet sites by category—Cars, Tours, U.S. Sites, World Sites, Airlines, Cruises, Hotels, Railroads, Theme Travel, Agencies, and Services. Whether you are going to Peoria or Sri Lanka, you will find destination-specific advice and intelligence here. Just about every tourist office in the world now has a web site. So does every major airline, cruise line, car-rental agency, and hotel chain. You will also find hundreds of agencies, consolidators, hotel chains, car-rental agencies, cruise lines, etc. offering discounts, rebates, and special deals.

Travelocity (http://www.travelocity.com) combines the same Sabre data bases used by EasySabre (see previous tip) with other destination-specific data bases. The result is a huge web site that gives you information on airline flights, fares, and availability as well as an enormous amount of information about thousands of travel destinations and special travel interests. As this edition was going to press, we found EasySabre easier to use than Travelocity for airline information, but expect it will become more user-friendly in the near future.

We also use area-specific travel forums on our on-line service and have gotten great answers to some specific questions. In one case, we went to a United Kingdom forum and asked about inexpensive lodging near the Manchester, England, airport. Within a day, we had responses from four different people who lived in or knew the area well—all just being helpful, not trying to sell us anything. One of the things we most enjoy about traveling is meeting and getting to know local people. With a computer and a modem, we can do that even before we leave home.

▶ OUT OF *WHOSE* SEASON?

The luxury Caribbean resort that charges $500 a day in March may reduce that price by as much as 50 percent six weeks later. By May, airlines flying to the Caribbean usually drop rates as well. Not much else has changed. The temperature may be 2 or 3 degrees hotter, but the prevailing island breezes make that difference barely perceptible. The tennis courts and golf course will be less crowded, and the duty-free stores often mark things down off-season.

You can also get terrific off-seasons bargains in most ski resorts. No snow, but you might not mind when you consider you can get summer mountain scenery, golf, tennis, lake swimming, hotel rooms, condo rentals, and restaurant meals at huge discounts from peak winter rates.

Is it really worth a 40 or 50 percent premium to go in season? Your answer may well be yes, if the choice is the Maine coast in January or July. But many choices aren't that dramatic. And sophisticated travelers, even those who aren't purposely penny pinching, avoid places like Paris in August, when the Parisians flee their city and busloads of tourists take it over.

▶ SHOP THE LOW-FARE AIRLINES

Low-fare, no-frills, start-up, or regional—whatever you call them, the new small airlines that have popped up in many parts of the country have become a major factor in penny-pinching travel plans. Many of them got their start when the majors pulled out of certain areas. Midway Airlines, for instance, moved into a vacuum in Raleigh-Durham, North Carolina, when American gave up its hub there. Midway's prices from New York to Raleigh-Durham usually beat the competition by at least 30 percent.

You will know if there is a small airline flying out of your area if you read the ads in your local newspaper. It is harder to keep track of them elsewhere, but *Consumer Reports Travel Letter* (see the introduction to this chapter) does a roundup of them from time to time, listing routes and 800 numbers. And you can search for them on the Internet (see previous tip). Among the names you should know: American Trans Air, Carnival, Kiwi, Frontier, and Tower.

Since the Valujet airliner crash in May of 1996, the FAA has become even more diligent about monitoring the pilots and equipment of these airlines, so we don't have any major concerns about their safety. Given the few planes in many of these fleets, however, any mechanical problems could cause more of a delay than on a major airline flight. Finally, to protect yourself in case one of them suddenly goes out of business, always use a credit card to purchase tickets.

▶ SHOP THE MAJOR AIRLINES' SALES

You can probably skip all of the tips that follow about saving money on airline tickets if you take advantage of the periodic sales on coach excursion tickets that all of the major airlines announce with full-page ads from time to time. The odds of your doing any better on prices— usually 30 to 50 percent under the normal coach fares— are slim. But you must be able to make a quick decision. Typically, the sales last only a week or ten days and only a limited number of tickets are available.

▶ BUY AIRLINE TICKETS FROM A CONSOLIDATOR

When airlines can't sell all the seats on a flight, despite their own promotions and special discounts, they may sell them to a ticket broker—a "consolidator"—at a wholesale price. The consolidator is then able to offer tickets for anywhere from 15 to 50 percent below normal prices. Some consolidators sell only to travel agents; others sell direct to the public as well.

Some consolidators specialize in international flights, but many also sell tickets for heavily traveled domestic routes. It's all perfectly legal, and quite safe to deal directly if it's a well-established, reputable company. Tickets are nearly always sold on a nonrefundable basis.

Although the companies listed below will hold your payment in escrow until your flight departs (not all consolidators will), it's a good idea to pay with a credit card so you can cancel easily if something goes wrong. Also, get your tickets as soon as possible after ordering so that you'll have time to correct any mistakes.

The downside: You may not fly at the most convenient time or by the most direct route. You may be told you can't get an advance seat assignment. You can't switch airlines at the last minute. You may not get frequent-flier credit for the miles flown (ask before you order). And don't take it for granted you are getting a discount; airlines often offer promotional fares that are better than what a consolidator can offer. In many such cases, however, that promotional fare may be loaded down with restrictions that you can't live with (travel only between Tuesday and Thursday and stay over one Saturday if the moon is full).

When you deal with a consolidator, make sure you are buying a discounted ticket and not a ticket on a charter flight. Some of them aren't too scrupulous about differentiating between the two. Too many charter flights pack customers into planes the way canneries pack sardines. They are also subject to extra delays if anything goes wrong. Unless you are part of an affinity group that is chartering the flight or have booked through a travel agent you trust, we suggest you avoid charter flights.

As usual, the number-one rule for an airline traveler who wants to save money is to shop all the alternatives before buying. A few consolidators to call for more information: *Uniglobe Access Travel* (800-938-5355; in CA 415-896-5333); *Travac* (800-872-8800); and *Cheap Tickets* (800-377-1000).

▶ CHECK ON NESTED FARES

The bizarre structure of airline fares sometimes makes it advantageous to throw tickets away. A regularly priced round-trip coach ticket that called for you to leave City A on Tuesday and return from City B on Thursday might cost $800. But *two* round-trip discount fares between the same two cities that called for a minimum stay of seven days, including one Saturday night, might cost only $300 each. You would save $200 by throwing away one of the tickets from each round trip. Especially if you are flying without a Saturday stay-over, ask your travel agent to look into this alternative.

▶ FLY VIA A "HIDDEN" CITY

When it comes to airline tickets, comparison shopping isn't always simply a matter of finding the lowest-priced ticket from City A to City B. It is entirely possible that if you buy a ticket for a flight that goes from City A to City C but stops at City B on the way, it will be cheaper than a ticket for the flight from City A to City B. You simply get off at City B and throw the rest of your ticket away.

If you do find a deal like this, make sure your luggage can be carried on the plane. Don't book on a round-trip basis, because you would be a "no-show" on the return flight from City C. And do things quietly; the airlines don't like this practice at all. In a few cases, they have actually billed travel agencies for the difference in fares.

▶ FLY VIA AN INTERMEDIATE CITY

Very often, a ticket for a direct flight between City A and City C is more expensive than two tickets, one that takes you from City A to City B, the other going from City B to City C. You may have to travel quite a few extra miles (in some cases, you may even have to go in the opposite direction of your eventual destination) and it will take some extra time. You may even fly two different airlines. But savings can be considerable.

How can you know when such a deal is possible? All the major airlines utilize "hub" airports. If you know that a cheap flight from City A to that hub is available, then check out flights from the hub to your destination— perhaps on a no-frills airline (see above). Major hubs include Atlanta (Delta), Chicago (United, American), Dallas (American), Minneapolis (Northwest), St. Louis (TWA), Pittsburgh (USAir), and Newark (Continental), but all major airlines have a few hubs each.

▶ USE A FREQUENT-FLIER CREDIT CARD

See Chapter 9.

▶ BE FLEXIBLE ABOUT AIRPORTS AND MORE

We wanted to fly from New York City to Toledo, Ohio. How did we actually get there? By flying from Newark,

New Jersey (thirty minutes farther away for us then La Guardia), to Detroit (less than an hour from Toledo). We saved hundreds of dollars by investigating the alternatives and being flexible.

This example is not at all unusual. Especially if you are flying a route in which there is little competition between airlines, go to your atlas and investigate possible alternatives. Also check into potential savings if you fly off-peak hours and/or off-peak days.

▶ GET BUMPED

Airlines routinely overbook flights to account for no-shows, and it isn't at all unusual for them to have to ask at the departure gate for volunteers who are willing to be bumped off a flight and take the next available one instead. To encourage volunteers, the most common award is a dollars-off certificate for any future flight, often of $100 or more. If you are in no hurry to get to your destination, check in early at the gate and ask to be put at the head of the volunteer's list (after you are reassured about the availability of an acceptable later flight).

▶ BEWARE THE COUPON BROKERS

When you see ads in newspaper travel sections offering 60 or 70 percent off on business and first-class airline tickets, chances are good they were placed by a coupon broker. These brokers buy free-travel award coupons from frequent fliers and resell them. The problem is, all of the airline frequent-flier programs specifically prohibit trading in such coupons. If you get caught—a possibility since the airlines are making some serious efforts to catch offenders—your tickets won't be honored.

▶ FLY AS A COURIER

If you can travel alone on a flexible schedule, the cheapest way to fly to many destinations in Europe, Asia, and South America is as a courier. Couriers have to make do with carry-on luggage, since their check-in baggage is supplied to them by a courier company. In return for a very low price on a round-trip ticket, couriers escort that baggage—usually business documents—from one airport to another. The day we called *Now Voyager,* a New York City–based courier booking agency (212-431-1616; $50 annual reservation fee), we could have gotten a round-trip ticket from New York to Amsterdam or Copenhagen for $199 or a round-trip ticket from Los Angeles to Sydney for $399.

If being a courier intrigues you, call Now Voyager for more information or *IBC-Pacific* in El Segundo, CA (310-607-0100; no fee). A book called *The Insider's Guide to Air Courier Bargains* by Kelly Monaghan ($14.95 from Inwood Training Publications, Box 438, New York, NY 10034; 800-356-9315) tells you everything you need to know about courier travel and includes a very complete directory of courier companies.

▶ EXCESS BAGGAGE? SEND IT AHEAD

If you are moving a season's wardrobe or a lot of household items, it can be cheaper—and certainly far more convenient—to send them ahead via UPS than to pay extra baggage charges to an airline.

▶ USE CORPORATE DISCOUNT RATES FOR PERSONAL TRAVEL

If corporate discounts are available when you are traveling for your company, there is usually no reason why you can't ask for them when traveling for personal reasons.

▶ ENROLL THE WHOLE FAMILY IN FREQUENT-FLIER PROGRAMS

It is foolish not to join an airline's frequent-flier program, even though most of them have instituted three-year expiration dates for miles earned. In an age of airline mergers and rapidly changing personal plans, who knows? It takes no effort at all to join most of the programs right at the airport. Maintain a file of what you've earned in each of the programs, and it may very well affect your choice of airline sometime in the future.

▶ USE FREQUENT-FLIER MILEAGE WISELY

The temptation is to use frequent-flier mileage for a free ticket as soon as you have enough saved up. That's not always the best strategy.

Always check first to see what special deals are possible. If the airlines are engaged in one of their periodic promotional price wars, you might be better off buying a ticket, collecting more frequent-flier mileage on that cheaper-than-usual flight, and using the mileage later when prices are back to normal. Keep expiration dates in mind, of course.

▶ BUY TRIP-CANCELLATION INSURANCE

We are not great believers in most forms of specialized insurance. But if you have paid a large sum months in advance for a tour or cruise, and something—a medical or business emergency or even the failure of the tour operator—prevents you from going, you'll be glad you bought trip-cancellation insurance. Read all the fine print to make sure you are fully covered and buy from a travel agent, not from the tour operator. If he goes out of business suddenly, his insurance will be worthless.

▶ TURN OFF THE HOT-WATER HEATER WHILE YOU'RE AWAY

Most people remember to turn the thermostat down when they're going to be away from an empty house for any length of time. But why pay to keep hot water available if nobody is there to use it? If you're going to be away long enough, also clean out the refrigerator and freezer and turn them off. When you do, leave the doors open a bit to prevent mold, and leave an open box of baking soda inside.   •

▶ CARRY A 100-WATT LIGHT BULB

Even luxury hotels often discourage inveterate readers by putting 40-watt bulbs in night-table lamps, and few hotel housekeepers in our experience have been able to supply brighter substitutes. After a midnight search a few years ago that finally resulted in the purchase of the world's most expensive single bulb, we've packed our own whenever we are headed for a hotel. We also bring along an extension cord.

A reader from Boston has another solution. She brings a flashlight and extra batteries. "It's like reading after lights-out at camp," she reports.

▶ WHAT YOU MUST KNOW ABOUT HOTEL RATES

Most important, you should know there is no such thing as a single rate for a hotel room anywhere in the world. Instead, there are at least a half-dozen rates on a room in even a moderately priced motel, and as many as 20 different rates on a room in a luxury hotel. What's more, these rates not only change daily; they may be different at 7:00 P.M. than they were at 3:00 P.M.

Confusing? Not even reservation desks can keep track of all the rates. The bottom line for you is simple: Unless you are desperate for a room in a hotel in a city jammed with convention guests, you should NEVER (well, hardly ever) pay the "rack" rate for a room. At a minimum, when you are first quoted a room rate, ask if that is the corporate rate. Oh, you are there on business? Of course you qualify, nearly always for at least a 10 percent discount. But that's just the beginning. Keep reading.

▶ CONSIDER BUDGET MOTELS

Our idea of penny pinching is not to sacrifice comfort or convenience for money. But when we are traveling in the United States and want only a clean, quiet, comfortable room for the night—knowing we will leave early the next morning and won't want room service or help with our luggage—we choose one of the budget chains. *Motel 6* and *Budget Host* are the least expensive we have tried and like; *Comfort Inn* and *Hampton Inn* are usually a bit pricier but still definitely in the budget range. The beds, bathrooms, and TVs are as good as they are in higher-priced motels. You won't be able to negotiate much of a discount (10 percent off for corporate or AARP membership is standard), but for $50 or less a night, we have never been disappointed.

▶ USE A CITY RESERVATION OFFICE

This is the no-hassle way to get decent discounts on hotel rooms in many major cities and resorts, both here and abroad. You may not get the best deal possible, but you will know you have a reservation. Also, many city reservation offices offer discounts on hotels that don't participate in travel club or discount-book deals. When you call one of these offices, you simply tell them where and when you are going; they will give you rates for different hotels and will make a reservation for you. You will pay the hotel directly.

Among those that deal with only one or two cities: *Capitol Reservations* (Washington, D.C.), 800-847-4832; *San Francisco Reservations,* 800-677-1550; *Hot Rooms* (Chicago), 800-468-3500; *Las Vegas Reservations,* 800-862-1155. There are also reservation offices that cover many different cities, sometimes including major cities abroad. Try *Hotel Reservations Network,* 800-964-6835; and *Central Reservation Service,* 800-548-3311.

▶ BOOK HOTEL ROOMS AT THE LAST MINUTE

It's risky if there's a big convention in town or it is "in season" for a particular city. But normally—and especially if there are stories in newspaper financial pages about low occupancy rates—you can negotiate a good rate when you call a few hotels on your arrival date. Simply ask for the lowest rate for the type of accommodations you want, and tell them you'll call back to confirm if you like what is offered.

This is a particularly effective strategy with smaller hotels. Before you leave, narrow your choices by checking guidebooks (*Frommer's, Fodor's,* etc.) that list and rate them.

▶ SPEND WEEKEND VACATIONS IN BIG CITIES

Deluxe and first-class hotels in major cities are highly dependent on business travelers, who tend to arrive on Monday morning and leave on Friday. That means a lot of expensive hotel rooms are difficult to fill on Friday, Saturday, and Sunday nights. Nearly all but the upper tier of big-city luxury hotels now offer some kind of promotional packages that can cut room rates by more than 50 percent and often include free breakfasts and other extras. Call the 800 line of any of the nationwide chains (*Hilton, Hyatt, Marriott, Ritz-Carlton, Westin,* etc.) for information about a city you are interested in, as well as chainwide promotions. The travel section of your newspaper and the travel magazines (*Travel and Leisure, Travel, Sunset,* etc.) will also feature ads about special weekend packages.

Except in resort areas and New York City, the same phenomenon makes car rentals from a big-city location a lot cheaper over the weekend.

▶ GO BACK TO COLLEGE

Because we could never seem to visit each other at home, we arranged to meet old friends for a weekend in the university town where two of us had gone to college, easy driving distance for both couples. By the time we left, we realized we had stumbled onto an incredible short-vacation bargain that can be duplicated in dozens of other university towns, regardless of whether you are an alumnus.

There was no alumni reunion going on (when prices for rooms more than double), but for less than a third of the cost in a major city, we saw an exciting Division I basketball game, visited a small but first-class art museum, attended a concert given by a world-renowned pianist, and had dinner at two good restaurants.

University towns all seem to have a lot of restaurant bargains, modestly priced accommodations, and a surprising variety of major cultural and sporting events. Our total bill for the weekend—two nights, motel room, six meals (two with wine), all tickets—was $242, about the cost of a New York City hotel room on a Tuesday night.

▶ JOIN A "HALF-PRICE" HOTEL PROGRAM

If you spend more than a few nights a year in hotels, the annual price of membership in a club that offers room discounts can be a good investment. Although most seem to promise 50 percent discounts off rack rate, that is always subject to availability and the occupancy level the hotel expects. Except during peak periods, though, the odds are good you'll get at least some kind of discount by joining one of these clubs.

When you enroll, you will be given a membership card and a directory of available hotels. Most directories include a variety of price ranges and also offer discounts on restaurants, car rentals, and tourist attractions. Using the directory, you call a hotel and tell them you are a member of the club and ask for a discounted price for the night you want. You can then make your reservation using your usual credit card; when you check in you will probably be asked for a membership card in the half-price club.

Among the largest half-price programs:

- *Entertainment Publications,* 800-445-4137, has a national hotel and dining directory that it sells for a $37.95 annual fee. It publishes many regional and international directories as well, which you can ask about when you call. The national directory includes more than 3,500 hotels and motels in the United States, Canada, and the Caribbean.

- *Great American Traveler,* 800-548-2812, $49.95 annual fee.
- *Encore,* 800-638-8976; $49.95 annual fee.

▶ GO ON THE SPUR OF THE MOMENT

Not everyone can afford to drop everything and fly off for a vacation on forty-eight hours' notice. If you can, though, and there are a lot of different places in the world you would love to visit, a last-minute travel club that offers members closeout prices on unsold cruises, tours, resorts, and air tickets may be worth the price of its annual dues.

Typically membership gives you access to a hotline telephone number with up-to-the-minute information on what travel bargains are available as well as a monthly newsletter. Have an unexpected long weekend coming up? The hotline might offer a five-day package tour to Acapulco for a 40 percent discount or round-trip air tickets to Las Vegas for half the lowest coach fare.

Among the last-minute clubs that operate nationally: *Worldwide Discount Travel* (305-534-2082; $50 annual dues) and, recommended if you can leave from New York: *Moment's Notice* (212-486-0500; $25 annual dues).

Spur-of-the moment travelers can also find great bargains on the Internet. Register with American Airlines Net SAAver program (http://www.americanair.com) and each Wednesday you will receive a list of bargain round-trip flights American has available for the upcoming weekend. Other airlines may follow American's example; check their web sites as well.

▶ ADD A VACATION TO THE END OF A BUSINESS TRIP

A very easy way to buy no-cost airline tickets is to switch from a direct route home on a business-class ticket to an alternate route with a stopover in a city you would like to visit. Instead of flying back to New York from San Francisco on a direct flight, you might find your ticket would buy you a San Francisco–Miami–New York or a San Francisco–Denver–New York route at an even lower price. Check your travel agent or call airlines direct.

▶ THROW AWAY PARTS OF PACKAGE DEALS

The big travel packagers buy at the best wholesale prices—charter airlines, hotels, restaurants, ground transportation, admission charges, etc.—and still make a profit even though they pass on some of the savings to you. Many people won't consider buying a package tour because they don't want to spend two weeks on a bus with a lot of potentially incompatible strangers. If you investigate certain packages carefully, however, you may discover you can throw away such elements as prepaid sightseeing buses and meals and still save money on what's left—usually airfare and accommodations.

▶ TRY A DISCOUNT CRUISE-ONLY AGENCY

Cruise Line and Cruises of Distinction (800-634-3445) is a travel agency that buys cruise accommodations in bulk at wholesale prices, then sells them at a discount. It is definitely one of the calls you should make when comparison shopping.

▶ HIRE OUT ON A CRUISE SHIP

If you have some special talent or expertise, you might be able to parlay it into an all- (or at least some-) expense-paid cruise. Many cruise lines offer guest lecturers or entertainers free room and board in return for magic tricks, fashion shows, investment counseling, bird-watching advice, and dozens of other services. College professors and retired diplomats have long known about this, but an advanced degree isn't always necessary.

Mature men with dancing and other social skills are also in demand, since a good percentage of customers paying full fare on many cruises tend to be single, older women. These men may pay something, but it is usually a small fraction of the usual price of the cruise.

It isn't easy to book a free or reduced-priced berth this way. If you think you may qualify, write the entertainment directors of the major lines including a résumé, references, and a video or audio sample of what you can do. It is a good idea first to familiarize yourself with the kinds of cruises offered by different lines. Check your library for references.

▶ DON'T RESERVE USING A HOTEL-CHAIN 800 NUMBER

The central reservations office of any big hotel or motel chain will frequently quote a higher rate than the desk clerk at the specific place you want to stay. You can also often negotiate a reduced price with the desk clerk, but can't with the central office. The best idea is to first get rates from the central office (a free 800 call), then call the desk clerk to make your actual reservations.

▶ DELAY CAR RENTALS . . .

If you arrive at the airport late in the day and, except for the drive to your hotel, don't need a car until the next day, why not wait and rent it then? The cost of a shuttle bus or train is bound to be less than the cost of renting the car for a day, and you'll save garage expenses as well.

You may also save a significant amount by checking the Yellow Pages in your hotel-room phone book and calling a local car-rental company. There are lots of these companies springing up around the country. Not burdened with the overhead expenses of the national chains, many of them offer better deals than you can get even with a corporate or other discount.

Finally, on the other end of the trip, even if you end up renting from a chain with an airport drop-off, why pay an extra day's rental charges if all you are going to do that day is drive the car to the airport?

▶ . . . BUT RESERVE ADVERTISED SPECIALS QUICKLY

When you see an ad for a special limited-time offer from a car-rental company, call and make your reservation at the special rate as quickly as you can. The companies change their rates frequently, and the special price may not be available in a day or two. Make sure you get a confirmation number.

▶ RENT YOUR CAR FROM AN OFF-AIRPORT LOCATION

Admittedly not quite as convenient, but you can nearly always save 20 to 30 percent by renting from an office outside the airport and taking a free shuttle bus to it.

▶ RENTING A CAR ABROAD? DO IT HERE

Reserve ahead with a U.S. travel agent. You'll get a better rate than if you wait and rent directly from a European agent. Ask about the airport surcharges in some countries; you may save up to 10 percent by picking the car up at a downtown office instead. If you will need the car for more than two weeks, compare the costs of leasing instead of renting.

For information, call the 800 numbers of the large American car-rental companies, all of whom have operations abroad. Also call *Auto Europe* (800-223-5555).

▶ DON'T TAKE THE FIRST CAR-RENTAL PRICE

However and wherever you rent a car, ask for a discount when quoted a price. Just about anyone can ask for a corporate discount. Maybe you have frequent-flier miles you can use, or an AARP card (see later tip in this chapter). If you manage to get the "advertised special" price, you probably won't get any discount, but it does no harm to ask.

▶ TRY FOR NO-FEE TRAVELER'S CHECKS

There is absolutely no reason—other than a desire for excess profits—why issuers of traveler's checks must charge a fee for the service. After all, you are giving them ready cash. They, in return, are giving you checks that will not be cashed until sometime in the future. The income issuers make by investing your money during that "float" period is more than enough to earn them a handsome profit on an average transaction.

Depending on competitive pressures at the time of purchase, however, your bank may insist that a fee is necessary. If you keep a reasonable balance in your accounts, ask them to waive the fee.

▶ LIMIT YOUR USE OF TRAVELER'S CHECKS ABROAD

When you use a traveler's check to pay a hotel, a restaurant, a car-rental agency, or just about anybody else when traveling abroad, you will nearly always be given an unfavorable exchange rate (which is why you'll usually get a delighted smile and a yes when you ask if your traveler's check will be accepted). Instead, use a credit card for all major expenses; the rate of exchange is usually much better.

Cash your traveler's checks only at a bank or an office of the company that issues the checks, and pay only minor expenses with cash in the local currency.

▶ USE ATM MACHINES INSTEAD OF TRAVELER'S CHECKS ABROAD

You'll find Automated Teller Machines just about everywhere in the world now. The two largest networks are

Cirrus, owned by MasterCard, and Plus, owned by Visa. Both will give you the wholesale exchange rate when you use your bank ATM card to withdraw cash in the local currency. That's a much better deal (a 5 to 10 percent difference) than the exchange rate you'll get with a traveler's check. Even if you have to pay a $2 or $3 fee per withdrawal (a typical charge), you'll save on a withdrawal of at least $100. Use your bank ATM card, which immediately debits your bank account, rather than a credit card; you'll pay much steeper fees and interest charges when you use a credit card for a cash advance.

Check your PIN number with your bank before you go. It has to be four digits abroad, and you'll have to memorize numbers, not letters.

As much as we dislike them, for safety's sake we still believe it is best to carry a few traveler's checks when abroad. If you can avoid using them, cash them in for their full, 100 percent dollar value when you return home.

▶ CHECK ON INSURANCE COVERAGE BEFORE TRAVELING ABROAD

It could prove to be an expensive mistake if you aren't sure your automobile or health insurance will cover you in the country you are visiting. Call your agent and/or talk to your benefits administrator. If you plan to drive while in a foreign country, call the American Automobile Association (AAA) to see if you'll need an international driver's license. You might also ask—even if you aren't a member—about supplemental insurance.

▶ SWAP HOUSES—VERY CAREFULLY

We've never swapped houses ourselves, but we have friends who have traded their condo in Hawaii for private houses or apartments in London, the south of France, and on two Caribbean islands. So far, they say, things have worked out well.

Most people use one of the three services that publish directories of homes for exchange. When you subscribe to one of these services, you pay a fee to list your own home in the directory, describing it and specifying where you are willing to go and when you can travel. Then, when the directory is published, subscribers who are interested in a swap call you directly. If you see a house you think you might like, you can also call its owner directly.

Don't expect overnight results. If you think you might want to swap houses in the summer, start the fall before so you can get a listing in a January directory. Your chances of a swap are obviously better if you are offering an East Side Manhattan apartment or a waterfront house in Malibu rather than a North Dakota farmhouse. In any case, you should be flexible about timing and accommodations.

If you are lucky enough to make contact with a promising potential swap, you will exchange references and ask and be asked a lot of questions. Before you trust someone to take over your home, make sure you are satisfied with their credentials. Having a trusted friend regularly stop in to "help" while you are away is a good idea.

The major directory services are *Intevac International* (800-756-4663); *Trading Homes International* (800-877-8723); and *Vacation Exchange Club* (800-638-3841). Prices for listings range from $50 to $65 plus the extra cost of including a photo, which is recommended.

▶ USE A 25 PERCENT DISCOUNT CREDIT CARD

The typical restaurant two-for-one deal in an Entertainment Publications discount book (see above) gives you the lower-priced of two entrées free. Cocktails, wine, appetizers, desserts, and coffee aren't included. Since the price of those items may exceed the price of the two entrées, it is easy to end up with a discount of less than 25 percent off the total restaurant bill.

The Transmedia Card (800-787-3463; $25 annual membership fee) gives you a full 25 percent off all charges (except for tax and tip) in over 6,000 participating restaurants, and you don't have to use a coupon to get your discount. When you apply for Transmedia-card membership, you give them your Visa, MasterCard, American Express, or Discover card information. Then, when paying the bill in a participating restaurant, you simply present your Transmedia card instead of your usual credit card. Your receipt will show the full price of the meal, but a credit of 25 percent will show up along with the charge on your next credit-card statement.

Dining à la Carte (same 800 number; $49.95 annual membership) gives you a 20 percent cash rebate on your total bill (including tax and tip) in some 4,500 participating restaurants (but only one visit a month to any one restaurant). You don't have to carry a special card. Instead, you simply register all of the credit cards you might possibly use in a restaurant with Dining à la Carte and use them as you normally would. Every month, you will get a cash rebate of 20 percent of whatever charges from participating restaurants appear on any of those cards.

In a number of areas around the country, groups of restaurants have banded together to offer discounts. These local plans often include popular restaurants that don't sign up for the national cards and many of them have been set up to reward regular customers.

▶ EAT YOUR BIG MEAL AT LUNCH

The menus may be exactly the same, but the price of lunch at most of the world's restaurants is invariably cheaper—often by 30 to 40 percent—than dinner.

▶ GET DINNER FOR THE PRICE OF A DRINK

We have a young friend who has systematically investigated the different free cocktail-hour appetizers at some of San Francisco's best known and, in some cases, most expensive hotels and restaurants. His favorite place charges an outrageously high price for drinks. But one glass of wine, he points out, can be sipped for the forty-five minutes it takes to eat what he considers quite a satisfying free six- or seven-course dinner. He strongly suggests you overtip if you like the place well enough to go back.

▶ EAT DINNER EARLY

In many restaurants, the difference between ordering the same dinner at 6:55 P.M. and 7:05 P.M. isn't just ten minutes. The earlier meal may be as much as 50 percent less expensive. Ask about "early bird" and pretheater specials when you call for reservations.

▶ GET PRICES ON SPECIALS

"Hello, my name is Dave. Let me tell you about our specials tonight." Too often, Dave skips one ingredient: the price. Knowing that most people are reluctant to ask their friendly waiter the price of specials, many restaurants overprice them. Ask before you order.

▶ TAKE HOME A FREE LUNCH

Until a few years ago, we were uncomfortable about asking for what is unfortunately called a "doggie bag." Then, as guests of a business associate during a wonderful dinner in New York City at Lutèce, perhaps America's finest French restaurant, we watched a celebrity multimillionaire at the next table beam as his doggie bag was graciously handed to him. We haven't given it a second thought since.

▶ ORDER THE ALL-INCLUSIVE DINNER

If you are going to have an appetizer, side dishes, and dessert as well as an entrée, you are nearly always better off ordering from the side of the menu offering complete meals. Ordering à la carte can easily increase the cost of a meal by 30 to 50 percent.

▶ SKIP THE ENTRÉE

If you are a light eater or aren't very hungry, order two appetizers and ask that one of them be served as your main course. Appetizers are usually priced at less than a third of the cost of a main course.

▶ SHARE COURSES

In many restaurants, one salad order is more than large enough for two. In Italian restaurants, we usually share a pasta course. And we invariably share one dessert.

▶ BEFORE YOU GO TO NEW YORK . . .

Given ticket prices of $100 for a new musical, going to the theater in New York City has become prohibitively expensive for people who aren't on expense accounts. But there are ways to find bargains:

- *The Hit Show Club* (630 Ninth Avenue, New York, NY 10036; 212-581-4211) prints and distributes "two-fer" coupons that you can redeem at the box office, usually for a third off the regular price of many Broadway and some off-Broadway shows. Send a SASE at least six weeks before your trip to get current discount tickets before you leave. You can stay on the club's mailing list from then on, if you like. If you call the above number, you will get a recorded message telling you what shows are currently offering discounts.
- *TKTS booths,* operated by the Theatre Development Fund, are located at Duffy Square (47th and Broadway) and 2 World Trade Center in Manhattan and in downtown Brooklyn at the intersection of Court and Montague streets. If you want to take a chance, you can go to one of these booths the day of the performance you want to attend and get half-price tickets (plus a small service charge). How good are your chances? Terrible for the hottest new shows, quite good for just about anything else, including many long-running hits. Call 212-768-1818 for information.
- *The Theatre Development Fund* (212-221-0013; 1501 Broadway, Suite 2110, New York, NY 10036) sends members periodic, usually monthly, offerings of discounted tickets, usually in the $14 to $16 price range, for a wide range of shows and events. Members can

also purchase TDF "vouchers" for about $15, which are good for additional discounts (sometimes even free admission) to a variety of performing-arts events. To join TDF, send a SASE with your request for an application. After you fill that out (there are vague restrictions, but you should find a way to qualify), return it with a $14 check.

▶ BEFORE YOU GO TO WASHINGTON, D.C. . . .

Call your congressman's or senator's local office and get free passes to the White House and Senate and House galleries. The White House tour is more extensive than the one tourists stand in line to pay for.

▶ UNDER 26? GET A CIEE CARD

The Council on International Educational Exchange (CIEE; 212-822-2600) is a nonprofit organization whose primary goal is to develop student exchanges and foster international understanding. For young travelers, especially those planning to travel, work, or study abroad, the CIEE is also a great penny-pinching resource.

The CIEE issues three International Identity Cards that will pay for themselves many times over on a trip abroad: *Student* ($18; proof needed that you are 12 or over and a junior-high, high-school, college, university, or vocational-school student); *Youth* ($18; proof needed that you are between 12 and 26); and *Teacher* ($19; proof needed that you are a full-time faculty member at an accredited institution).

The cards make you eligible for discounts on transportation (local mass transit as well as airlines and railroads), accommodations, tourist attractions, cultural events, etc. They also include sickness, accident, life, and emergency medical insurance coverage as well as access to a 24-hour toll-free Traveler's Assistance Service.

▶ CHECK OUT FARES FROM COUNCIL TRAVEL

Council Travel (800-226-8624) is the travel division of the CIEE and has 40 offices nationwide. It is a good place for any budget-minded traveler to check for discounted airfares, railroad passes, and low-cost accommodations and car rentals. Some, but not all, of their discounts are available to anyone, not just students. Even students, however, shouldn't take for granted that Council Travel rates are the lowest available. They are nearly always competitive, but you should compare them with other consolidators and charter operators as well as with special airline promotional fares.

▶ STAY IN YOUTH HOSTELS

At any age, hostels, which offer dormitorylike rooms, are the lowest-cost way to spend a night unless you are a camper. Prices range from as low as $5 to $25, and accommodations range from primitive barracks to authentic castles. Many serve meals and have recreational facilities. To stay at one of the more than 5,000 *Hostels International* worldwide, you must first purchase an HI membership card (under 18, $10; 18–54, $25; over 54, $15; family membership, $35). Cards are available at any Council Travel office. Call 800-226-8624 for the nearest location.

▶ OVER 50? JOIN THE AARP

See page 245 for other reasons, but quick-and-easy travel discounts alone make the $8 annual membership fee of the American Association of Retired Persons a must for anyone over 50. Nearly all hotel and motel chains offer at least a 10 percent discount to AARP card holders. Some offer discounts as high as 50 percent. Car-rental and some restaurant chains also give AARP members discounts, as do individually owned motels, bed-and-breakfasts, and resorts.

Once you have an AARP card, get in the habit of always asking about a possible AARP discount when you make any kind of travel purchase. You will often be pleasantly surprised. But negotiate for the best deal possible first, and only then ask for your AARP discount.

▶ OVER 62? BUY AIRLINE SENIOR COUPON BOOKS

Most of the major domestic airlines sell books of discount coupons to travelers over 62. Typically, the books have four coupons, good for two round-trip coach flights anywhere the airline flies in the U.S. (plus a few places in the Caribbean and Canada). As of this writing, a book of coupons from American, Delta, United, or Northwest costs $596; America West, TWA, and Continental offered even better deals. A round-trip fare of $298 may not make sense on some flights, but it could represent a significant discount on others. Most airlines allow standby travel with senior coupons as well as frequent-flier credits. You must use all of the coupons within one year and there may be other restrictions as well, including advance reservations. If you qualify for a senior coupon book, first consider where you want to go and which airline offers the best service to those places from your home airport.

▶ OVER 55? CHECK OUT ELDERHOSTEL

Elderhostel (to get a catalog, call 617-426-7788 or write 75 Federal Street, Boston, MA 02110) is a nonprofit program that sponsors weeklong educational vacations at hundreds of different locations (often college campuses) in the U.S., Canada, and in Europe. Prices, including rooms (often in dormitories), meals, classes, and other activities average about $350 per person. If you go as a couple, only one of you must be over 55.

(See Chapter 5 for tips on shopping for travelers.)

8

Saving on Quality Clothing

We have made an effort throughout this book to offer money-saving tips that don't involve a lot of extra time or effort. But when it comes to shopping for clothing, there are not too many time-efficient ways to get the very best bargains. Most of those are found by people who don't mind spending hours checking on sales, love to read and compare catalogs, and can spend a full day at an outlet mall and then happily repeat the experience a week later.

If you hate to shop, you can still manage to save money with some of the tips in this chapter. Tips you will probably want to avoid are labeled FSO—For Shopaholics Only.

The transformation of the retail landscape in the past few years has changed the way all of us shop for clothes. Many of the great department stores and traditional specialty stores that dominated the apparel scene for generations have disappeared. The survivors have had to adopt aggressive new selling strategies to hold on to old customers and attract new ones. The competition is fiercer than ever for your clothing dollar—among department stores, specialty stores, discount stores, off-price retailers, designer and factory outlet stores, mass merchandisers, mail-order sellers, and even wholesale clubs. The opportunities for bargain hunters have never been greater, but neither has the potential for confusion.

Fewer and fewer stores can be relied on completely for quality and for knowledgeable service. Those that can usually cater to people who can afford the best at any cost. When you shop anywhere else, including many traditional department and speciality stores that now stock merchandise they might once have shunned, it is important to know how to recognize quality and a proper fit.

Nowhere in this chapter will you find advice on saving money by buying inexpensively produced clothing. Our philosophy is simple: Cheap isn't cheap if you wear it once. Expensive isn't expensive if you wear it forever. The goal is to buy "expensive" for as little as possible.

▶ WHO DESIGNS DESIGNER LABELS?

Usually not the designer who has lent his or her name to the clothing label. In most cases, the rights to the name have been sold to a manufacturer who then pays a royalty, a percentage of the manufacturer's cost, to the designer.

With a few honorable and usually high-priced exceptions, a designer label is not a guarantee of quality. Three checklists in this chapter will help you avoid shoddy merchandise and spot a well-made garment. Use them no matter what the label is.

▶ DESIGNER VERSUS BRAND NAME VERSUS PRIVATE LABELS

If you suspect the industry may be out to confuse you on purpose, you aren't far wrong. What's in a label? Not much. Is Christian Dior, who died quite a few years ago, a designer label or a brand name? Certainly, in cases like this, you can at least be positive that Monsieur Dior himself had nothing to do with the hemline. Famous models and movie stars lend their names to labels, too, although this is usually seen mainly in mass merchandisers like Kmart.

Private labels are one way department stores have fought back against their dependence on designer-label clothing. If you know you may be able to buy a famous designer label cheaper at an off-price or designer outlet store, why buy at a department store? Realizing that too many people have come to this conclusion, many department stores have devoted a lot of their resources to establishing their own private labels.

Because department stores and specialty chains have so much at stake in their private labels, you will often find very good buys in quality clothing at certain stores. Stores as different as The Limited, Barney's, Neiman Marcus, and The Gap have developed private-label lines that offer a consistent fit and a sense of fashion that reflects each store's image.

You should also know, however, that some private-label apparel is bought from a manufacturer who may be selling exactly the same apparel to another department or specialty store in the same area. Only the labels will be different. And the prices. It is entirely possible that the same suit will cost $600 at a department store and $350 at a second-floor walk-up discount specialty store across town.

What to do? Use the kind of quality checklists you'll find in this chapter and shop around.

▶ SAVE 50 PERCENT! BUT IS IT ON SALE?

Not always. More and more often, whether you are shopping in a department store, an off-price store, a factory or designer outlet, a mass merchandiser, or a mail-order catalog, a "sale" is not a sale but a cynical marketing gimmick. "Originally $100, not $49.95" is meaningless if the garment was never bought by anyone for $100, and, in fact, gives the retailer a handsome markup at the $49.95 price.

Some states have laws against this kind of deception, but there are few efforts to prosecute any but the most blatant abuses. When you see a price tag stating "suggested retail price $100, our price $39.95," your first thought should be: "Suggested by whom?"

Unfortunately, there are fewer and fewer retailers who don't resort at least occasionally to such tactics. If you want to save money as well as buy quality clothing, you simply have to know how to examine every prospective purchase.

▶ ARE THERE STILL BARGAINS IN TRADITIONAL DEPARTMENT STORES?

With all the different kinds of retailers now competing for your clothing dollar, are there still bargains available in traditional department stores? Absolutely, but usually only at certain times of the year.

Department stores sell seasonally. Because they anticipate what you will want to wear next season, you can't walk into a department store in the Northeast on a 98-degree day in August and expect to find a good selection of bathing suits or summer dresses. That's when winter coats and wool dresses are featured.

To make room for next winter's clothing, summer clothes are now routinely put on sale in traditional department stores at just about the time you may want to wear them, in June. And winter clothing, on sale everywhere in January, has in recent years been put on sale by nervous retailers well before Christmas.

▶ GET DEPARTMENT STORE CREDIT CARDS

It is far more convenient to use one Visa or MasterCard for all of your purchases, and virtually every store now

A Quick Quality Checklist for All Clothing

■ Stitching. Small stiches usually mean longer-lasting apparel. Stitches should be neat, straight, and even, although in a very well made garment slightly uneven stitches indicate hand-sewing, always an indication of quality.

■ Seams should be flat. The seam formed where two pieces of fabric meet should be straight. Even slight puckering should be avoided.

■ Puckering at darts (the short, stitched folds that make a garment fit more closely) also indicates lower quality.

■ Patterns (stripes, plaids, checks) should "shake hands" at the seams; if two pieces aren't matched exactly, it is a sure sign of a poorly made garment.

■ Armholes and shoulders of jackets should fit smoothly, without any wrinkles.

■ Linings are not supposed to be attached all the way around.

■ Pockets should be large enough to use comfortably and should have reinforced stitching.

■ Few cheap garments use 100 percent natural fiber fabrics, so an all-cotton men's shirt, for example, is probably well constructed. This isn't to suggest that a lot of quality clothing isn't made of synthetic fibers.

■ Check the grain of the fabric. It is important that every garment be cut "on-grain," meaning that lengthwise yarns hang perpendicular to the floor and crosswise yarns at a perfect 90-degree angle. This is much easier to spot in a plaid or a stripe; if these are cut "off-grain," horizontal and vertical lines won't match. But no garment will hang well if cut slightly "off-grain." They are getting hard to find, but a knowledgeable salesperson or a good tailor can point out examples of how important the grain of the fabric is.

■ Look for flaws and variations in the fabric, but remember that some are normal and desirable in some natural fabrics.

■ Buttonholes should be evenly spaced and neatly and securely stitched.

takes them. The only reason to go to the bother of opening credit-card accounts with individual stores is so that you get advance notice of "private" cardholder sales. If the sale involves using only the store credit card to get the savings you want, do so. Otherwise, keep all of these cards in a safe place and never use them at all.

▶ SHOP OFF-PRICE STORES

They won't always have your size or the color you want. Some of the clothing will be marked "irregular" or "imperfect." Buttons may be missing, and a thread may be loose. Service is either bad or nonexistent. But you can't think of yourself as a penny pincher unless you at least look into off-price stores from time to time. Quality is uneven, but you can definitely find quality clothing, often with designer labels, at very attractive prices—up to 80 percent off.

Off-price stores are where manufacturers dump slow sellers returned by traditional stores (nothing to do with quality), irregulars (defects are sometimes hard to find and usually nothing that affects wearability), and overstock. When credit crunches hit and a manufacturer needs cash quick, first-run merchandise may also turn up in off-price stores.

You've got to be careful when you find a bargain in an off-price store. Seconds (more serious flaws) and irregulars (minor ones) are supposed to be marked, but that doesn't always happen. Sizes aren't dependable either; the garments may have been incorrectly sized originally and that's the only reason they're in the off-price store. Try everything on.

Finally, make sure you know what the return policies of the store are.

These are the leading off-price chains that we have found most likely to offer at least some quality clothing at very attractive discounts (phone numbers for "location nearest you" information):

■ *Marshall's* (800-MARSHAL). Men's, women's, children's clothing. Among labels you'll find from time to

A Quick Quality and Fit Checklist for Women

■ When you try on a coat or jacket, bend your arms; the sleeves should still come to your wrists.

■ Do the shoulder pads stay in place? Take the jacket off and put it back on a couple of times. It's a telltale sign of a poorly constructed garment if you have to keep adjusting the shoulder pads.

■ Jacket lapels that seem to be pressed flat or are stiff should be avoided. Lapels should be soft and rounded and should spring back into shape after you crumple or squeeze them.

■ When trying on a coat, wear the bulkiest jacket or sweater you intend to wear under it. The armholes should still feel comfortably roomy.

■ Sit down when you try on a skirt. It should have enough room in it to avoid creases across the front from sitting.

■ Pleats in a skirt should hang smoothly, without parting at the hip area.

■ The waistbands of all types of skirts should fit snugly, but without any indication that they will roll.

■ No matter how they are finished (hand-rolled, blindstitched, etc.), hems on a well-made garment will fall smoothly, without any signs of unevenness, puckering, or rippling. Hems are easy to alter, though, so if everything else is okay, consider buying the garment.

■ Hemline stitches should always be invisible from the outside.

■ Zippers should be dyed to match the fabric and completely covered.

■ Buttons should be functional. Sticking a button on for decoration is a sign of cheap design. If buttons are supposed to match the color of the garment, they should match exactly.

■ No matter what you buy, make certain you can move easily while you have it on. "It looks great, so I don't mind being uncomfortable" is never a successful long-term strategy.

time: Calvin Klein, Perry Ellis, Armani, Anne Klein. Two Marshall's stores, twenty miles away from each other, may have quite different mixes of clothing.

- *T.J. Maxx* (800-926-6299). T.J. Maxx bought Marshall's in late 1995, but is keeping both names. Together, with more than 1,150 stores nationwide, they have enormous buying clout. T.J. Maxx sells men's and women's clothing, including Donna Karan, Anne Klein, Esprit, and Armani labels. Clothing here tends to be a bit younger and perhaps more stylish than in Marshall's.
- *Loehmann's* (718-409-2000). More than 80 stores nationwide, and, with Filene's Basement, the originator of the off-price concept. Women's clothing only. You'll never find all sizes, colors, etc., but legendary buys are still possible here. More likely for sizes 4 and 6.
- *Burlington Coat Factory* (800-444-COAT). More than 230 stores nationwide. "We're more than great coats" is the slogan, and these stores do sell men and women's clothing of all kinds. We haven't bought anything but coats yet, though.
- *Filene's Basement* (800-666-4045). More than 50 stores, still confined to the Northeast and Midwest. Men's and women's clothing. Recent find: men's dress shirts with a Brooks Brothers label for $15.

▶ SHOP DEPARTMENT-STORE CLEARANCE CENTERS

Some top-line department stores, including Nordstrom, Saks Fifth Avenue, and Neiman Marcus, ship unsold clothing from main stores to their own clearance centers. You won't find current-season clothing at these locations, but the quality is usually dependable and markdowns of up to 75 percent are possible.

▶ SHOP OFF-PRICE STORES AND EVERYWHERE ELSE [FSO]

Now let's discuss the tactics used by shopaholics. They don't "look into off-price stores from time to time." They haunt them. They make special trips to factory and designer outlet centers—and repeat the trip a couple of weeks later.

If you have guessed that we don't shop this way, you are right. But there's no question that those who do find the greatest bargains. And a true shopaholic loves the game, which involves such tactics as these:

- Visiting the store just before the announced sale day. Sometimes salespeople will bend the rules and allow early sale shopping. If not, the shopaholic locates every potential buy beforehand and is the first in line the morning of the sale.

- Being constantly on the lookout for clothing that isn't marked "as is," but has some easily correctable flaw (a missing button, a broken stitch, etc.). Shopaholics immediately ask for a much lower price. They also look for and, more often than you would imagine, find mismarked items early in a sale, before the manager is aware of the mistake made by some harried clerk. This is sheer shopaholic bliss.

- Getting to know clerks and managers at different stores and calling from time to time about big-ticket items. "Any change in the price of that suede coat you've never had on sale?"

- Getting on every mailing list possible and tracking prices in different catalogs.

▶ SHOP DESIGNER OUTLETS

Off-price stores are still a hit-or-miss proposition. You've got to be lucky, your timing has to be right, or you have to be a relentless repeat shopper. That's less true of the designer outlets now found throughout the country, usually off a main highway in malls that include a number of designer and factory outlet stores. *Donna Karan, Polo/Ralph Lauren, Calvin Klein, Anne Klein, Liz Claiborne,* and *Harvé Bernard* are among the leading designers who operate outlet stores, selling their clothing at discounts of up to 75 percent.

What's sold in these stores keeps changing, depend-

A Quick Quality and Fit Checklist for Men

- Make certain there is felt backing stitched under the collar of any suit or sport jacket.

- Zippers should be sewn in absolutely straight and should lie flat.

- Every well-made shirt has two rows of stitching under the armholes.

- Extra fabric often indicates quality, since the manufacturer isn't cutting close to save a few cents. There should be a minimum of ⅜″ of fabric on both sides of the center seam in a pair of pants. Even if you don't need the extra length, be suspicious if a jacket doesn't have an inch or two of extra fabric under the cuff to allow for lengthening.

- The edges of fabric inside a jacket should be stitched. If you see a piece of fabric that looks like it could unravel, avoid the jacket.

- Buttonholes should be strongly reinforced with thread and jacket buttonholes should have a slight "keyhole" effect on the lapel side. Buttons should button easily; if the hole is too small, it is a sign of a hastily made garment.

- Check to make sure the sleeve lining is neatly stitched to the jacket lining and the coat itself at the armpit. If it looks uneven or badly stitched, avoid the jacket.

- Squeeze the lapels for a couple of seconds. If they don't spring back to their original shape immediately, avoid the jacket.

- The waistbands of pants should be reinforced with a stiffening fabric inside the lining. All well-made pants also have a second button inside the fly on the left, just below the waist button, to ensure a better fit and relieve pressure on the waist button.

- Don't even bother to go into the fitting room if a jacket doesn't lie flat on your shoulders; this is nearly always extremely difficult to alter. So is the length of the jacket.

ing on economic conditions in the retail business. Originally, designer outlet stores were supposed to sell end-of-season leftovers that hadn't been shipped to department and full-price specialty stores. Troubled times for many traditional stores, however, have widened the assortment of newer apparel in many designer outlets. Some outlets are likely to have a very substantial assortment of their designer's newer apparel. Others, like the thirty Ann Taylor Loft stores, sell less expensive clothes manufactured specifically for the designer outlets.

The clothing in most of these stores is often prime quality, although some also include seconds and irregulars, not always clearly marked. Unlike the off-price stores, most are well furnished and are pleasant places to shop. It is a good idea to know beforehand what the designer label clothing is selling for in department and full-price specialty stores. As designer outlets have become more popular, prices have tended to rise. Not everything is necessarily a great bargain or even a good buy.

▶ SHOP OUTLET STORES

A step down in chic from designer outlets, outlet stores are nevertheless a good place to bargain-hunt for clothing and footwear. The first factory outlets were actually attached to the factories and sold seconds, damaged goods, and irregulars. Because these factories were usually in the old textile and leather centers on the East Coast, the factory outlet phenomenon was limited to that part of the country until the last decade.

What happened, of course, is that factory outlets became so profitable that manufacturers opened new stores and started producing perfectly sound, first-line merchandise for them. There are now outlet stores nationwide, most of them grouped into outlet centers. There are also quite a few retail operations that try to pass themselves off as factory outlets, but are usually just discounters of second-rate merchandise.

Long-standing agreements between manufacturers

and regular retail customers, although under some pressure these days, make it unlikely that you will find the very newest lines or fashions in outlet stores. But a lot of good-quality merchandise is sold in them. As with designer outlets, it helps to know beforehand the normal retail-sale price of an item you might buy in an outlet store; too often, there is little difference or the outlet is actually more expensive. The outlets of some manufacturers are more dependable than others, and you will get a sense of this as you spend time in them.

If you have never visited a large outlet center, be prepared to be somewhat overwhelmed by the number of stores and the variety of the merchandise offered. If you are fairly close to one, you might want to devote a first trip mainly to looking around and eliminating stores you know you aren't interested in. Then go back and shop the others.

Many outlet centers are located in vacation or resort areas, and you might want to know about them if you are planning a trip. You can get a magazine ($6.95 plus shipping) with helpful information on more than 350 outlet centers nationwide by calling *The Joy of Outlet Shopping* (800-344-6397). This magazine includes information on 11,500 outlet stores, and cross-references stores and malls—not only listing all the stores in each mall, but also describing all the major mall retailers and listing the malls in which they have stores. It also includes maps, phone numbers, helpful tips and lists, and $200 worth of coupons.

▶ ARMY-NAVY STORES STILL HAVE BARGAINS

Sure, the variety is limited, but check out prices on basics like jeans and T-shirts at an army-navy store.

▶ ASK FOR "ALTERATION DISCOUNTS"

Our Bantam editor reports that a short (5′0″) friend almost always has to have pants, skirts, and dresses altered. Often, when she points this out to the salesperson who has been helping her, she gets an "alteration discount" of up to 10 percent.

▶ COMPARISON-SHOP IN THE BOYS' DEPARTMENT

Our editor's friend and other small women have an opportunity to save much more than 10 percent on sweats, windbreakers, knit shirts, and other clothing items. Comparison-shop for items like these in any store's

---

Questions to Ask Before You Buy Anything

■ Would I like this just as much if the label read "Sears" instead of "Famous Designer"?

■ Do I really believe I'll be able to wear this next year . . . five years from now?

■ Is this garment well made enough to last that long?

■ How much will dry cleaning cost?

■ Am I prepared to wash and iron this every time I wear it?

■ Does it really fit, or am I tempted to buy it because it fits pretty well and is a size smaller than I usually buy?

■ How does this fit into my wardrobe? What can I wear it with that I own now?

■ What else will I have to buy to make full use of this garment? Will I need special accessories? Do I really want to spend that much more?

■ Where will I be able to wear this—given my actual (as opposed to my fantasy) lifestyle?

■ Does it go with the coat I intend to wear it with? If it is a coat—does it coordinate with everything else I own?

■ Can I use this year-round if I add or subtract a layer? If it is a one-season garment, ask once again where and when you can wear it. Do you go there/do that in summer/winter?

■ Am I at least fairly confident I've shopped enough elsewhere to be sure this is a good value?

boys' department. Invariably, the prices are far less than in the woman's department for the same or even better-quality items.

Actually, certain unisex items like knit shirts are almost always less expensive in the men's department, so women of any size should do some comparison shopping there.

▶ THE TWO-PANTS STRATEGY FOR MEN

Years ago, sales of two-pants suits were limited to low-quality bargain stores. No more. If you wear a suit to work every day, and are reasonably sure you'll wear the same size for a few years to come, consider taking advantage of the increasing number of stores and mail-order retailers that sell perfectly matched jackets and pants separately. It will cost you more in the short run to buy two pairs of pants, but jackets are far more expensive and pants invariably wear out long before jackets.

A suit with a three-year life span might have a six-year life span this way. The trick is to make certain that you alternate wearing the different pants from the very beginning and dry-clean all three pieces at the same time. That way, both pairs of pants will match the jacket after five years as well as they did when you bought them.

▶ BUY CLOTHES WITH YOUR PASTA

We wouldn't join a warehouse club (see Chapter 1) for its clothing section alone, but we do check the section out whenever we make one of our periodic trips to buy groceries in bulk. There's no telling what kind of clothes will be there, but on a couple of occasions in the past year we have found a terrific buy.

▶ BUY AND SELL AT CONSIGNMENT SHOPS

A number of readers of prior editions wrote to tell us how well they do buying and selling clothes at consignment shops. The best consignment shops buy only good-quality used clothing that is still in style and in excellent condition.

When an article of clothing is sold in the shop, the original owner typically gets 40 to 50 percent of the sale price.

Although some women use consignment shops only to sell clothing they no longer want, many sellers are also regular buyers. You can find top designer-label clothing in many consignment shops, often at a small fraction of original prices. And once you become a regular customer, some shops will call to tell you when something special turns up in your size.

▶ SHOP IN BAD WEATHER [FSO]

Store managers get lonely during a snowstorm at the end of January or on the hottest day in August. Those are particularly good shopping months in any case, but if you are one of the few customers in sight on a bad day and are serious about buying something, ask about the price tag. On-the-spot markdowns are possible.

▶ BEWARE THE 90 PERCENT DISCOUNT

For as long as world-famous designers have shown their new collections at openings attended by the rich and the high-fashion elite, there have been frantic efforts starting the next day to copy the new line by manufacturers who have no intention of paying the designer a penny.

This is perfectly legal. "Knockoffs" are an accepted part of the industry. In fact, many designers "knock off" their own high-priced designs in lower-priced lines of clothing, using less expensive fabrics and mass production methods but still producing good-quality garments.

What is not legal is counterfeiting, which is putting a fake label in a copy of an item of apparel or an accessory and then selling it as the real thing. In addition to being illegal, a counterfeit is nearly always a shoddily produced piece of merchandise.

If you see a $500 Gucci bag for $39.95 and think it is too good to be true, it is.

▶ THINK JANUARY AND JULY

Sales are routine year-round these days, but it is still true that stores are anxious to get rid of winter clothing that didn't sell during the Christmas shopping season. Doing some serious shopping during the first week of January can be especially rewarding. July is not only the slowest month of the year for stores in most areas, it is also when retailers are making room for winter lines and slashing prices on summer clothing.

▶ BUY "SLIGHTLY IMPERFECT" HOSIERY BY MAIL

So slight are the imperfections in the hosiery we've seen ordered from the free *L'Eggs, Hanes, Bali, Playtex* catalog (800-300-2600) that we'd probably use it even if it didn't offer an unconditional 100 percent money-back guarantee. With that guarantee, and the opportunity to save 50 percent on the brand we use (all the popular Hanes brands available), the catalog is a basic annual resource.

If you prefer *No Nonsense* brands of panty hose, they also offer "practically perfect" hosiery at 50 percent to 60 percent off retail prices. For a free catalog, call 800-677-5995.

▶ CHECK OUT SPIEGEL'S CATALOG

Spiegel (800-345-4500) is a mail-order giant, but its clothing seems to be a cut or two above the competition's in terms of fashion. The big Spiegel catalog ($3.00, money back with first order) includes much more than clothing; it is a good resource to check in other areas as well.

Spiegel's special sales catalog of men's and women's clothing is called *The Ultimate Outlet* ($2.00) and includes discounts as high as 70 percent.

If your computer has a CD-ROM drive, Spiegel also offers a catalog in that format.

▶ BUY MEN'S DRESS SHIRTS BY MAIL

Paul Frederick (610-944-0909; 223 West Poplar Street, Fleetwood, PA 19522) is a manufacturer of quality shirts that you will find in better stores, often with their private labels. The same shirts are available direct from the company for discounts that can be as high as 50 percent off store prices. Send $1.00 check or money order for the catalog.

▶ BUY FROM LANDS' END OR L. L. BEAN

There are other general mail-order catalogs, but we continue to find these two the most reliable for both men's and women's casual clothing. Discounts off retail prices can't be quoted because you won't find this clothing in retail outlets, but savings of from 20 to 35 percent off comparable apparel are likely.

Once you are on their mailing lists and buy even occasionally, you'll get seasonal catalogs. Both feature a few pages of marked down, discontinued merchandise at very large discounts off previous prices. We nearly always find something to buy, and have never been disappointed.

Lands' End (800-356-4444, or try its Internet store: http://www.landsend.com); *L. L. Bean* (800-221-4221).

▶ RENT INSTEAD OF BUYING

Want a knock-'em-dead evening dress for a once-in-a-lifetime occasion? At least check on what's available at rental shops in your area. Typically, you might spend as much as $250 to rent a $2,000 dress, and the odds get better every day that you won't be the only one at the affair with a money-saving secret. Check the Yellow Pages under "formal wear."

▶ MAKE A BUYER'S TRIP TO NEW YORK CITY [FSO]

Although not much clothing is actually manufactured in New York anymore, it is still the capital of the garment industry and a must stop for retail buyers from everywhere in the country. You can't get into the wholesale showrooms the buyers do, but savvy city shoppers know that not all of them are "for the trade only." *The Bargain Hotline,* 540-0123, is updated weekly (on Friday nights) and lists upcoming sample and overstock sales in garment-center showrooms—complete with what kind of merchandise is on sale at each showroom, their addresses, and information about what kind of payment will be accepted.

The number can only be dialed from a phone within the New York metropolitan area (212, 516, 718, and 914 area codes) and the call will cost $1.95 for the first minute, 75 cents a minute after that.

Also check out the "Sales and Bargains" section in the back of the latest issue of *New York* magazine. It does a good job of keeping up with what stores and manufacturers have new and notable sales.

The famous Garment District (roughly between Fifth and Eighth avenues from 34th to 41st Street) is filled with storefronts that say "trade only" or "wholesale only." But some of these places will sell direct. There are a number of showrooms in the area that welcome retail customers.

One of the best areas to explore for all kinds of discounted clothing is Orchard Street in the Lower East Side.

When you buy anything in New York, skip the city's huge sales tax by having your purchases shipped to your home.

▶ BUY MATERNITY CLOTHES BY MAIL

Mother's Place (800-829-0080) doesn't offer discounts, but it does offer a free catalog of its own-label maternity clothing at very attractive prices.

▶ BUY KIDS' CLOTHES BY MAIL

- *Olsen Mill Direct* (800-537-4979) sells the OshKosh line of children's clothing at factory outlet prices.

- *Children's Connection* (516-798-0142) sells many top brands by the dozen as well as by the piece, always at large discounts.
- *After the Stork* (800-333-5437) sells quality kids' cottons at very competitive discount prices.
- *Lands' End* (800-356-4444), better known for adult casual clothes, has a terrific children's catalog.

The malls compete with mail-order operations quite successfully in this category. *Sears* and *JCPenney* sell clothing for everyone, but their prices on good-quality children's clothes are especially hard to beat. They get stiff competition from the *Kids "R" Us* chain.

▶ DON'T JUST BUY CLOTHES, PLAN A WARDROBE

Impulse shopping in clothing stores is as dangerous as it is in supermarkets. To get the most from your clothing dollar year after year, you must discipline yourself. Certain styles of clothes and colors look good on you; stick to them. Never buy anything unless you can coordinate it within your basic wardrobe. A pair of shoes that goes with only one dress or a shirt that goes with only one sport jacket are expensive mistakes.

The best way to avoid impulse shopping for clothes is to make up a very definite list of what you need. Keep this list in a small notebook that you can always carry with you, and update it constantly. It may be months before you find exactly the summer jacket you are looking for, but if you have a coordinated wardrobe it may be worth the wait.

See page 185 for a list of questions to ask yourself before you make a final purchase decision on any garment or accessory. If you keep them in mind, you'll avoid a lot of mistakes.

▶ DON'T JUST BUY CLOTHES, INVEST IN THEM

If you always buy clothes to become part of an evolving but carefully coordinated wardrobe, you will need fewer items than if you buy the latest fashion fads or follow short-term trends. You will begin to think in terms of investing in clothes, not just buying them. While few of us can afford the very finest quality for every item in our wardrobe, investing in a few classic garments that fit that description becomes a realistic strategy.

You will seldom find the best for sale under signs that proclaim "60 percent off," but the exclusive specialty men's and women's stores that carry such merchandise all have sales, too. Look for their often sedate sale ads and stop in. There are clothing bargains at every price level, and the most satisfying in the long run may be the ones that were initially the most expensive.

▶ WORRY ABOUT BUTTONS

What happens if you lose one of the seven unusual buttons that "make" the outfit? Try to buy an extra button or two with the garment.

Alternatively, what if you find a quality garment ruined only by cheap buttons? It often pays to buy the garment anyway, and purchase top-grade horn or natural buttons elsewhere.

▶ REMEMBER "DRY CLEAN ONLY" COSTS EXTRA

A woman who dresses for an executive job in a city office fifty weeks of the year can easily spend $1,500 a year on dry cleaning. Buying some clothes that need to be dry-cleaned is unavoidable, but searching out summer blouses that can be washed is worth the effort.

As for clothes that must be dry-cleaned, avoid silk, because it is the most expensive fabric to have dry-cleaned as well as the most delicate, and pleated skirts and dresses of any fabric, because most dry cleaners will charge extra to press each pleat.

▶ LEAVE A NOTE FOR YOUR DRY CLEANER

If you know what caused a stain (even if you think it is obvious), pin a note over it when you send the garment to your dry cleaner. Helping him choose certain solutions and avoid others can make all the difference.

▶ BUT DON'T USE HIM TOO OFTEN

Dry cleaning isn't just expensive. It is also hard on fabrics and can fade colors. Unless the garment is stained, get it pressed instead—and save at least 50 percent.

▶ USE A SPRAY TIE PROTECTOR

Men who dress in a suit and tie every day often find themselves spending hundreds of dollars a year on what they wrap around their necks. Few have not had the experience of buying a $30 tie and seeing it destroyed at lunch the next day by an errant drop of sauce. Spray tie protectors actually work. Try a can on a couple of your favorites.

One more tip: If you water-spot a silk tie, wait for it to dry and then simply rub the spot with another part of the tie. Nine times out of ten, you'll remove the spot.

▶ USE "SHOE GOO" ON SNEAKERS

After a couple of months, an otherwise perfectly good pair of sneakers may begin to wear out in just one or two small areas of the sole. Instead of throwing them away, repair them overnight using an inexpensive tube of "Shoe Goo," available in most sporting-goods and many hardware stores. You can easily triple the life of a pair of sneakers this way.

9

Dealing with Banks, Mortgages, and Credit

All of the services offered by your bank, credit-card company, and any other kind of lender are considered "products" by these organizations. Just like cans of soup on a supermarket shelf, these financial products—from checking accounts and home-equity loans to trust services and annuities—are conceived, priced, and marketed to make a profit.

Some people have trouble accepting this. After all, they trust their banks with their money, with their most precious and valuable documents if they have a safe-deposit box, and with their complete financial histories if they take out a loan. Banks have grave fiduciary responsibilities that make them more than mere marketers of different financial products.

While this is true, and true that banks are subject to strict regulation by both state and federal laws and agencies, it is also a fact that banks must make a profit to survive, and fierce competition has eroded many traditional sources of profitability. So services that were given away to loyal customers in earlier generations have been turned into mini–profit centers.

To put it bluntly, your friendly 1990s banker is likely to do anything legal to part you from as much of your money as possible. You can't protect yourself against some abuses. All banks, for instance, make you wait longer than is actually necessary to draw on a check deposited into your account. If you can imagine how much they earn a year by having the use of billions of dollars for an extra day or two, you can understand why.

Keep these three principles in mind when dealing with banks, other lenders, credit-card organizations, and other credit-granting organizations (department stores, auto dealers, etc.):

- Don't pay interest on a loan unless you have to. *The best way to earn 18 percent tax free on your money is to pay off any 18 percent loans you have outstanding.* With the exception of a home mortgage and perhaps loans to start a business or invest in an education, it is always better (barring the return of double-digit inflation) to save first, then spend.
- Take advantage of the competition among banks and among credit-card organizations for your business. Shop around for the best deals you can get. A long-term relationship with one bank can be of some importance, but in these days of bank mergers and impersonal, computerized banking, it doesn't mean as much as it once did.
- Learn a few basics about how interest rates on loans are calculated. (Tips in this chapter will help.) Most important, make sure you understand all the fine print in a loan or credit agreement before you sign it.

▶ KEEP SHOPPING FOR BETTER BANKING DEALS

Differences in geography, state laws, and changing competition within markets make it difficult to set minimum standards that can be applied to all the different kinds of checking accounts available. But the easiest way for banks to increase profits from their retail operations is to raise the fees and minimum balance requirements of current customers. At the same time they are doing this, they may be advertising special introductory deals to attract new accounts. That's why it's a good idea to read the ads from different banks about minimum balances, fees, and services. At least once a year, make sure you review what you are paying versus what's offered elsewhere. If your bank is involved in a merger, pay special attention to new fees and changes in services and balance requirements.

This isn't to suggest that you continually switch banks to save a dollar a month or to escape an extra $500 minimum requirement. But if you let your bank take your business for granted, they will. When you see a better deal elsewhere, get the details and show them to an officer of your current bank. Every bank gives its officers at least some flexibility to make fee and other concessions to good customers. If you are one of them, your bank won't want you to leave.

▶ COMBINE ACCOUNTS AT ONE BANK

The best way to eliminate most fees and become the kind of customer a bank wants to keep happy is to deposit enough money to be perceived as a significant customer. That may mean trading off an extra percentage point or so of interest on a couple of thousand dollars, keeping it in a bank's federally insured money-market deposit account, for instance, instead of a higher-paying money-market mutual fund.

Keeping that kind of money in such an account will usually mean you won't need a minimum balance in your checking account to escape fees. Since the very first rule of saving and investing is to have a minimum of three months' salary readily available for emergencies, a bank money-market account makes sense.

Another way to eliminate fees and become a more significant customer is to establish an IRA (Investment Retirement Account) with your bank. Many banks will now include IRA balances when determining what kind of deal you'll get on your checking account. It is perfectly legal to have more than one custodian for your IRA funds, so it is possible to keep just a small portion at your bank.

▶ CLOSE EXPENSIVE SAVINGS ACCOUNTS

How can a savings account be expensive, when it pays you interest? Simple. If your bank charges you a monthly fee or per-check fees for your checking account, you will nearly always be better off keeping in that account whatever minimum balance the bank requires for no-fee checking. If that means shifting funds out of a savings account, do it.

▶ CHECK THE APY ON SAVINGS ACCOUNTS

The Truth in Savings Act of 1993 requires that all banks use the same formula to calculate the yield you earn—the "Annual Percentage Yield" or APY. Previously, banks were allowed to advertise an interest rate that didn't take into account whether interest was being compounded daily, monthly, or quarterly. How interest is compounded makes a big difference in how much you really earn. When you compare rates on CDs or savings accounts, no matter what the interest rates are, choose the account with the higher APY.

As we write this, it seems possible that Congress may actually repeal some of the provisions of the 1993 legislation. If this happens, in some states your only protection will be vigilance on your part. Make certain you know exactly how your bank calculates interest rates and compare their formulas with other banks in your area.

▶ SHOP FOR THE BEST CD RATES

Before you buy or renew a Certificate of Deposit at your bank, check its rates against the competition via *Banx-Quote* (800-765-3000; Internet: http://www.banx.com). It is easy to purchase a federally insured CD by mail, and rates vary significantly in different parts of the country.

Before you go to the trouble of sending CD money out-of-state, though, ask your bank's branch manager to match (or come close) to the higher rate. If you are a good customer and the bank wants to keep your business, it may be willing to negotiate.

▶ DON'T BUY CHECKS FROM YOUR BANK

Banks that once supplied good customers with free checks now mark up the checks they sell you by 300 percent or more over the price they pay their printers.

Deal direct with specialized check printers and save 60 to 75 percent. All they need is a sample check from you (write "canceled" on it before mailing) to match any bank's necessary computer codes. Among reputable sources to contact for catalogs and prices: *Checks in the Mail Inc.* (800-733-4443); *The Check Store* (800-424-3257); *Current* (800-426-0822).

▶ USE DIRECT DEPOSIT FOR YOUR SALARY CHECK

Not only is it a waste of time to stand in endless bank lines every week or two, you also get the use of your money faster when the company you work for sends your salary check to your bank electronically. If your employer offers direct deposit, have your salary deposited automatically into a money-market or interest-bearing account.

▶ BEWARE OF ATM SURCHARGES

Until 1996, the Plus and Cirrus networks, which link ATMs nationwide, banned individual banks from charging fees to noncustomers who used their automated teller machines to get cash. That ban has been lifted, and some banks are now imposing fees, typically $1 per withdrawal but as high as $2 or even $4 per withdrawal at nonbank locations such as airports.

By the time you read this, a law may have been passed making it mandatory that fee schedules be posted on the first screen you encounter on any ATM. If you don't see such a schedule, beware. And whether the law has been passed or not, running out of cash in a strange place has become more expensive. Stick to your own bank's machines whenever possible. When you are traveling, use your credit card whenever you can to cut back on cash needs.

▶ CHECK OUT BANKING BY COMPUTER OR TELEPHONE

Security First Network Bank of Bell County, Kentucky (http://www.sfnb.com) is the only bank we know of offering full services on the Internet, but many others are gearing up to do so. It requires only a $100 minimum deposit, gives you free checks, and charges no fees if you pay twenty or fewer bills each month electronically.

You can also use one of the many banks that offer free or low-fee electronic banking if you maintain a minimum balance and access the bank through either the *Quicken* or *Microsoft Money* software programs (see Chapter 10). Other banks will provide you with their own software. If you have not yet heard from your bank about what computer banking alternatives it offers, chances are good that you soon will.

What is it like to bank electronically? We have been using *Citibank Direct Access* for the past six years. We pay 95 percent of our bills electronically, rather than with paper checks, thus avoiding postage costs. After the initial setup of recurring accounts, paying bills this way is much faster than writing a check and addressing an envelope. We transfer money from our interest-paying money-market account into our checking account only as needed. We access balances and send electronic messages to Citibank service people. And we do all of this from home, whenever we like.

Citibank doesn't charge its electronic banking customers any fees, but there is a hidden charge—the loss of the "float" on each electronic check. When we write a paper check and mail it, a few days usually elapse before the check is deposited and the money is drawn from our account. When we make an electronic payment, our account is debited on the date that electronic "check" is posted. This means that Citibank has the use of our money until the check it sends out in our name clears. Nevertheless, we estimate that our savings in postage probably outweigh the cost of the float we lose.

Overall, we think banking this way is wonderfully convenient. Banks like Citibank are beginning to use their capabilities in this area to attract new accounts, and we expect other banks to fight back. The competition ought to provide some good penny-pinching opportunities.

Many banks also allow you to pay bills by telephone. The plans we have investigated offered significant savings, essentially because a local telephone call is cheaper than a postage stamp and you can pay a number of bills with one call. Check out what your bank has to offer.

▶ JOIN A CREDIT UNION

Credit unions, which offer many of the same services as banks, are nonprofit organizations and often are able to offer members cheaper checking accounts and loans.

If your employer offers a credit union or you have a good community credit union in your area, you should certainly compare its prices and services with local banks. Many people use both, mainly because they can get a free checking account at their credit union. Some credit unions don't have automatic teller machines, however, a disadvantage if ready cash at any hour is a priority for you.

▶ THE PENNY PINCHER'S MORTGAGE

Unless you are certain you will own your home for only a few years and want to take a chance on changing interest rates, usually the best way to finance it is with a conventional fixed-rate mortgage amortized over as few years as possible. Since most people do sell their homes before the mortgage is paid off, make sure you or your accountant includes the points and origination fees in your calculations. A loan with a quarter-point-higher rate might be preferable to a loan with high up-front costs.

ARMs (Adjustable Rate Mortgages) can be dangerous; they shift the risk of interest-rate changes from the lender to you. Don't listen to expert opinions: No one knows which way interest rates are headed in the future. In the early 1990s, when interest rates declined significantly, people who had ARMS benefited. One reader of the second edition of this book, Joe Tufo of Alamo, California, showed us how well an ARM has worked for him. He bought his house in November 1991, got an ARM at a $7^{1}/_{2}$ percent start rate, and renewed at 6 percent in 1993. If he had instead chosen a fixed-rate mortgage in 1991, he would have been paying over 10 percent. There is no question that Joe has saved many thousands of dollars so far. Also, since he intends to pay off his loan as quickly as possible and is rapidly prepaying his mortgage principal (see following tip), he feels comfortable with the risks of the ARM.

Of course, people who chose ARMs over fixed-rate mortgages fifteen years before Joe bought his house saw the opposite happen. Back then, rates on some ARMs approached 20 percent.

Will this ever happen again? Nobody knows. Joe has persuaded us that an ARM can be the preferred choice for some people. Nevertheless, even if you choose an ARM, we believe that if you are doing so because you can't afford a fixed-rate mortgage, you probably can't afford the house. Also, before you take on an ARM, make sure you work up a worst-case scenario to see what you would be faced with if interest rates go sky-high again. Make doubly certain you understand all of the small print in an ARM agreement.

Why pay off your mortgage as quickly as you can? Few people ever calculate just how much more interest is involved in longer-term loans. Here's one example, using a fixed-rate mortgage of $100,000 at 8 percent:

	15-year loan	25-year loan	30-year loan
Monthly payments	$ 955.65	$ 771.82	$ 733.76
Amount owed after:			
5 years	$ 79,193	$ 92,429	$ 95,169
10 years	47,131	80,985	87,872
15 years	PAID	63,959	77,001
20 years		38,579	60,806
25 years		PAID	36,677
30 years			PAID
Total Amount Paid:	$ 172,017	$ 231,545	$ 264,155
Total Interest Paid:	$ 72,017	$ 131,545	$164,155

The $221.89 difference in monthly payments between a fifteen-year and a thirty-year loan is significant to anyone with a $100,000 mortgage. But so is the $92,138 difference in the amount of interest paid. And if you can manage just another $38.06 in payments (the difference between twenty-five-year and thirty-year loans), you'll save $32,610 and be able to burn the mortgage agreement five years sooner.

For most people, most of the time, paying the highest monthly payments possible for the shortest period of time possible is a sound investment decision.

▶ IF YOU MUST BUY MORTGAGE INSURANCE . . .

Unless you make a down payment of at least 15 percent on your house, the lender will insist that you buy mort-

gage insurance. It may sound harsh, but we think anyone who has to buy mortgage insurance to buy a house
would be better off waiting and saving until a 15 percent
down payment is possible. If you do take out mortgage
insurance, however, make certain before you sign any
agreement that you will be able to cancel it after your
equity in the house is more than 20 percent of its market
value.

RENEGOTIATE YOUR MORTGAGE

As a general rule, it pays to look into refinancing if you
plan to stay in your house for a minimum of five years
and if the rate on your current mortgage is at least one
percentage point above the going rate for a thirty-year
fixed-rate mortgage.

Depending on where you live, prevailing conditions,
and the competition among mortgage lenders, you may
have to pay up to 3 percent of the amount borrowed in
up-front points and closing costs. Your present lender
certainly isn't going to encourage you to cancel a loan
whose terms are now very favorable to him. On the
other hand, if your lender is convinced you are going to
shop elsewhere, he may want to give you an attractive
deal since he already knows you are creditworthy.

Here's an easy way to figure out how long it will be
before it pays off to refinance. Just substitute your own
numbers for those used in this example:

Suppose your present thirty-year $150,000 mortgage
at 10.5 percent has a principal balance of $137,601 after
exactly ten years. Your monthly payment is $1,372. It
will cost you $3,000 in up-front points and penalties to
refinance a twenty-year mortgage at 8 percent. Your new
principal amount will be $140,601 ($137,601 + $3,000)
and your new monthly payment $1,176. The numbers
look like this:

Mortgage balance	$ 137,601
Plus points and penalties	3,000
Total new mortgage principal	$ 140,601

Present monthly payment	$	1,372
New monthly payment	−	1,176
Difference	$	196

$3,000 refinancing costs
divided by $196 = 15.3 months.

If it takes 15.3 months before you pay off the cost of points and penalties, after that you will be saving the full $196 a month difference in monthly payments for the life of the mortgage. Total savings: $196 × 224.7 months (12 months × 20 years minus 15.3 months) = $44,041.

▶ PREPAY YOUR MORTGAGE PRINCIPAL

If you bought your home when interest rates were higher, prepaying your mortgage or adding to your monthly principal payments can make a lot of sense. Suppose you have a thirty-year fixed-rate mortgage of $200,000 at 9 percent. Your monthly payment is $1,609.25 and you will pay a whopping $379,328 in interest charges over the thirty-year life of the loan.

Now suppose that after five years, you raise your monthly payment to $1,800 a month, instructing the lender to apply the $190.75 difference to the principal of the loan. You can always change your mind when you voluntarily make such prepayments. But if you continue to make that relatively small extra payment, it will mean a saving of $95,506 in total interest charges and your mortgage will be paid off nearly eight years early.

One last calculation: If, instead of making that regular prepayment after five years, you saved $190.75 a month at 6 1/2 percent interest, tax free, for the next seventeen years, you would have only about $56,678 in total savings.

An accountant can help you factor in all the variables that pertain to you, including the deductibility of mort gage interest on your income tax. A mortgage prepayment strategy shouldn't be considered until you have paid off any other debts, have at least three months' salary in an emergency account, and have adequate disability insurance. You should also make sure the strategy doesn't interfere with saving for retirement or future college expenses.

Finally, if you do make prepayments, watch your mortgage statements like a hawk. Many mortgage lenders haven't set up computer programs that easily handle prepayments, and have to be forced to credit them correctly.

▶ EXPECT A MORTGAGE ESCROW ACCOUNT REFUND?

New 1995 federal rules put an end to some creative accounting that many lenders used to inflate the amount of money they required mortgage borrowers to keep in the escrow accounts from which their real-estate taxes and (sometimes) homeowner's insurance premiums are paid. If your mortgage lender was one of them, it was unfairly getting the use of money on which you could otherwise have been earning interest. (Even when, by state law or bank policy, interest is paid on an escrow account, the rate is never competitive with current money-market rates.)

If your mortgage closed after April 24, 1995, you are protected by the new regulations. If you have an older mortgage, however, your lender has until April 1998 to switch to the newly required accounting system. At some point before then, if your lender used so-called single-item accounting, you will get a refund from your escrow fund. The Department of Housing and Urban Development estimates that consumers will receive a total of over $1.5 billion.

If you haven't received a refund yet, and are unsure of what accounting method your lender had been using, ask if you should expect a refund—and when.

▶ GET RID OF HIGH-INTEREST CREDIT-CARD DEBT

Probably the worse sin a penny pincher can commit is to get in the habit of using credit cards as a way to borrow money. The rates are exorbitant—typically 12 to 19 percent—and the temptation to keep adding to the principal amount gets millions of people in real trouble every year.

The only smart times to use credit cards are (1) when you can't save money by paying cash; (2) when you want to have recourse to a third party—the credit-card company—to guard against the possibility of a merchant not delivering as promised; (3) as a way to take advantage of the "float"—the period of time between the date of purchase and when you have to pay the credit-card company the full amount in order to avoid any interest payments; and (4) when you use a card that rewards you in some way for dollars charged on it.

If you are carrying credit-card debt, get rid of it as fast as you can. If necessary, and if you also have other high-interest debt such as a car loan, visit your bank or credit union and talk about one new "consolidator" loan at a lower rate that will enable you to pay off all your higher-interest debt. Homeowners can do this with home-equity loans, a particularly good deal because interest payments on home-equity loans are still fully tax deductible. Just remember that you are putting your home up as collateral.

▶ GET A FREE REVIEW OF YOUR CREDIT RATING

Until a few years ago, you couldn't get a look at the credit reports maintained on you by credit bureaus without paying them a fee. One of the major bureaus, TRW, will now send you a free copy of your report once a year. Many, if not most, credit reports have erroneous information in them. Especially if you are applying for a new mortgage or considering another major loan, it is a good idea to insist that any negative errors be corrected. To request a free report, call TRW at 800-392-1122.

▶ IN TROUBLE? GET HELP

It's easy enough to give advice about staying out of trouble with credit card and other debt, but if you think you are already there, get help immediately. *The National Foundation for Consumer Credit* (800-388-2227) will tell you the location of the nearest regional office that offers credit counseling.

▶ DROP "AFFINITY" CREDIT CARDS

Millions of people feel good about their Visa or Master-Card credit cards because they know that by using them, they are helping their favorite charity or their college alma mater. The fact is, though, that only a small percentage of your money actually ends up with the affinity organization and you can nearly always get a better deal on the card elsewhere. Besides, whatever donation you are making isn't tax deductible. Write a check to your favorite cause instead.

▶ THE PENNY PINCHER'S BANK CREDIT CARD

There are interesting bells and whistles attached to different credit cards. The tips following this one discuss them. But the single most important question you should answer before you decide which card is best for you is whether or not you are going to pay your full balance each month, thereby never incurring interest charges.

If you can do this, and it is a goal every penny pincher should have, you really don't *care* how high the interest rate on your card is set. You can concentrate on finding a card that (1) has no membership fee; (2) offers a twenty-five-day grace period from the time of billing until payment is due; (3) offers some valuable supplemental benefits.

We've switched, dropped, and added cards over the past few years but always keep those three features in mind. To us, a bank credit card it both a great convenience (it is easier to account for expenditures by budget category this way than by keeping track of cash expenditures) and a way to postpone putting out cash for from thirty to forty-five days (and thus get the interest on that money ourselves).

On the other hand, before some purchases, especially in smaller stores, we ask how much we can save by paying cash. Green is quickly substituted for plastic when we like the answer.

What would we do if we were just starting out, couldn't get a low-interest bank loan, and had to buy a few high-ticket items before we had the ready cash to pay for them? First we would put off buying anything that wasn't absolutely necessary. Then we would pay the membership fee, if necessary, for a *second* bank card. Our first card, especially since it had no membership fee, might charge a high interest rate on unpaid balances. This second card would charge the lowest interest rates available. We would then use this second card *only* for the high-ticket items. Each month thereafter we would pay off as much as possible of the principal owed until we had no debt left. Finally, we would cut the card in two and hope never to use it again.

If you haven't gotten to the point of cutting up your second card and still carry a balance on it, don't fall into the trap of thinking that interest rates on different cards are fairly consistent, so it doesn't make any difference which one you use. As this book went to press, rates ranged from 7.75 percent to over 19 percent. If you carry a balance of $2,000 a month, the difference in interest charges can add up to over $150 a year.

Barron's (a weekly financial newspaper) and *Money* magazine (a monthly) both list credit cards with the lowest current interest rates in each issue. For more comprehensive information, send a $4 check to *Bankcard Holders of America,* 524 Branch Drive, Salem, VA 22070.

Ask for information on currently available low-interest, no-fee, and gold cards.

▶ THE FREQUENT FLIER'S CREDIT CARD

Paying no annual fee for a credit card isn't always the best penny-pinching strategy. If you travel by plane frequently and also charge more than $1,000 a month on the card, you will be better off with an airline card that credits you with one frequent-flier mile for every dollar you spend. Naturally, you should choose a card sponsored by the airline you fly on most often.

In a typical frequent-flier program, you need at least 25,000 miles to qualify for a free round-trip domestic ticket. That ticket might cost more or less than $375, but let's use that number to arrive at a value of 1.5 cents for a frequent-flier mile ($375 divided by 25,000). Now let's say you pay a $50 annual fee for a card and charge $12,000 on it during the year. The 12,000 frequent-flier miles you have earned are worth $180, so you are $130 ahead of the game.

This works only if you pay off your balance each month. The airline cards never offer the lowest interest rates, and if you pay their rates on unpaid balances, there is no way an award of 1.5 cents per dollar will make up the difference. Also, most airline cards require that the miles you earn be used within three years. If you earn only a couple of thousand miles a year through card use and don't also earn a lot of miles by flying on the airline, you may never get a chance to cash your miles in.

Among the airlines sponsoring Visa or MasterCards are *American* (800-359-4444), *United* (800-537-7783), TWA (800-322-8921), and *Continental* (800-446-5336). If you fly on another airline frequently, call and ask about any cards they sponsor.

If you don't want to be restricted to one airline, look into Bank One's *TravelPlus* Visa card (800-945-2023). This card allows you to use the mileage you earn on any domestic airline. *American Express* and *Diner's Club* have had similar all-airline cards for years, but the TravelPlus card's annual fee is much lower and Visa is accepted in more places. What's more, unlike the airline cards, there are no blackout days (usually around holidays) when you can't use your miles. You must book 14 days in advance and stay over a Saturday night, but if a seat is available on the flight you want, you will get it. Finally, for many flights you need fewer miles using this card than you do with an airline card.

▶ OTHER CARDS THAT OFFER AWARDS

Both *Ford* (800-374-7777) and *General Motors* (800-846-2273) sponsor cards that offer a 5 percent rebate on each dollar charged toward the purchase or lease of a new car. GM's maximum annual rebate is $500 ($1,000 with its gold card) for up to seven years. Ford's limit is $700 a year for up to five years. So both allow you to take as much as $3,500 off the price of a new car.

Exxon (800-554-6914), *Gulf* (800-367-4853), and *Phillips 66* (800-884-1930) are among the major oil companies that sponsor no-fee cards offering rebates on gas purchases and other merchandise. *General Electric* (800-437-3927) offers a no-fee card that gives users rebates of up to 2 percent a year on all purchases.

There are many other rebate cards available, and there will no doubt be more by the time you read this. Competitive pressures may affect the deals you can get with existing cards. Read the ads and check them out with the information sources cited in the previous tip. Keep in mind that the interest rates on all cards that offer rebates are invariably higher than no-frills cards issued by some banks. They make sense *only* if you pay off your balance each month.

For an up-to-date report on all rebate cards available, send $5 to Bankcard Holders of America (see address in previous tip) and ask for their Rebate/Frequent Flier Credit Card Guide.

▶ DON'T FALL FOR CREDIT-CARD "INTRODUCTORY OFFERS"

The interest rates on all cards can change at any time. If you pay interest charges on your balance, monitor any changes monthly. Don't fall for the "introductory offer" rate often featured in huge type in the direct-mail promotions of various cards. It makes no sense to switch to a card that offers a 5 percent interest rate for three months if you will pay 18 percent after that.

▶ PAYING A FEE FOR YOUR CARD? MAYBE YOU DON'T HAVE TO

As competition heats up between card issuers, many of them offer no-annual-fee cards to new customers, but conveniently forget to do the same for existing customers. The next time you are billed for an annual fee on your card, pick up the phone and ask the bank to waive it. They may very well be willing to do so.

▶ WHAT ABOUT GOLD-CARD ENHANCEMENTS?

Do you really think you will ever use one of those "exclusive private clubs in London" offered as one of the reasons to pay extra for a gold or platinum card? Do you really think your waiter will be impressed if you use a gold card?

Do you really care? Of course not. There are standard gold-card-enhancement packages on Visa and Master-Cards nationwide, and you may want to check them out (see information sources on page 208). Most of us want only the enhancements that are also available on many standard cards—particularly automatic collision insurance when we use the card to rent a car and some kind of automatic extension of product warranty when we use the card to buy that product. Shop among them first before paying extra for a showy piece of plastic.

▶ WATCH OUT FOR TWO-CYCLE BILLING

If, despite all of our sermonizing, you do carry a balance on your credit car from time to time, make sure your issuer is not using "two-cycle billing." The insidious thing about this accounting dodge is that it doesn't affect the card's stated interest rate, but it can effectively increase the actual rate you pay dramatically. Cards using two-cycle billing retroactively impose finance charges on the *previous* month's balance when (even after many consecutive months of paying up in full) you decide to carry a balance.

Since even people who always pay full balances have been known to forget to mail a payment in time, every credit-card user should avoid cards using this billing method. Read the fine print on the back of your statement and call your card issuer if you are still not sure.

▶ YES. PILE ON CREDIT-CARD CHARGES

Only, *only* (the penny pincher's broken record) if you are *absolutely certain* you will pay the full balance every month. If you do, and you use an airline or other card that rewards you based on charges, why not use it wherever possible unless you can get a discount for using cash?

Many colleges accept credit cards for tuition bills. You can buy postage stamps with a card and make most of your charitable contributions that way. There are a lot of people sitting in free airplane seats because they used a credit card at supermarkets and at doctors' and dentists' offices. Where else? Before you use cash or your checkbook, ask.

▶ CANCEL OLD CARDS

When you do switch from card to card, don't just cut the old one up and throw it away. Make sure you write the card issuer telling them to terminate your account and to notify all credit bureaus that your account was closed in good standing. If you don't do this, a lender or credit-card company may check your records and turn you down because they see you have too many cards.

▶ DEBIT CARD OR CREDIT CARD?

When you use a debit card issued by your bank, whatever you charge is immediately deducted from your checking account. When you use a credit card, you have a grace period of at least 25 days before you have to write a check. Furthermore, a credit-card purchase gives you some protection if the merchandise you buy isn't delivered or is defective. For anyone who pays balances in full each month, a credit card (even more so a frequent-flier or rebate credit card) is a better choice.

The exception is at an ATM machine, where a debit card is always a better choice.

▶ THE BEST SOURCE OF A LOAN

As a general rule, the worst possible source of a loan is the seller of the product. When you borrow money from an automobile dealer, the most common of many loans made by sellers of products, he gets a kickback (which you pay for) from the ultimate source of the money. Even if the seller is self-financing the loan, you can bet you'll be paying a far higher rate than you would had you borrowed from a bank.

Finance companies deal with the most unsophisticated borrowers, which is how they get away with borrowing money themselves and then relending it at a much higher rate.

The best source of a loan? Your own resources. If you've got $20,000 in a money-market fund, and need to buy a new car, take it out of the fund and pay cash. You'll still have some emergency funds left over (you have no business buying a car for more than $15,000 if all you've got saved is $20,000), and no money-market fund is paying you as much in interest as you'll pay to a lender.

With that lecture over, a few other alternatives, none as good:

If you have a cash-value insurance policy, check out a loan from your insurance company. If you are fortunate enough to be a member of an active credit union, you will probably be able to get a low-cost loan there. You may also be able to borrow money from your profit-sharing fund where you work; check with your benefits or personnel department. After that, banks are still your best choice. See the next few tips for what to look for and what to avoid.

▶ A ROSE IS A ROSE IS A ROSE, BUT A LENDER'S INTEREST RATE ISN'T

Your bank agrees to lend you $10,000 at 10 percent for one year. How much will you pay in interest?

The obvious answer is 10 percent of $10,000, or $1,000. The actual answer will almost certainly be different, and higher. Unfortunately, the interest rates quoted by lenders don't tell the whole story. The next few tips do.

▶ SIMPLE-INTEREST/SINGLE-PAYMENT LOANS

This is the least expensive way to borrow money. You pay interest only on the money you still owe. Using a single-payment method, you would take the $10,000 and at the end of the year make one payment to the lender of $11,000. You have had the use of the full $10,000 for the entire twelve months and have paid $1,000—10 percent—in interest.

Alternatively, if you pay off a 10 percent simple-interest loan in twelve monthly installments, your total interest payments will be only $550. Why? Because you will not have had the use of $10,000 for the full twelve months. Your first monthly payment of $879 would include interest charges of $83 and a partial payment of

$796 on the principal. Your second monthly payment of $879 would consist of a smaller interest payment and a larger partial payment on the principal because you would now have the use of only $9,204 ($10,000 minus $796) of the principal. And so on, for each of the next eleven months. As the amount of the principal still outstanding diminishes, so does the interest payment.

Either kind of simple-interest loan is highly desirable, but don't count on getting one from any lender unless you are a highly preferred or corporate customer.

▶ DISCOUNTED INTEREST LOANS

Still using our example of a $10,000 one-year loan at 10 percent, with this type of loan the lender deducts the 10 percent interest up front and therefore lends you only $9,000. At the end of the year, you will pay back $10,000 in a single payment.

Not so bad? Let's calculate your true interest rate. You have really borrowed only $9,000 and paid $1,000 in interest. When calculated ($1,000 divided by $9,000), this comes to a true interest rate of 11.11 percent.

It gets much worse. If you take the $9,000 and agree to make twelve monthly payments of $833.30 ($10,000 divided by 12), your effective annual interest rate on the money you have actually had use of comes to almost 20 percent!

You are beginning to understand some of the mysteries of banking. Read on.

▶ ADD-ON INTEREST LOANS

You may also be offered this method by a lender. The $1,000 interest on your $10,000 loan is added on to the principal in the beginning. Then you repay $11,000 in twelve monthly installments. True annual interest: almost 18 percent.

If you are quoted either an "add-on" or "discounted" interest rate, then the true annual interest you will pay will be almost *double* the percentage quoted.

▶ KNOW THE APR—AND MORE

Lenders can and still will quote you an add-on or discounted interest rate, but for the past fifteen years they have also been legally required to tell you the true annual percentage rate (the APR). Unfortunately, too many people still commit to overly expensive loans because the APR isn't mentioned until all the papers are about to be signed. Do not ever commit to a loan until you have seen, in writing, the federally required APR interest on it.

Even then, especially in the case of a complicated loan such as a mortgage, the APR quoted may not take into account some of the expenses you have to incur to get the loan (title insurance fees, credit-report fees, application fees, etc.). It gets very complicated indeed, but if you are repaying a loan over a thirty-year period, a difference of $1/2$ percent on a principal of $100,000 can amount to thousands of dollars. If you aren't comfortable doing it yourself, have a good accountant review the figures to arrive at your true loan costs.

▶ SECURED VERSUS UNSECURED LOANS

A secured loan means that you have given the bank some form of collateral as security. If you don't pay the money back, they get to keep the collateral. Your home mortgage is a secured loan, but you can also use stocks, bonds, a car, or any other hard asset as collateral.

An unsecured loan means the bank has extended credit to you without collateral. When you get an approved line of credit up to a certain amount at your bank and write checks against it, you are in effect taking out an unsecured loan. Banks are careful about the credit ratings of people approved for unsecured loans, but even so you will pay a higher interest rate than if the loan were secured by collateral. You've got to pay it back anyway, so why not secure the loan?

▶ BEWARE THE FLOATING RATE

Banks and other credit institutions love to shift risk from themselves to you. That's why you may be offered a "floating rate" loan, usually tied to the "prime rate" charged by banks to their best corporate customers. You might be offered a loan at "prime plus 3," for instance, meaning your interest payments would always be 3 percent over the current prime rate.

The danger here is the same as it is with an adjustable-rate mortgage. Avoid it if at all possible.

▶ THE PENNY PINCHER'S BANK LOAN

Despite the previous example of simple-interest/single-payment loans, you should know one thing about them: Banks rarely if ever offer simple-interest/single-payment loans to retail customers. Installment loans of any kind are more profitable. But you can at least try to negotiate. Here's how:

Dealing (ideally) with a bank officer you already know (your branch manager, perhaps), don't say anything about the single-payment method until after you have the bank's agreement on the amount and term of the loan as well as the APR. The bank, of course, will be planning to charge you monthly installments with a fixed monthly payment in which interest payments will gradually decline and payments to principal will gradually increase.

Once you have the commitment, tell your banker you will be willing to pay off the loan in monthly payments over the term agreed upon, and at the APR the bank has quoted. But you want the loan structured as a single-payment loan that allows monthly payments. In other words, you will pay the same amount each month toward the principal, as well as interest at the agreed-upon APR on the principal outstanding.

The result will be that you will pay more than you would under the usual installment method at the beginning of the loan, and less at the end. More important, you will pay less in interest over the term of the loan.

Your banker won't be thrilled with your suggestion, but you'll have a good argument: She has agreed to amount, to term, and to APR, and there's no additional risk to the bank. Why not do it your way?

▶ PAYING OFF EARLY: BEWARE THE RULE OF 78s

Although illegal in many states, some still allow lenders to use an accounting method called "the rule of 78s" when a loan is paid off early. If you decide to prepay a loan that uses this method—even if there is no prepayment penalty in your loan agreement—you will end up paying a much higher interest rate than the agreement calls for. Here's how it works in a loan with a one-year term:

The first month, you would pay $12/78$ of the interest, the second month $11/78$, the third $10/78$, and so on down to $1/78$ in the final month. If you pay the loan off at the end of the sixth month, and the lender activates the rule of 78s, you will have already paid $57/78$ $(12 + 11 + 10 + 9 + 8 + 7 = 57)$ in interest—not half the amount owed, but nearly three quarters of the total.

When you read a loan agreement, look carefully for references to prepayment penalties, the rule of 78s, or the term "the sum of the digits." What you want instead is a simple-interest loan or an agreement that uses the actuarial method for computing interest due on prepayments. *Ask for it.*

▶ NO INTEREST CHARGES! BUY NOW! 24 MONTHS TO PAY!

And maybe you believe in the tooth fairy. The interest charges are hidden in the bloated price of the car or whatever else you are buying. It is still an installment loan, and the dealer can still sell it to a bank for a profit. In practice, because such offers are particularly attractive to unsophisticated borrowers and no APR need be declared, what you end up paying is higher than what you would have paid by buying the car for an honest price and paying interest on the loan.

Making Money
with Your
Money

Penny pinching is easier when you have extra dollars to pinch. This chapter will suggest a few ways to make the money you earn work harder to make you more money.

The word "tip" has a deservedly negative reputation when it comes to investment advice. But unlike the tips your brother-in-law gives you about hot stocks, ours concentrate on the decisions you must make among saving and investing methods and techniques. (Tip #1: Avoid hot stock tips.) Or they suggest cheaper ways to make different kinds of investments.

As a brief checklist, they are useful. For complete investment advice, go elsewhere. Where? That's not an easy question, so we'll start with a couple of basic rules.

▶ DON'T BLINDLY TRUST EXPERTS

Yes, you can hire a financial planner to take complete charge of every aspect of your life that involves money—your household budget, savings plans, investments, and retirement. You can take your allowance like a teenager and not worry about a thing. Naturally you will have less money to manage, since the fees for this kind of all-encompassing financial planing don't come cheap. And what happens if you choose an adviser who is inept, unlucky, or even dishonest?

Year after year, there are new stories about rich and famous athletes and show-business personalities who lose millions or are even bankrupted because they trusted an adviser to make all their financial decisions. The media seldom report on the millions of middle-class people who rely on other people and end up paying big fees for terrible results.

The first and most important tip about saving and investing is to learn enough about the subject so that you can trust the one person who is ultimately responsible: yourself. You don't have to become an expert, but you have to know enough to decide what you want to hire experts for, how to choose good ones, and when it is just as easy—and cheaper—to do it yourself.

▶ GET INTERESTED IN YOUR MONEY

That's different than getting interest *on* your money. If you have enough penny-pinching instincts to save hundreds of dollars a year by shopping wisely and saving on energy bills, you can't afford to skip the financial pages of your newspaper. What's happening to interest rates, federal budget deficits, the value of the dollar, and the economy has a direct bearing on your money and your future.

To get comfortable with the idea of being responsible for your money, first read the tips in this chapter. Frankly, if you have no background at all in money management, you're likely to be a bit confused, even though the tips may help you with specific questions or problems. So turn next to a book on basic investing principles. Among the good ones at your library, Andrew Tobias's *The Only Other Investment Guide You'll Ever*

Need is sensible, quite comprehensive, and more fun to read than most.

After you've read one or two books, begin spending a couple of hours a week reading newspapers (nothing beats *The Wall Street Journal*) and magazines (*Money* and *Kiplinger's Personal Finance Magazine* are fine, but working your way up to *Forbes* and *Barron's* is a reasonable goal).

Keeping up with a rapidly changing world and new investment possibilities is essential. The days of putting your money in "safe" investments and never worrying about them are over.

▶ BUY A PERSONAL-FINANCE SOFTWARE PROGRAM

If you have a computer, personal-finance software can be one of the best buys you will ever make. The top programs cost less than $40 in discount outlets and all offer comprehensive, well-organized ways to manage your money. You can use them to track your investments and your family budget, pay your bills electronically, figure out how much insurance you need, how much you'll owe in taxes, and much more. There is no better way to "get interested in your money" with a minimum expenditure of time and effort.

Quicken, from Intuit, is the most popular all-inclusive personal-finance software program and is especially easy to use in setting up a budget. *Microsoft Money* is another good program. As of this writing, our longtime favorite, *Managing Your Money,* from Meca, had not done a good job of updating for Windows and was running a distant third.

▶ SURF THE INTERNET'S INVESTMENT SITES

A few months ago, if we had had to choose between *The Wall Street Journal* and all the sites about investing on the Internet, CompuServe, or America Online, the *Jour-*

nal would have won hands down. Then the *Journal* started its own very good web site (http://www.wsj. com), which offers subscribers not only a lot of what is in the print version but also access to breaking news. The print version is still a lot easier to "access" and read, so we prefer it. By 1998? Who knows? There are probably hundreds of other worthwhile sites as we write this, new ones are being added daily, and you can definitely learn a great deal visiting some of them for the price of your hourly access rate. You can use any full-scale search service such as Yahoo (http://yahoo.com) to see what sites are devoted to different aspects of investing. Or start with these sites and move on from them:

■ *Money Personal Finance Center* (http://pathfinder. com/money) also directs you to other pertinent web sites and gives you access to many *Money* magazine articles and features.

■ *NETworth* (http://networth.galt.com) provides daily quotes on all major mutual funds and allows you to access its database of 5,000 funds to research those appropriate for you.

▶ PAY OFF HIGH-INTEREST DEBTS

It is silly to keep $2,000 in a money-market account paying 4 percent taxable interest at the same time you owe $2,000 on your bank credit card and are paying 17 percent in non-tax-deductible interest. The first way to get more income from your income is to pay off any high-interest debt—normally everything but your home mortgage and home-equity loans, which are tax-deductible.

▶ OWN A HOME

Is this an investment strategy? And if so, is it still a good one? For decades, as residential real-estate prices in most parts of the country rose every year, it was virtually an article of faith among personal financial advisers that owning a home was the single best investment anyone could make. Then the end of the boom came. In the late 1980s, houses in some areas declined in value by 30 percent or more in one year. Throughout the first years of the 1990s, housing prices in some parts of the country have either declined or been flat. A lot of people have good reason to question the old conventional wisdom.

It is possible they are right. But there have been other periods of depressed real-estate prices in American history. In the long run, prices have rebounded. In the long run, the odds are still high that the value of your home will at least keep pace with inflation.

"In the long run" doesn't help much if you buy at a market high and are forced to sell in a depressed market a couple of years later. If you don't plan on staying in your area for a minimum of five years, renting might be safer. Otherwise, home ownership is still a sound investment. You have to live somewhere, and paying rent is a certain way not to build any equity. The one major tax shelter left to most people is the deduction of mortgage-interest payments and real-estate taxes on their federal income-tax returns. Perhaps we will see some form of a flat tax eventually, but our guess is that it will be difficult politically to tamper too much with these deductions.

Finally, if the real-estate market in your area still hasn't recovered as you are reading this, if the gloom and doomsday predictions are shared by just about everybody, you just may have the buying opportunity of a lifetime. Historically, the best buys are made when there are more eager sellers than buyers. Just as the best time to sell is usually when everyone else is jumping on the bandwagon to buy.

▶ TAKE ADVANTAGE OF TAX-DEFERRED INVESTMENT PLANS

You have certain investment goals—money for a child's college education, a new house, a wedding, redecorating, etc.—that probably can't be achieved with tax-deferred investments. That's because the government assesses a big penalty if you withdraw money from a tax-deferred plan before you are fifty-nine and a half.

When your investment goal is a comfortable retirement, though, your first and best decision is to take maximum advantage of tax-deferred investment opportunities. "Tax-deferred" means that no taxes are collected on the money you make until you withdraw it. By avoiding annual taxes for many years, a lot more of your money stays invested, earning interest and appreciating in value.

Any personal-finance guide will explain the ins and outs of IRAs, Keogh plans, 401(k) and 403 (b) plans, and SEPs (Simplified Employee Pension plans, which allow employers to contribute to employees' individual IRAs). These are all tax-advantaged ways to invest, and you should understand how each works. The next tip offers a few guidelines for people fortunate enough to have an employer-sponsored 401(k) plan.

▶ TAKE FULL ADVANTAGE OF YOUR 401(k)

Fewer and fewer companies are offering "defined benefit plans"—plans that guarantee employees a monthly lifetime income upon retirement depending upon years of service and annual income. The very strong trend has been to switch to 401(k) plans, which shift the responsibility for retirement planning from the company to its individual employees. Employees who don't take full advantage of 401(k) plans from an early age may find that retirement is a glum prospect. Even today, Social Security provides less than 30 percent of the income of retired people living on $25,000 a year or more. Most experts expect Social Security retirement benefits to diminish in terms of actual spending power in the next century.

If you can't depend on Social Security and you aren't part of a defined benefit plan, you must face the hard fact that your future is in your own hands. This isn't necessarily bad news. Take a look at how much you would save at various rates of return after 30 years of contributing to a 401(k) with employer's matching funds equal to 50 percent:

Annual Employee Contribution	6%	8%	10%	12%
$1,000	$118,587	$ 169,925	$ 246,741	$ 361,999
$2,000	$237,175	$ 339,850	$ 493,482	$ 723,998
$4,000	$474,349	$ 679,699	$ 986,964	$1,447,996
$8,000	$948,698	$1,359,399	$1,973,928	$2,895,992

In a 401(k) plan, you contribute pretax dollars. Whatever matching funds your employer puts into your account are also free of any tax that year. Then all of the earnings of these contributions compound free of any tax until you retire. At that point, you pay tax at normal rates as your money is withdrawn.

This is by far the best deal you will ever have to save and invest for a comfortable retirement. To take full advantage of it, do the following:

■ *Start now.* Stop procrastinating, delaying, and dreaming about winning the lottery. The sooner you start, the better. The magic of compounding makes dollars you save at age 25 much greater nest-egg builders than dollars saved at 45. Given an annual rate of return of 10 percent, a 25-year-old would have to save only $180 a month for the next 40 years to have $1,000,000 at age 65. A 45-year-old would have to save $1,392 a month to achieve the same result. A thousand dollars saved at 25 and compounding at 10 percent a year grows to $45,269 at age 65. A thousand dollars saved at 45 grows only to $6,728.

■ *Save as much as your plan allows.* Putting every penny of your own money into a 401(k) is important for two reasons. First, because this is the only way to save pretax dollars and to put them into a tax-deferred account. Second, because only this way can you take maximum advantage of your employer's matching amount. If your employer puts in 50 cents for every dollar you put in, you are getting an instant return of 50 percent on your money. Where else can you do that?

- *Don't borrow from your plan.* The temptation is great when money is needed, and you see that great lump sum that is all yours. But look elsewhere, a home-equity loan perhaps. Remember that any money you withdraw would no longer be compounding tax-free, and that interest payments would not be tax-deductible, as they would with the home-equity loan.
- *Don't play it "safe."* The biggest mistake made by most people when they look at the investment options offered by their 401(k) plans is to choose a Guaranteed Investment Contract or some other "safe" low-return short-term bond or money-market fund. When you have a lot of years left before retirement, history says you will be much better off investing in the stock market. Since 1926, long-term bonds had compound average total returns of about $5^1/_2$ percent, shorter-term treasury bills returned about $3^1/_2$ percent, and common stocks returned over 10 percent. If you settle for a 4 percent return and inflation averages 5 percent a year during the life of your 401(k) plan, your money will actually lose purchasing power. Look at the difference over a 30-year-period in the table on page 225 between a 10 percent and a 6 percent return, and you have to conclude that avoiding the stock market with long-term investments is not playing it safe at all.

This is not an argument for staking all of your 401(k) money in the most aggressive funds offered by your plan, or for investing all of it in the company you work for. The advice in the next tip applies to 401(k) investing as well as every other kind.

▶ NEVER BET IT ALL ON ONE SCENARIO

No one can predict the future. Not your brother-in-law with a hot tip about a stock that can't miss, not the chairman of the Federal Reserve Bank, not the most successful money managers in the world. Trust no one who is absolutely certain about what will happen to the stock market in the next few months, or where interest rates will be next year. *No one knows.*

In the long run (yes, again), although they may invest huge sums based on a certain future scenario, most money managers who stay in business always diversify their assets in some form or another. They may think the economy will boom and the stock market will go up 500 points in the next year, but they don't bet everything on that one outcome.

Most of us should diversify our investments in two ways. First, we should own different categories of assets: real estate (usually just our homes), equities (stocks and stock mutual funds), fixed-income investments (bonds and certificates of deposit), and cash equivalents (money-market funds and savings accounts).

As a general rule, the younger you are the more heavily weighted your long-term investments should be in equities and real estate. That's because, historically, over a long period of time those investments have produced a greater return than bonds. If you are five years away from retirement, you may want to become more conservative, shifting some assets into investments that will pay you a fixed income and protecting yourself from the possibility of a long slump in the stock market. Even then, as a hedge against future inflation, you should own some equities or some real estate that may appreciate in value as well as produce income.

The second way you should diversify is within asset categories. Don't invest all of your equity money in one stock or buy the bonds of just one company. In fact, don't even invest in just one kind of stock or bond—the oil industry, for example, or computers or airlines. You will reduce your risks considerably by owning a portfolio that isn't completely dependent on one future scenario coming true.

If you have $100,000 or more to invest and can establish a good relationship with a knowledgeable broker, you can diversify by investing in individual stocks and bonds. Otherwise, except for investments in U.S. Treasuries (see page 237), your best alternative is to invest in mutual funds. The different types of funds give you a way to diversify categories (stocks or bonds) as well as to own widely diversified portfolios within those categories.

▶ HOW TO CHOOSE A MUTUAL FUND

Since 400-page books are written on this topic and we cover the subject in about that many words, don't expect much detail in what follows. But there is an easy, three-step way to narrow your choices down from thousands of funds to a few that will meet your objectives.

(1) Exactly what are you looking for in a fund? Growth? Income? What kind of risk are you willing to take? Do you want a fund that invests all or part of your money outside the United States? Only you can decide what investment philosophy and strategies suit you best, although some of those 400-page books may help you clarify your thoughts. There is no one mutual fund that is right for everyone, and if your portfolio is large enough, you should diversify into funds with different objectives and/or investing techniques.

When you feel comfortable with your objectives, it is time to go to the library. Take a look at the annual and/or quarterly mutual-fund issues of *Money, Barron's, Kiplinger's Personal Finance Magazine, Business Week,* and *Forbes.* Each uses somewhat different criteria in examining and ranking funds, but all include data about past performance, investment objectives, and 800 numbers to call for prospectuses. For the most comprehensive coverage of funds, ask the librarian for *Morningstar Mutual Funds.* By this point, you will be able to concentrate on the funds whose objectives match your own.

(2) Now narrow your choices to "no-load" or very "low-load" funds. All the magazines above tell you which funds are no-load. A no-load fund charges no commission on the up-front sale and no fee for the back-end redemption. There have been countless studies of the performance of no-load funds versus load funds, which

can charge up to an 8.5 percent commission. None of them has yet made a compelling case that there's any difference in how the funds perform. There are many load funds with superior long-term records, but there are no-load funds that have performed just as well. An initial investment of $1,000 instead of $915 ($1,000 minus an 8.5 percent commission) gives you a head start.

(3)   Finally, choose no-load funds with low fees. The best source of this information is *Morningstar Mutual Funds*. Or check *Money* magazine's annual mutual-fund issue (February) for a projection of expenses for the leading 1,000 or so funds. If your choice is between a fund with a terrible record whose five-year expenses per $1,000 are projected by *Money* at $50 per thousand and another with a superior record with projected expenses of $100, you might want to pay the higher expenses. But higher expenses don't guarantee better results, so if everything else is equal, why not opt for the savings?

By this point you will find your choices narrowed down to a very few funds. Get their prospectuses and read them. Remember that superior past performance is not a guarantee for the future. In fact, we suggest you stay away from the hottest funds of the previous year—the ones ranked at the very top for one-year performance. So much money is flowing into them that their managers may have a hard time investing it as wisely as they did in the past. Find a fund with a good long-term record over five or ten years, take the plunge, and monitor performance against the competition from then on.

You can skip a lot of this research when you invest in index funds. See page 231.

▶ **BUY MUTUAL FUNDS USING DOLLAR COST AVERAGING**

No matter what else is happening in the world, you will always be able to find one expert predicting that stock prices will double in the next year and another one predicting the opposite. Nor can you rely on consensus opinions; historically, when a vast majority of experts have agreed it was time to buy, it was usually a good time to sell. And vice versa. Except, of course, that once this became known, everyone became a "contrarian" investor and all bets were off about what majority opinions actually meant.

Confusing? Of course. That's what makes a market a market. At any given time, one party to a transaction is convinced it is a good idea to sell at a certain price and another party is equally sure it is a good idea to buy at the same price. There are thousands of professionals who make a living trying to "time" the market, selling and buying at just the right times. Yet over the long term, very few market timers manage to beat the stock market averages.

You simply can't be certain you'll always buy at the best possible time. So many people believe the best strategy is not to worry about timing at all. They use dollar cost averaging, an especially effective technique if you are investing for long-term results. The example on pages 232 and 233 shows you why.

▶ WHY MARKET TIMING DOESN'T WORK

We added this explanation because dozens of readers of the first editions questioned our brief advice in the previous tip about guessing which way the stock and bond markets are headed.

The appeal of market timing is understandable. If you could always buy when the markets are at their lows and sell when they are at their highs, you would never lose any money in a market decline. Your returns would be incredible. Doesn't Expert X on *Wall Street Week* predict an imminent collapse of the stock market? Why not sell everything on his advice?

First, because if you are a wise penny-pinching investor, you are not betting money needed in the short term in the stock market or in volatile bonds. You are investing for the long term. And in the long term, you are better taking losses during a decline than you are trying to guess which way the market is going. Why? Because you can't know when the decline will halt and the market will rebound.

When the stock market does rebound, it tends to make a large percentage of its gains in a very few days. One study showed that a dollar continually invested in stocks from 1980 to 1992 would have grown to over $7. If you had taken your money out of the market and missed just the top five performing months in those years (out of 156 months total), your return would have dropped to below $3. Every study made of the stock market in the past 50 years confirms this phenomenon.

▶ BUY INDEX FUNDS

An index fund is a "passively managed" mutual fund that owns stocks that exactly replicate an index such as the Standard & Poor's 500 Composite Stock Price Index. That is, an S&P 500 index fund owns all 500 stocks in the index in exactly the same proportions as they are weighted in the index itself. The fund manager isn't trying to decide whether GE is a better buy than IBM or AT&T or Coca-Cola. He doesn't care. The performance of the index fund exactly tracks the performance of the index, less expenses incurred in running the fund.

Because the fund conducts no expensive research, its expenses are much lower than an "actively managed" fund, one in which the manager picks stocks he believes will outperform the market. Why would anyone choose to put money in a fund where nobody is even trying to "beat the market"? The answer, based on historical data, is that—in the long run—*very few actively managed funds outperform the indexes.*

Furthermore, in an example cited by John Bogle in *Bogle on Mutual Funds* (Dell Books, $12.95), the annual rate of return from the total stock market (which can be replicated by an index fund) was 12 percent between 1970 and 1992. For the average actively managed equity

Why Dollar Cost Averaging Works

You've decided that all the arguments about investing in stocks for long-term results make sense. But you've also heard horror stories about buying shares in a mutual fund for $10 and seeing them sink to $8 in less than a week's time. How do you guard against that?

You don't, because you can't. The stock market averages are always going up or down, and a long bear market (when stock prices fall nearly continuously for months at a time) is no fun for anyone. The fact is, though, that the biggest gains made in stock investments are usually those made by buying in the depths of a bear market when hardly anyone wants to own stocks.

The best investment technique available to people who are putting their money in the stock market for the long term (at least seven to ten years, preferably longer) is dollar cost averaging. You invest a fixed amount of money each month (or each quarter) in a particular mutual fund. You keep doing this year after year, on exactly the same dates, whether the experts are predicting eternal prosperity or an imminent doomsday. By investing *the same amount each time* you will buy more shares of the fund when prices are low and fewer shares when prices are high.

It's that simple, but it works. Here's an example, exaggerating the price movement of the fund's shares in just one year's time to illustrate the effects of dollar cost averaging (realistically, it takes a lot longer than this for such a dramatic effect to be apparent):

WITH DOLLAR COST AVERAGING

Date of purchase	Price per share	Number of shares purchased	Amount invested
Dec 31	$ 6	150	$ 900
Mar 30	$ 3	300	$ 900
Jun 30	$ 9	100	$ 900
Sep 30	$15	60	$ 900
Dec 31	$12	75	$ 900
Totals		685	$4,500

WITHOUT DOLLAR COST AVERAGING

Price per share	Number of shares purchased	Amount invested
$ 6	100	$ 600
$ 3	100	$ 300
$ 9	100	$ 900
$15	100	$1,500
$12	100	$1,200
	500	$4,500

The same $4,500 invested with dollar cost averaging gives you 185 more shares than you would have gotten by purchasing a fixed number of shares on the same dates.

mutual fund, it was 10.8 percent. Remember, that is an average; *half of all funds did worse.*

Index funds are detested and reviled by many Wall Street professionals, but nobody can argue with the historical data. The reason index funds do so well, in addition to penny-pinching low expense ratios, has to do with the "efficient market theory" propounded by some Nobel Prize–winning economists. If you are intrigued, by all means read John Bogle's brilliant book, which explains all this and much more. All good libraries have a copy.

Many investors own one or more index funds as long-term cornerstones in their mutual-fund portfolios but also own actively managed funds to pursue specific asset-allocation strategies. This gets too complicated for a book about penny pinching, but you'll learn more from books like Bogle's.

One last word about index funds: If you buy one, pay special attention to how its expense ratios compare with funds tracking exactly the same index. Believe it or not, the annual difference can be as much as 300 percent. *The Vanguard Group* has always offered funds with extremely low expense ratios.

▶ CHECK OUT DRIPs

More than 1,000 U.S. companies, including most of the bluest of blue-chip stocks, offer Dividend Reinvestment Programs. DRIPs allow stockholders automatically to reinvest the dividends they earn in additional shares or fractional shares, without incurring brokerage fees. In addition, many of these corporations allow existing stockholders to make additional stock purchases directly from the company without paying brokerage fees, although some charge small fees of their own.

For long-term investors making regular, periodic investments in individual stocks, especially in odd lots of fewer than 100 shares, DRIPs are a great way to stretch every investment dollar. To find out if a company you are interested in offers a DRIP (and what its limitations and costs are), you can write or call its investor relations department at corporate headquarters.

Although some companies (including Proctor & Gamble, McDonald's, and Exxon) now sell shares direct to anybody, most won't allow you into their programs unless you own at least one share. And buying one or ten shares from even a discount broker can be expensive. One good alternative is to call *The National Association of Investors Corporation* (810-583-6242) in Madison Heights, Michigan. They will give you a list of companies with DRIP plans and, for a modest fee, buy one share in your name in any of 100 companies. Once you own that, you simply notify the issuing company that you want to enroll in its DRIP.

You can also call the *Direct Stock Purchase Plan Clearinghouse* (800-774-4117). They will send prospectuses for a maximum of five stocks along with a list of companies offering DRIPs. On the Internet, *No-Load Stock Information* (http://www.calweb.com/~mkeller/noload/) includes links to many companies that sell stock direct or offer DRIPs.

Saving money by avoiding brokerage fees is a good strategy only if you would have bought the stock in any case. DRIPs are suitable only for long-term investors because you have no control over when or at what price you purchase more stock. Selling isn't easy, either; most companies take at least ten days to comply with a sell request. Finally, if you decide to use DRIPs in a major way, keep in mind the advice in a previous tip about the need for diversification.

▶ **THINK TWICE ABOUT VARIABLE ANNUITIES**

Variable annuities have become a "hot" investment, pushed by banks, insurance companies, brokerage companies, and mutual-fund groups. Although they include a life insurance component, the real reason to buy a variable annuity is to escape the tax on its investment gains until withdrawal. Over a long period of time—a minimum of 15 years for most people, in our opinion—that single reason might make a variable annuity a good investment vehicle for you. You must also keep in mind that if you withdraw the money before age 59½, you will pay a stiff penalty. Also, the annuity is just as risky as whatever it is invested in—stocks, bonds, or money-market funds. Finally, most variable annuities have very high fee schedules, sometimes adding up to more than 2 percent a year.

Don't even think about buying a variable annuity until you have put every cent possible in other tax-advantaged accounts—401(k) plans at work, IRAs, etc. And don't ever buy one without either having it checked out by an independent financial advisor you trust (someone who is not selling it to you) or doing some solid research of your own. *Morningstar* publishes a guide to variable annuities that is available in many libraries.

▶ START A TEENAGER'S IRA

Putting money away for your child's college education and your own retirement are first priorities, but the long-term benefits of starting an Individual Retirement Account as early as possible are so compelling that they should be considered by every investor with children.

If your child has any earned income, from a summer job or after-school work, she can start an IRA with an annual contribution equal to the amount earned up to $2,000. Suppose she earns $1,000 at age 16 and you make a $1,000 gift to her that year, putting it into a mutual fund IRA in her name. By the time she is 65 years old, that $1,000 will have grown to $133,000, assuming a growth rate of 10.5 percent a year. If she waits until she is 25 to make the same $1,000 contribution, it will grow to only $54,000 by the time she is 65.

If you put $1,000 into her IRA annually from age 16 to 20—a total of just $5,000—she will have a nest egg of $499,000 by the time she is 65. Quite an inheritance from a farsighted penny pincher.

▶ BUY U.S. TREASURIES DIRECT

Except for DRIPs, you don't have any choice when you want to buy stocks. You either pay a brokerage commission or you pay a mutual fund its annual fees as well as any up-front or back-end redemption fees it charges.

But why pay a broker—even a discount broker—as much as $30 to $90 each time you invest in super-safe U.S. treasury bills, notes, or bonds? Unless you think you will want to sell the note before it matures, it is actually easier, more convenient, and completely free (except for the price of a stamp) to deal directly with the seller of the bonds—the U.S. government. Call Treasury Direct at 202-874-4000 or look in the phone book for the number of a Federal Reserve Bank or branch near you (there are thirty-six of them nationwide). Ask for an application to set up a Treasury Direct account. All you need is your Social Security number and a bank account where you want your future interest payments and principal deposited. From then on, using the very brief and easily understood forms provided, you can buy any denomination of new treasury offerings by mail—at exactly the same price a broker would pay.

You can get information about Treasury Direct and download all necessary forms from the New York Federal Reserve Bank on the Internet (http://www.ny.frb.org/pihome/treasdir/).

▶ CHECK OUT OLD U.S. SAVINGS BONDS

Do you still have that $25 Series E U.S. Savings Bond Grandpa gave you for your birthday back in 1950 or 1960? If you do, you probably keep it in a safe-deposit box, glance at it once a year, and take for granted that it is still earning interest.

Holders of almost $2 billion of old savings bonds are presently making that mistake. Their bonds are no longer earning any interest at all because the bonds have reached final maturity.

Check the dates in the top right-hand corner of your bonds. If you have a Series E bond that is over 40 years old, it has stopped earning interest. If your E bonds were purchased after November 1965, they will stop earning interest after 30 years. If you have a Series H bond that is over 30 years old, it has stopped earning interest.

What should you do? Once Series E bonds stop earning interest, you have a one-year period during which you can still exchange them for HH bonds, which are issued at full face value and pay regular semiannual interest. This allows you to defer reporting the interest earned on the E bonds until you redeem the HH bonds. If you miss the one-year deadline, or hold H bonds that have matured, of course you should redeem them (otherwise, it is like keeping cash in a mattress), but you'll have to pay taxes on the earned interest.

There are some other important facts to keep in mind about savings bonds. Each bond you own has a unique interest rate, increase schedule, value, and maturity date. Don't assume all of your bonds are the same; they're not. For instance, on most Series E and EE bonds, you can forfeit up to six months of interest if you redeem them even one day prior to a scheduled increase.

Although banks are supposed to have information about current values, timing issues (when specific bonds increase), interest rates, and dates of final and extended maturity periods, many don't. Others may not have accurate information. If you have questions about bonds you hold, your best source of free information is a Federal Reserve Bank (see previous tip). A much easier way to get complete and accurate information is to call *The Savings Bond Informer* (800-927-1901). For a small fee (they'll tell you how much when you call), this company will provide an easy-to-understand written statement outlining the timing issues, values, maturity dates, and interest rates for each of your bonds.

▶ COMPARE TAX-EXEMPT ALTERNATIVES

The interest on municipal bonds (bonds issued by states, cities, school districts, and other local and state authorities) is generally not subject to federal income taxation. If you live in the state in which they are issued, you also won't have to pay state income taxes on the interest. This can make municipal bonds and mutual funds that invest in them an attractive alternative to other fixed-income investments, especially if you live in a state with high income taxes.

The mistake many people make is to avoid taxes just for the sake of avoiding them. What you are interested in is the after-tax return, and there is a quick way to compare the after-tax return of a tax-exempt bond or fund.

Suppose you are in a 28 percent federal and 8 percent state tax bracket. Here's how you would analyze a yield of $6^1/_2$ percent that was tax-exempt in your state:

(1)   Because state taxes are exempt from federal taxes, calculate your "effective" state tax. To do that, multiply 8 percent by 72 percent (100 percent minus your federal tax rate of 28 percent). That calculation is $.08 \times .72 = .057$.

(2)   Add your "effective" state tax rate to your federal tax rate. That calculation is 28 percent + 5.7 percent = 33.7 percent.

(3)   Subtract 33.7 percent from 100 percent to get 66.3 percent.

(4)   Divide the after-tax yield of $6^1/_2$ percent by 66.3 percent (.065 / .663) to get 9.8 percent.

All other things being equal, only if you can get a taxable yield of more than 9.8 percent are you better off than with the $6^1/_2$ percent tax-free yield.

Penny Pinching on Everything Else

College Expenses, Medicine, Cosmetics, Pets, Kids, and More

Here is a final grab bag of tips that didn't seem to fit under any of the previous chapter headings—in no particular order, and covering prescription drugs, cosmetics, college expenses, pets, kids, movies, lawn mowers, and more.

▶ DON'T TRUST ANYBODY'S BILLS

Keep good enough records of credit-card purchases to be able to check monthly bills for errors. Computers don't often make mistakes, but the people who punch in the numbers do.

▶ STRETCH REGULAR EXPENSES OUT

Many well-organized people get into a spending rut when it comes to certain regular expenses. If you get your hair cut every two weeks at $12 an appointment, that's $312 a year. If you stretch those fourteen-day intervals by just four days, you'll spend only $240 a year. One of us wears disposable contact lenses that have to be changed every week. By wearing glasses for two or three days in between lens changes, we use only forty week's worth of disposable lens a year—reducing our annual costs by nearly 25 percent.

Reexamine every expense you make regularly. You may be surprised at how easy it is to cut back by stretching out.

▶ BUY HALF SHARES WITH OTHER PENNY PINCHERS

You use your lawn mower once a week and get it serviced once a year. If you buy your next one cooperatively with your next-door neighbor, it will probably last just as long, you'll still service it just once a year, and only one of you will be stuck with storing it. Most important, you'll cut your costs by 50 percent.

There are a number of things you need but don't use very often that can be bought cooperatively with trustworthy friends or neighbors. Garden tools are the most obvious examples, but sewing machines, magazine subscriptions, indoor power tools, and many other items are possibilities to consider.

▶ BARTER SERVICES WITH NEIGHBORS

A retired friend is an avid gardener with too small a yard to keep him happy. His accountant neighbor, who always hated any kind of gardening, now gets complete, loving care of his grounds—free. In return, he buys all the garden supplies for both houses and prepares the gardener's annual tax forms.

Given the increasing costs and decreasing availability of baby-sitters, you may also want to reach a barter agreement with other parents in the neighborhood. You'll keep their kids if they'll keep yours. Especially if your schedules are compatible (you have a class every Tuesday night, they bowl every Friday) this really does work out and can save enormous amounts of money over a year's time.

▶ TRY BARTER OPTIONS ELSEWHERE

If you like the idea of bartering, you don't have to limit it to neighbors. It's anybody's guess how many accountants regularly barter free tax services with dentists for free dental work, or how many garage owners barter automobile maintenance for carpentry work on their houses. Hundreds of millions of barter transactions take place in the United States every year between people who trade goods and/or services with no exchange of money. Especially if you have a special skill, barter is something to consider whenever you are buying goods or services from an owner/manager or a professional. *Caveat:* IRS regulations make most barter transactions taxable.

▶ WAIT THREE MONTHS FOR MOVIES

Except for the biggest hits, most new movies are now available on video within three to five months. Renting a movie for $3 instead of paying $12 for tickets for two makes sense, unless there are special production values lost on the small home screen. Just as sensible: Borrow videos, particularly classic films, from your library, which also usually has records, cassettes, and CDs.

▶ FACE THE TRUTH ABOUT COSMETICS? NOT LIKELY

Deep down, you know the cosmetics makers sell hope, dreams, and fantasies. You know the ingredients in a $100 bottle of perfume may cost less than the $3 cost of the fancy bottle the perfume comes in. You know that nothing that comes in a box is really going to make you instantly beautiful, desirable, or younger.

So what? Life is not a matter of penny pinching alone. But even if you don't give up that expensive fragrance or switch to a cheaper brand of lipstick, perhaps you might consider the few money-saving tips that follow.

▶ DEEP-CONDITION YOUR HAIR FOR PENNIES

You can spend a lot of dollars on expensively packaged potions, but none will do a better job than this:

Beat together one egg and equal amounts—about one-third cup—of water and olive oil. Work the mixture into dry hair, leave on for one hour, then rinse thoroughly before shampooing and conditioning hair as usual.

▶ SAVE ON SKIN MOISTURIZERS

There is nothing a $20 skin moisturizer can do for you that won't be accomplished just as well by a $3 product. Or a 49-cent one—Vaseline petroleum jelly.

It *is* likely you may find the oil in some other moisturizer more pleasant. But all moisturizers contain some kind of oil, even those that claim to be oil-free; they are simply defining "oil" differently. The only thing that really moisturizes your skin is water, best applied through proper humidity in your house, by cutting back on hot water (which dehydrates the skin) in baths and showers, and by just splashing it on. All any moisturizer does is help hold water on your skin, and the only ingredient in any of them that does that is some form of oil.

If you want to use Vaseline, don't towel-dry after a bath or shower. Wait a minute or two and, while still damp, apply the Vaseline. Too messy? At least switch to something inexpensive that has a fragrance you like. And don't bother with different mixtures for hands, feet, elbow, neck, etc. They are interchangeable, but avoid using too oily a product on your face.

▶ SAVE ON ASTRINGENTS AND TONERS

The problem with penny-pinching advice about cosmetics is that nobody wants to hear it. The beautiful packages and ads insist that the $20 8-ounce bottles of astringents or toners, used to clean and tighten pores after washing your face, perform some kind of magic.

Witch hazel ($1.99 a quart at drugstores) feels good, has no unpleasant odor, and works every bit as well. Some things haven't improved since your great-grandmother's time.

▶ GET FREE SAMPLES AT THE COSMETICS COUNTER

They are seldom offered, but when you buy something at a department-store cosmetics counter, ask about free samples. The more you buy, the more generous the saleswoman will be.

Don't forget the ubiquitous "gift with purchase" offers either. Even if you refuse to give up those $20 moisturizers, at least you can get something free with them.

▶ BUY KNOCKOFF SCENTS

There is nothing illegal about copying a fragrance, and a company called *Parfums de Coeur* is doing exactly that with some of the world's most famous and expensive perfumes. You'll find their knockoffs in discount drugstores and chains such as Kmart. Even experts are fooled, and you'll pay a fraction of the cost of the real thing.

▶ SAVE ON DRUGS IN THE DOCTOR'S OFFICE

- Too many busy doctors still automatically use a brand name when writing a prescription. When you see your doctor pick up a pen to write your prescription, quickly ask if he will write it generically. Nine times out of ten, there's no reason not to save the money.
- Don't be shy about asking the doctor if she has any free samples of the drug being prescribed, especially if it is for very short-term use. The drug companies

flood doctors' offices with samples and many doctors are happy to get rid of them.

- If the doctor is prescribing a daily 10-milligram pill, ask him if he will write the prescription for 20 milligrams. You can cut the pill in half, and the double dose will usually cost less than two single pills.

- Quite a few drugs are now sold over-the-counter that could be bought only by prescription until recently. The over-the-counter cost is always lower *unless* you have an insurance plan that covers prescriptions. We have a policy that allows us to buy a three-month supply of a prescription drug for a flat price of $5. So if our doctor says "you can buy it without a prescription," we may ask him to write one anyway.

▶ JOIN THE AARP

Probably a majority of people celebrating (well, *observing*) a fiftieth birthday get what some younger friend thinks is a great joke gift—an $8 membership in the American Association of Retired Persons. The joke, of course, turns out to be that membership in the AARP (202-434-2277 for information) is one of the great penny-pinching bargains of the century.

In addition to a quite readable bimonthly magazine, membership entitles you to 10 to 15 percent discounts at many hotels and car rentals (and higher discounts at a few others), as well as excursion rates on some airlines that are 10 percent less than their cheapest published rates. You will also probably want to buy prescription and nonprescription drugs from the AARP's very efficient and very cheap discount mail-order pharmacy.

▶ BUY PRESCRIPTION DRUGS BY MAIL

You don't have to be an AARP member to use its pharmacy service. And there are other discount mail-order pharmacies whose prices you should check out, especially if you must take some medication over a long period of time. (Obviously, if your doctor prescribes an antibiotic, you can't wait ten days to have it delivered.) Because these companies buy in bulk quantities and have low overhead, they can offer prices on both brand-name and generic drugs that are often lower than those of discount drugstores. All of the companies listed here also sell over-the-counter medications such as aspirin, sunblocks, and cold remedies at low discount prices. They will quote prices by mail and will also send you catalogs. Comparison-shop all of them before making a major purchase; prices vary greatly for different drugs. *AARP Pharmacy* (800-456-2226); *Action-Mail Order* (800-452-1976); *Medi-Mail* (800-331-1458).

▶ CHECK YOUR BENEFITS DEPARTMENT FOR DISCOUNT PRESCRIPTIONS

An increasing number of corporations have set up programs that allow employees to buy drugs at discounted prices from participating drugstores or from a special mail-order supplier.

However you buy a prescription drug, and especially if it is one that you will have to refill on a regular basis, compare prices from a number of sources. Then compare them again three months later. There are wide discrepancies even among discount suppliers, and prices are constantly changing. Finally, if you use a pharmacy regularly, ask them to match the best prices you find elsewhere.

▶ USE FLEX BENEFITS IF YOU HAVE THEM

If your company allows you to contribute pretax dollars, deducted from your salary, into a flexible benefits plan that reimburses you for all out-of-pocket medical expenses, sign up right away. Virtually everyone has some out-of-pocket medical expenses, even if they are just small copayments for drugs or doctor's visits covered by insurance. If these expenses are paid out of your flex account, instead of from your after-tax income, you have automatically saved 28 percent on whatever your tax bracket is. Be careful not to overestimate these expenses; you won't get back whatever isn't used at the end of the year.

▶ MAKE YOUR OWN FROZEN GEL PACKS

Applying a frozen gel pack to a muscle injury is easier than using an ice pack, but the blue gel packs sold in pharmacies are expensive. You can make your own for less than 25 cents. Partially fill a large heavy duty plastic freezer bag with a mixture of $1/4$ rubbing alcohol and $3/4$ water. Seal and place in a second bag. Seal and put in freezer.

▶ BUY READING GLASSES, SUNGLASSES, AND CONTACT LENSES BY MAIL

There are mail-order services offering prescription eyeglasses (see *The Wholesale-By-Mail Catalog,* described on page 106), but we prefer the convenience of trying on different frames at nearby discount optical stores. Reading glasses, sunglasses, and contacts are a different matter. If you need simple magnification, nonprescription reading glasses are available in our area either in discount drugstores, where we've never been able to find an acceptable style, or in optical stores, where even the "discount" prices seem inordinately high.

- *Precision Optical* (for a free catalog, write them at 507 Second Ave., Rochelle, IL 61068; or call 815-562-2174) offers a very good mail-order alternative. In addition to half frames, clear bifocals, and other magnifiers, they sell sunglasses and other nonprescription optical devices at very reasonable prices.
- *Sunglasses USA* (800-872-7297) has a free catalog offering big discounts on Bausch & Lomb, Ray•Ban, and other brand-name sunglasses.
- *Dial a Contact Lens* (800-233-5367), *Lens Express* (800-

666-5367), and *Lens Direct* (800-772-5367) will give you quick discounted price quotes on any contact-lens prescription. Prices will vary; check all three before ordering. Check your wholesale club, discount drug and optical stores, and Wal-Mart as well; all are aggressively discounting contact lenses.

▶ GET PETS FREE

It is possible you will find a purebred cat or dog at an animal shelter. More likely you'll choose from mixed-breed animals. Either way, good shelters give away (sometimes charging a small fee or donation) healthy, vaccinated dogs and cats that are often in better shape than animals sold by pet stores.

▶ MAKE OWNING A PET LESS EXPENSIVE

It is easy to spend $1,000 a year on food, medical care, grooming, and other needs of a dog or cat. It is also easy to cut some of those expenses by ordering pet supplies from one of the national mail-order discounters. Among those that offer savings of from 35 to 75 percent:

- *The Pet Warehouse,* 800-443-1160. Just about everything for owners of tropical fish, dogs, cats, birds, gerbils, etc. Good discounts and a very good catalog.
- *R. C. Steele,* 800-872-3773. Mainly a supplier for dogs—big savings and great service. Free catalog.
- *Doctors Foster & Smith,* 800-826-7206. Veterinary products and more, for cats, dogs, horses.

▶ TRY STORE-BRAND FILM

The film with your discount drug chain's name on it was produced by a manufacturer that also markets under its own brand name. Same film, but the store brand will be 15 to 20 percent cheaper. Once you decide you like that film, buy it in multipaks and save even more. Just be certain you will use the film before its expiration date.

Whatever film you buy, you will pay more for higher

speeds. If you are taking snapshots outdoors on a reasonably sunny day, you probably don't need more than 100-speed film.

▶ BUY GOLF AND TENNIS EQUIPMENT BY MAIL

There are a number of discount sources for golf and tennis equipment; they all advertise monthly in *Tennis, Golf Digest,* and the other magazines that cover the sports. Your best bet is to call a few of them for prices, because they constantly change.

▶ JOIN THE Y

Prices vary, and so does what is offered. But in many cities and towns across America, the Ys have wonderful facilities and offer incredible bargains to swimmers, runners, racquet-sports players, and fitness enthusiasts.

▶ EXERCISE AND DIET ON COMPANY TIME AND MONEY

More and more companies are offering exercise and diet programs to their workers, on premises and either free or well below the costs of comparable programs outside the office. If your company isn't one of them, you might canvass coworkers to build up interest and then talk to a benefits or personnel manager. The principle that healthier workers cost companies less is generally accepted today, so you may well get the program you want.

▶ CALL FOR HOUSEPLANT BARGAINS

Companies that rent houseplants to offices often sell those they can't use at a fraction of their usual retail price. If you are in the market for some new houseplants, check the Yellow Pages (under "plants") and make a few telephone calls.

▶ REDUCE A CHILD'S ASSETS BEFORE FINANCIAL AID FOR COLLEGE

More than 75 percent of students attending college today receive some kind of financial aid, and most of that aid is based on need. Even families with incomes over $100,000 a year can get financial assistance under certain circumstances, but they have to prove need based on what is called "Congressional Methodology Need Analysis."

When you apply for financial aid, you will fill out a very complicated form that lays bare your income and assets as well as any assets your child has. It is important to know that only 5.65 percent of your assets are considered available for the costs of college, but 35 percent of your child's assets are.

What this means is that you have good reason to reduce any assets your child has *before* you file the financial aid documents. Buy the computer that will be needed in college—as well as clothes, airline tickets, etc.—using his or her assets, not yours.

If grandparents want to make gifts of money to your college-bound child, ask them to wait and instead pay tuition bills, or part of them, directly to the school. They can do this in any amount without incurring any gift tax.

▶ PLAN WAY AHEAD FOR COLLEGE FINANCIAL AID

The process of applying for and receiving grants and loans for a college education is always time-consuming and usually frustrating. But it is not as mysterious as it seems to those confronting all the forms and choices for the first time. Your library has books that tell you everything you need to know. If you don't have a home computer, your child probably has access to one at school, and information about financial aid is readily available on the Internet. One good place to start a search is at the Yahoo education site (http://www. yahoo.com/Education/). More specifically, you can get

forms, advice on how to fill them out, and other information from the Department of Education's Student Aid Information Center (800-433-3243; http://www.ed.gov/
money.html).

Even if your child is years away from college, if you
think you will need or want financial aid when the time
comes, visit your library or the Internet now. What you
learn may very well affect your saving, investing, and
tax strategies in the ensuing years.

Here's one specific example: Suppose your child
plans to enter college as a freshman in September 1998.
The financial-aid package he or she gets will depend on
what your income was in 1997. That gives you a big incentive to defer income from that year (see Chapter 4).

Also, you want to be ready to file for financial aid as
early as possible. Most colleges accept forms as early as
January 1; mail yours the day after Christmas. The reason: Many colleges make grants (which you don't have
to repay) on a first-come, first-served basis. The later
you file, the more likely you'll be getting a higher ratio
of loans (which you do have to repay) in your package.

▶ FIND A SCHOLARSHIP

High-school guidance counselors are the primary starting point for most people, but your bookstore and library have a number of good books about scholarships
and financial aid. One of the best Internet sites we have
seen is *fastWeb* (http://www.studentservices.com/
fastweb), a free service that allows you to set up a per-
sonalized search and get feedback about it on an address you set up on the site. The site also has up-to-date
information about financial aid and an on-line calculator
that computes an estimate of a student's expected family
contribution and financial need using the Federal Need
Analysis Methodology.

▶ CASH IN U.S. SAVINGS BONDS TO PAY
TUITION

All the interest you earn on Series EE U.S. Savings
Bonds is excluded from taxes when the bonds are re-

deemed to pay any part of your child's college tuition bills. This exclusion can't be claimed by higher-income families; if your adjusted gross income in the year bonds are redeemed exceeds a certain amount (currently around $66,000), the tax-free amount begins to be phased out and is phased out completely at around $96,000. See Chapter 10 for more about U.S. Savings Bonds.

▶ PAY TUITION IN ADVANCE

A number of states sponsor prepaid tuition plans, which in effect let you pay in advance—at today's prices—for college expenses that won't be incurred for a number of years. If you want to explore this option, use the resources mentioned in previous tips to check out what your state offers. In addition to knowing exactly what options your child would have when it comes time to choose a school (most of the plans allow for a transfer of funds to pay for tuition in nonstate schools), also look into the latest tax rulings on such plans. As of this writing, it was unclear how—or if—the IRS would tax prepaid tuition plans.

▶ START COLLEGE IN HIGH SCHOOL

One of the best ways to cut college expenses is to reduce the time period it takes to get a degree. The first way to do that is by enrolling in college-level courses while still in high school. To earn credits accepted by most colleges, you then have to pass an Advanced Placement exam administered by the College Board. High-school guidance offices have full information.

▶ ENROLL IN AN ACCELERATED DEGREE PROGRAM

Many colleges have programs that make it possible to earn a bachelor's degree in three years instead of four. Such programs are arduous, demanding heavier course loads during the regular school year as well as summer school, but they can cut the cost of a degree by 20 to 30 percent.

▶ GO TO A COMMUNITY COLLEGE FIRST

You can cut the costs of a degree by as much as 40 percent if you spend the first two years at a local community or junior college and then transfer to a residential four-year college for your final two years. You'll save money by living at home; more important, the costs of a community college are usually at least 75 percent lower than a private four-year college.

▶ CHECK OUT COLLEGE DISCOUNTS

To attract good students, many colleges now offer various discounts on tuition. Among them: discounts if more than one family member attends the college at the same time; discounts for the children of alumni; older-student (25 or over) discounts; evening and weekend discounts for classes held outside regular hours; and campus-activity discounts for certain student leaders.

▶ CHECK OUT COMPANY BENEFITS

Many corporations have assistance plans to help employees pay for their children's college educations. Ask your benefits department.

▶ TRIM THE COSTS OF COLLEGE HOUSING

This is not a strategy for everyone, but if you have sufficient assets and are confident that your son or daughter is mature enough to help manage the property, there is a compelling case to be made for buying a residence for your college-bound youngster instead of paying for dormitory space.

Here's how it works: You buy an off-campus house or condo and then rent it to your child at the going market rate. He or she in turn takes in student roommates to help pay the rent—perhaps generating enough income to pay all or nearly all the rent owed to you.

Not only is your son or daughter living close to rent-free (although he or she will have all the headaches of managing the property), you can deduct the costs of mortgage interest expenses, taxes, insurance, maintenance, depreciation, etc. You can also probably deduct the costs of visiting the college because it will be a "property inspection trip." Finally, because the depreciation allowance added to all other expenses will no doubt mean you will take a paper loss on the property, you will be able to deduct up to $25,000 of the loss each year against nonpassive income—including your wages.

The allowance is phased out for higher-income taxpayers, and you must meet some easy standards that prove you "actively participate" in managing the property. Over a three-year period (starting in your child's sophomore year), you could easily save not only thousands on room and board but also thousands more on your taxes.

You need much more information than we've given you here. Check out the real-estate investment section of your library and a good income tax handbook for full details.

▶ SHIP COLLEGE-BOUND KIDS OFF EARLY

This is a bit radical, but worth mentioning. A few years ago, the son of friends of ours, then a junior in high school, decided he wanted to go to a state university outside his own state. Tuition fees there were far higher for out-of-state residents. He went to live with an uncle and aunt during his senior year, establishing a new residence, and qualified for the far lower in-state tuition. His family saved at least $24,000 over a four-year period.

▶ STOP BUYING LOTTERY TICKETS

If you want to dream about being a multimillionaire, fantasize instead about an unknown relative dying and leaving his riches to you. It is a likelier scenario than a lottery win. State lotteries are nothing but another form of tax, and unfortunately this tax falls most heavily on those who can least afford it.

Here are some numbers to inspire you: Instead of throwing away $100 a year on lottery tickets for the next fifty years, invest that money in an aggressive-growth mutual fund that averages a 16 percent return a year. At the end of fifty years, you will have $1,043,565 instead of a pile of worthless tickets.

▶ GET FREE CONSUMER ADVICE FROM THE GOVERNMENT

We've mentioned a couple of specific booklets available from the Government Printing Office in this book, but there are hundreds of them. Many are free and few cost more than a couple of dollars (unless you take into account the taxes you pay to write, produce, and print millions of copies a year).

One of the most useful is an $8^{1}/_{2} \times 11$-inch 96-page booklet called *The Consumer's Resource Catalog.* In addition to some reasonable (if not exactly streetwise) advice on how to be a smart consumer, this catalog lists addresses and telephone numbers of whom to write to at different corporations, including car companies, with a complaint. It also gives addresses and telephone numbers of different state and federal agencies, regulators, authorities, and commissions. It is a very handy book to have, and it is free.

The government will give you advice on buying a used car (50 cents), choosing a nursing home (free), and traveling abroad ($1.25). It will tell you what to do about depression (free), asbestos in the home (50 cents), or a child with a speech disorder (50 cents). It has booklets on careers and education, exercise and weight control, federal programs, food and nutrition, health, housing, money management, parenting, small business, travel, and hobbies.

You may not find every answer you want, but at these

prices you may at least want to know what's available. You can get a free copy of the catalog that describes all the booklets, *Consumer Information Catalog,* as well as a copy of *Consumer's Resource Handbook* by calling 800-664-4435.

▶ LOOK FOR BARGAINS EVERYWHERE

They exist. No matter what you are buying, there are nearly always alternative sources and quick ways to find them. There are usually ways to negotiate better deals. Strategies that work in one area can often be adapted to work well in others. Use the tips you've read in these pages, but don't stop there.

If you are lucky, one of the things your taxes pay for is a good free library system. Use it. Ask librarians where to find information that will help you make major purchase decisions. Borrow cookbooks, travel guides, how-to references, and books on investing and saving. When you discover you are using a book constantly, go to a bookstore and buy it.

Things change. If you want to make your dollar go as far as possible, you've got to keep up. We know very well that the day after this book goes to press, someone will share with us a terrific new money-saving tip that should have been included. We'll keep looking. You should, too.

▶ PINCH PENNIES, NOT KIDS, FRIENDS, OR YOUR SENSE OF HUMOR

Saving money and not wasting any are worthwhile activities, but only if they don't interfere with more important things in your life. Wasting a few dollars is better than jumping on your kids every time they forget to turn out the lights. And saving money should never get in the way of enjoying what you spend it on.

Keep things in perspective. Penny pinching is a rewarding means to an end, not the definition of a complete, well-rounded lifestyle.